The AI Engineer's Guide to Surviving the EU AI Act

Navigating the EU Regulatory Requirements

Larysa Visengeriyeva

O'REILLY®

The AI Engineer's Guide to Surviving the EU AI Act

by Larysa Visengeriyeva

Published by O'Reilly Media, Inc., 1005 Gravenstein Highway North, Sebastopol, CA 95472.

O'Reilly books may be purchased for educational, business, or sales promotional use. Online editions are also available for most titles (*http://oreilly.com*). For more information, contact our corporate/institutional sales department: 800-998-9938 or *corporate@oreilly.com*.

Acquisitions Editor: Nicole Butterfield
Development Editor: Sara Hunter
Production Editor: Kristen Brown
Copyeditor: Rachel Head
Proofreader: Kim Cofer
Indexer: Krsta Technology Solutions
Cover Designer: Susan Brown
Cover Illustrator: Monica Kaamsvaag
Interior Designer: David Futato
Interior Illustrator: Kate Dullea

July 2025: First Edition

Revision History for the First Edition

2025-06-27: First Release

See *http://oreilly.com/catalog/errata.csp?isbn=9781098172497* for release details.

978-1-098-17249-7

[LSI]

Table of Contents

Preface

The European Union's Artificial Intelligence Act, which came into full effect in August 2024, represents a watershed moment in the global regulation of artificial intelligence. As the first comprehensive legal framework for AI, its stated purpose is clear: to foster innovation and development within the EU while effectively mitigating the potential risks posed by AI systems. This ambitious regulation establishes a uniform legal framework governing the development, placement on the market, putting into service, and use of AI systems across the EU.

Navigating the complexities of the EU AI Act might, at first glance, seem like a task exclusively for legal teams and policy experts. The Act is indeed complex, featuring 113 articles that address highly technical issues, complemented by 13 annexes that detail implementation specifics and 180 recitals (introductory statements providing context and guidance for interpretation). However, as the practical requirements of the EU AI Act reveal, *achieving and maintaining compliance with the Act is fundamentally an engineering problem*. This is the core message of this book.

Operationalizing EU AI Act compliance goes far beyond legal interpretation. It requires establishing roles, processes, structures, and AI engineering practices. Post-market compliance, for instance, directly necessitates the implementation of machine learning operations (MLOps) practices such as monitoring and alerting. Successfully achieving EU AI Act compliance is linked to understanding the design, development, and maintenance of AI systems.

Compliance is not a legal stamp applied at the end of the development lifecycle, but a continuous process that must be engineered into the core of AI systems from the beginning. The Act's foundation on the concept of "trustworthy AI" mandates that systems be lawful, ethical, and robust throughout their entire lifecycle. This necessitates embedding ethical and compliance aspects directly into the AI system development process.

This book serves as your guide to tackling EU AI Act compliance as the engineering challenge it is. We'll explore various practical methodologies and frameworks essential for this task, including:

AI engineering
: Defined as the application of software engineering principles to the end-to-end lifecycle of AI systems—including design, development, deployment, and maintenance.

CRISP-ML(Q)
: This structured machine learning development process provides a blueprint for designing, developing, and maintaining AI systems with compliance in mind. Its emphasis on quality assurance and continuous risk management throughout the AI lifecycle is directly aligned with the EU AI Act's risk-based approach. CRISP-ML(Q) requires documentation of the entire development process, including risk management measures, which is crucial for meeting the Act's technical documentation and transparency obligations.

MLOps Stack Canvas
: The MLOps Stack Canvas is a comprehensive and practical framework designed to guide organizations in architecting and managing their machine learning operations infrastructure. The canvas is structured around three core domains: Data and Code Management, Model Management, and Metadata Management. It provides a holistic view of the components necessary for successful ML deployment. By aligning with the CRISP-ML(Q) process model, the canvas ensures that each phase of the ML lifecycle is addressed, from data sourcing and versioning to model deployment and monitoring. It emphasizes critical aspects such as reproducibility, reliability, and efficiency, helping teams to plan infrastructure costs, select appropriate tools, and establish robust workflows. Serving as both a strategic and an operational tool, the MLOps Stack Canvas facilitates clearer communication among stakeholders for all ML and AI initiatives across the organization.

SMACTR (Scoping, Mapping, Artifact Collection, Testing, and Reflection)
: Introduced as an internal audit framework to guide the practical implementation of ethical AI development throughout its lifecycle, SMACTR promotes a proactive and preventive approach for AI development. Embedding audit processes into the design and development phases allows engineers to anticipate and address potential risks before deployment, aligning perfectly with the Act's emphasis on risk mitigation. SMACTR's focus on generating detailed documentation at each stage is also essential for meeting the Act's technical documentation requirements for high-risk AI systems.

The synergy between CRISP-ML(Q) and AI engineering offers a powerful framework for addressing EU AI Act compliance. Furthermore, the integration of SMACTR with the CRISP-ML(Q) methodology provides a robust and auditable process for responsibly developing AI systems. This combination allows for proactively engineering compliance into the ML lifecycle, from data collection through monitoring, rather than treating it as an afterthought.

The book also explores how these engineering principles apply across the Act's risk classifications—prohibited, high risk, limited risk, and low risk. While high-risk systems face the most stringent requirements, Article 50 introduces transparency obligations that apply to all AI systems designed to interact directly with humans, regardless of their risk level. These obligations, such as informing users of AI interaction and marking synthetic content, demand practical engineering solutions for proactive compliance. Aligning AI engineering practices with SMACTR and CRISP-ML(Q) provides a structured and automated approach to managing the AI system lifecycle for transparency.

This book also addresses the particular challenges posed by general-purpose AI (GPAI) and generative AI (GenAI), late but significant additions to the Act. The concept of generative AI operations (GenAIOps) is introduced as an extension of traditional MLOps principles to handle the unique complexities of GPAI and generative AI applications. Applying AI engineering principles to implement transparency obligations for GPAI and integrating CRISP-ML(Q), SMACTR, and GenAIOps are crucial for navigating this evolving landscape.

Who Should Read This Book

This book is intended for AI engineers, MLOps practitioners, data scientists, AI product managers, and anyone involved in the hands-on development and deployment of AI systems. It demonstrates how, through the application of robust methodologies, disciplined documentation, and continuous integration of ethical considerations, AI teams can build systems that are not only technically innovative but also demonstrably compliant, trustworthy, and aligned with societal expectations. I have tried to make this book as actionable as possible by introducing a comprehensive framework and practical checklists for aligning AI engineering practices with the EU AI Act articles throughout the CRISP-ML(Q) lifecycle.

As ImageNet creator Fei-Fei Li, known as the Godmother of AI, noted recently (*https://oreil.ly/_PUIb*): "Now more than ever, AI needs a governance framework." This book provides the practical engineering foundation for implementing such a framework, enabling practitioners to build trustworthy AI systems that meet the stringent requirements of the EU AI Act through empirical validation, risk-aware development, and collaborative practices. The law sets the requirements, but it is the engineering that delivers compliance.

Navigating This Book

This book has been designed as a reference for you, a guide to practicing proactive EU AI Act compliance through AI engineering and integrating it into the AI lifecycle, from data collection through monitoring. Each chapter is fairly self-contained, with appropriate references to other chapters identified. The chapters are organized as follows:

- Chapter 1, "Understanding the AI Regulations", provides a foundational understanding of the EU AI Act and the need for trustworthy AI systems. It outlines seven essential requirements for building such systems: human agency and oversight; technical robustness and safety; privacy and data governance; transparency; diversity, non-discrimination, and fairness; societal and environmental well-being; and accountability. This chapter describes the structure of the Act, including definitions, key players, risk classifications, and the implementation timeline, and provides an overview of this significant regulatory framework.
- Chapter 2, "AI Engineering: A Proactive Compliance Catalyst", explains how combining CRISP-ML(Q) with AI engineering helps organizations meet the compliance requirements of the EU AI Act. CRISP-ML(Q) guides the AI lifecycle through distinct phases, such as data preparation and model evaluation, while MLOps principles including automation, versioning, testing, and monitoring provide the operational backbone for ensuring AI systems are reliable, reproducible, and continuously compliant. In this chapter, you will also learn about the MLOps Stack Canvas as a framework for defining the necessary technical infrastructure, covering data, code, and model management, to support proactive compliance engineering.
- Chapter 3, "Data and AI Governance and AI Engineering", explains the critical roles of data governance and AI governance within the context of the EU AI Act. In this chapter, you will learn about how these governance concepts can be practically integrated into the AI system development lifecycle to ensure trustworthy and compliant AI.
- Chapter 4, "AI System Assessment and Tailoring AI Engineering for Different Risk Levels", focuses on the crucial initial steps for organizations to achieve compliance with the EU AI Act. You will learn about creating an inventory of your existing AI systems and how to classify their risk level to determine the applicable obligations. The chapter also explains the different roles organizations can take (provider or deployer), which further tailors compliance requirements.
- Chapter 5, "AI Engineering for High-Risk AI Systems", offers a comprehensive guide to implementing the EU AI Act's requirements for high-risk AI systems through AI engineering practices. It breaks down key articles of the Act (Articles 9–15), focusing on topics like risk management, data governance,

documentation, recordkeeping, transparency, human oversight, accuracy, robustness, and security. You will learn how to map the Act's legal requirements to specific quality attributes and how to integrate them into the CRISP-ML(Q) lifecycle. This chapter shows why documentation and metadata management are crucial for demonstrating compliance and ensuring the trustworthiness of high-risk AI systems.

- Chapter 6, "AI Engineering for Limited-Risk AI Systems", focuses on how to develop AI systems that meet the EU AI Act's transparency obligations, which differ from the stricter conformity assessments required for high-risk systems. Here, you will learn about integrating the SMACTR framework with the CRISP-ML(Q) lifecycle. This chapter also highlights the emerging role of AI governance platforms and various technical tools in facilitating compliance and responsible AI deployment.
- Chapter 7, "Toward Trustworthy General-Purpose AI and Generative AI", explains how the Act aims to balance AI innovation with risk mitigation, introducing concepts like GPAI and systemic risk. It outlines the specific transparency obligations for generative AI systems, such as informing users of AI interactions and marking synthetic content, and details the regulations for GPAI models, including documentation and risk management requirements for providers and deployers. You will also learn about GenAIOps, a framework for operationalizing the transparency and compliance aspects of GenAI development and deployment by integrating them with established methodologies like CRISP-ML(Q) and the SMACTR framework.

Conventions Used in This Book

This element signifies a tip or suggestion.

This element signifies a general note.

This element indicates a warning or caution.

O'Reilly Online Learning

O'REILLY® For more than 40 years, *O'Reilly Media* has provided technology and business training, knowledge, and insight to help companies succeed.

Our unique network of experts and innovators share their knowledge and expertise through books, articles, and our online learning platform. O'Reilly's online learning platform gives you on-demand access to live training courses, in-depth learning paths, interactive coding environments, and a vast collection of text and video from O'Reilly and 200+ other publishers. For more information, visit *https://oreilly.com*.

How to Contact Us

Please address comments and questions concerning this book to the publisher:

O'Reilly Media, Inc.
1005 Gravenstein Highway North
Sebastopol, CA 95472
800-889-8969 (in the United States or Canada)
707-827-7019 (international or local)
707-829-0104 (fax)
support@oreilly.com
https://oreilly.com/about/contact.html

We have a web page for this book, where we list errata, examples, and any additional information. You can access this page at *https://oreil.ly/AI-engineer-EU-AI-Act*.

For news and information about our books and courses, visit *https://oreilly.com*.

Find us on LinkedIn: *https://linkedin.com/company/oreilly-media*.

Watch us on YouTube: *https://youtube.com/oreillymedia*.

Acknowledgments

Bringing this book to life has been a truly fulfilling experience. I've had so much support from so many people throughout the process of writing the book—thank you so much to everyone who helped make it a reality!

I would like to give an especially big thank you to the book's technical reviewers: Una Galyeva, Katharine Jarmul, Janna Lipenkova, Anil Sood, and Debmalya Biswas. Their time and effort in reading through the initial draft and providing comments, suggestions, and corrections were invaluable, and they made significant contributions to improving the book's overall quality.

Everyone at O'Reilly has been fantastic to work with throughout the book's lifecycle, starting with Nicole Butterfield, who immediately saw the potential of the core message that EU AI Act compliance is fundamentally an engineering challenge. Sara Hunter worked intensively with me to shape and edit the book, and when I was ready to move to the production process, Kristen Brown was just amazing. A big thank you to the entire O'Reilly team, including copyeditor Rachel Head, proofreader Kim Cofer, indexer Ben Hurst, illustrator Kate Dullea, and the cover design team of Monica Kaamsvaag and Susan Brown. You are all heroes!

CHAPTER 1

Understanding the AI Regulations

As people, organizations, and the public sector increasingly rely on AI to drive decision making, the technology must be trustworthy. The EU AI Act (*https://oreil.ly/-8wI7*) aims to provide a legal framework for developing, deploying, and using AI technologies within the European Union, emphasizing safety, transparency, and ethical considerations. It is a regulatory framework for artificial intelligence that includes specific requirements for AI systems of different risk categories within the EU. This book is focused on understanding and implementing the regulatory requirements set by the European Union's legislation on artificial intelligence. Please note that the guidance it provides is not intended as a substitute for obtaining professional legal advice.

This chapter begins by outlining the motivation behind the EU AI Act, emphasizing the idea of "trustworthy AI," and identifying the essential requirements for ensuring AI is trustworthy. It then describes the structure of the EU AI Act, including its definitions, key stakeholders, risk classifications (prohibited, high risk, limited risk, and minimal risk), and the implementation timeline. Finally, it briefly compares the EU AI Act with other international regulations and standards related to AI.

> The author is not a lawyer, and this book does not provide legal advice. The intersection of law and artificial intelligence is a complex subject that requires expertise beyond the scope of AI, data science, and machine learning. Legal considerations surrounding AI systems can be complex and far-reaching. If you have any legal concerns related to the AI systems you are working on, seek professional legal advice from qualified experts in the field.

The Motivation for the EU AI Act: Trustworthy AI

As AI becomes increasingly intertwined with our daily lives, one of the challenges we face is learning to navigate the uncertainty that comes with it. This uncertainty is inherent to AI. AI models' predictive accuracy has long been considered a core evaluation criterion when building an AI system. However, with the widespread use of AI in critical areas such as human resources, transportation, finance, medicine, and security, there is a growing need for these systems to be trustworthy—and traditional predictive accuracy alone is not sufficient to build trustworthy AI applications.

To better understand trustworthy AI, let's start with its definition. *Trustworthy AI* is an umbrella term that refers to artificial intelligence systems that are designed and developed with principles such as fairness, privacy, and non-discrimination in mind, and with robust mechanisms to ensure reliability, security, and resilience. Within the AI community, this term is used interchangeably with *responsible AI*, *ethical AI*, *reliable AI*, and *values-driven AI*. Trustworthy AI systems must be adaptable to diverse and changing environments and robust against various types of disruptions, including cyber threats, data variability, and operational changes. They should operate transparently and be held accountable, with continuous monitoring and evaluation to respect human rights, including privacy and freedom from discrimination, and to ensure adherence to democratic values.

Trustworthy AI is a complex term that incorporates a long list of concepts and principles, which are visualized in Figure 1-1. These concepts lay the foundation for understanding the EU AI Act.

Trustworthiness in AI is grounded in the three pillars of *lawfulness*, *ethics*, and *robustness*. First, AI systems should be lawful, meaning they must comply with all relevant regulations to ensure a fair market, promote economic benefits, and protect citizens' rights. Second, they must be built on ethical principles and values, incorporating input from all stakeholders and establishing appropriate feedback mechanisms. Finally, they must be robust, accounting for potential risks and ensuring safety at every stage of development and deployment.

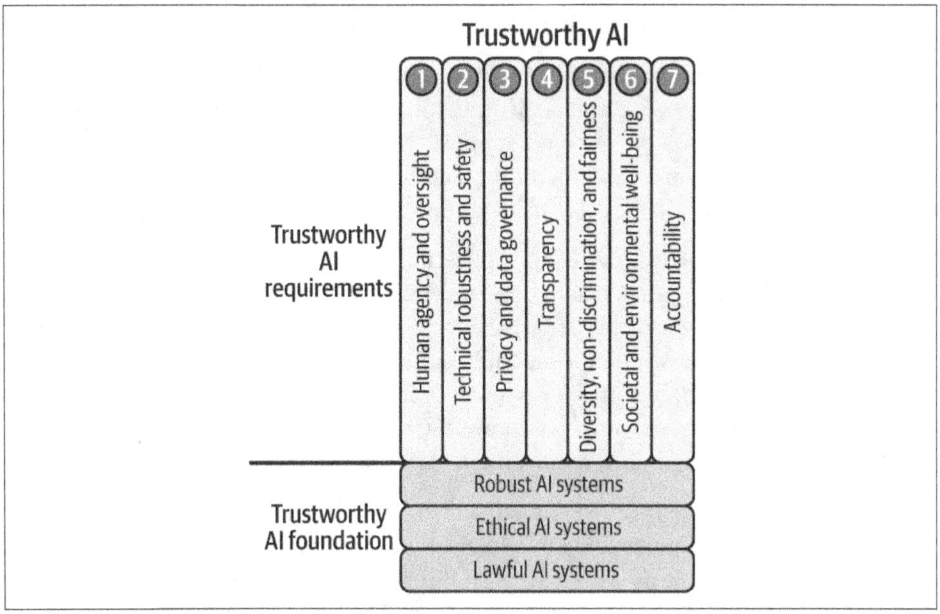

Figure 1-1. The foundation and seven requirements of trustworthy AI

Standing on these three pillars are seven key requirements that AI systems must implement to be deemed trustworthy:

1. Human agency and oversight
2. Technical robustness and safety
3. Privacy and data governance
4. Transparency
5. Diversity, non-discrimination, and fairness
6. Societal and environmental well-being
7. Accountability

These come directly from the requirements outlined in the Ethics Guidelines for Trustworthy AI (*https://oreil.ly/nBhE6*) developed by the European Commission's High-Level Expert Group on AI (AI HLEG). In the following sections, I provide an explanation of each.

Human Agency and Oversight

Human agency and oversight are crucial in developing and operating AI systems. *Human agency* refers to the ability of individuals to make informed decisions and maintain control. AI systems should support this by providing transparency, interpretability, and mechanisms for control and intervention that enable humans to understand and influence the system's decisions and actions.

Human oversight involves establishing governance processes and mechanisms that allow for human monitoring, evaluation, and intervention in the operation of AI systems. This includes ensuring transparency and interpretability of the systems' decision-making processes based on the results produced by the AI models. Additionally, AI systems should provide human control mechanisms (e.g., the ability to override, adjust, or shut down the system when necessary). As depicted in Figure 1-2, I distinguish between four different modes of human oversight:

Human-in-command
: This mode represents the highest level of human control, where humans maintain ultimate authority and responsibility over the AI system. Humans must explicitly authorize any AI system action. They are at the core of decision-making processes and always make the final decisions. In this mode, humans oversee the AI system's overall activity and can decide when and how to use the system in specific situations. For example, the "AI cockpit" concept (*https://oreil.ly/HFlbo*) demonstrates the human-in-command approach by providing a central user interface that enables operators to monitor AI systems' effects on different user groups, evaluate results against technical and ethical criteria, and exercise the authority to disable the systems when necessary.

Human-in-the-loop
: AI systems require human interaction at critical points in the decision-making process to add a layer of human experience and contextual understanding that AI currently lacks. Often, this involvement entails guiding the direction of decisions based on AI-generated predictions. The level of intervention and control might depend on the risk level of the system. Medical AI applications, for example, will typically require more intensive human intervention and control than less critical AI applications.

Human-on-the-loop
: The human plays an observer role, monitoring the actions of the AI system and intervening if necessary.

Human-out-of-the-loop

The AI system operates independently, without human intervention or real-time supervision. This scenario is possible when decisions based on the system's predictions can be programmatically implemented. Often, this mode is applied in trading applications that require data processing at speed, where human oversight is not realistic.

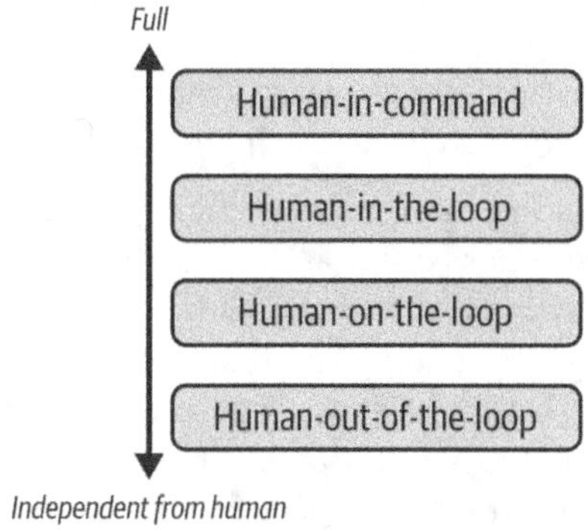

Figure 1-2. The different levels of human oversight in AI

The modes described here are each suitable for different AI use cases. Regardless of the one you use, proper implementation of the human agency and oversight requirement is crucial for designing and developing ethical AI systems that benefit from the strengths of AI while mitigating potential risks.

Technical Robustness and Safety

To be trustworthy, AI systems need to be accurate, reliable, and able to repeat their results. They should also have a "backup plan" if something goes wrong. In computer science, *robustness* means a system can keep working correctly even when there are mistakes, unusual inputs, or unexpected situations. For AI, robustness means that a machine learning (ML) model can keep making good, reliable predictions despite facing different conditions, tricky inputs, or changes in the type of data it sees.

In simpler terms, a robust ML model can still give you the correct answers even if the information it receives is somewhat noisy, messy, or comes from a different source than the model was originally trained on. If these differences cause its performance to drop suddenly, then it's not considered robust anymore. Achieving robustness is essential for building trust in AI—especially in areas like self-driving cars, cybersecurity systems, and healthcare, where a single mistake can have serious consequences.

There are three core layers to an AI system: the data it's trained on, the algorithm it uses, and the software that puts them to use. Correspondingly, there are three levels of robustness:

- *Data robustness* requires training the system on a wide variety of data types and scenarios. This allows the model to "learn" to handle different situations and ensures it is less likely to fail when confronted with new or unexpected conditions. For example, a self-driving car's AI should be trained on data from different weather conditions to handle rain, snow, and fog. In cybersecurity, an intrusion detection system should learn from many different types of network traffic and attack methods, so it can catch new threats as they emerge.
- *Algorithmic robustness* focuses on defending against attacks that try to trick the AI model itself. Some attacks occur at the moment of decision making by slightly altering the input to confuse the model. Others are executed during the training phase by introducing "poisoned" data that causes the model to make incorrect predictions later. A robust algorithm should be able to handle noisy or altered inputs, changes in data types, and even deliberately manipulated inputs designed to fool it. For example, a robust language model can deal with misspellings, slang, or strange grammar without losing accuracy.
- *System-level robustness* looks at the bigger picture—the entire lifecycle of the AI product, from how data is collected to how the model is built, tested, and finally used in the real world. By examining every step, we can spot risks before they lead to serious problems. This holistic approach ensures the entire AI pipeline, and its interaction with other systems, remains steady and secure.

In research, we often differentiate two types of robustness:

Non-adversarial robustness
: Can the model handle everyday challenges, like noisy inputs or slight changes in the environment, without losing accuracy?

Adversarial robustness
: Can the model resist "tricks" that attackers use intentionally to confuse it, such as subtly modified inputs designed to produce the wrong answer?

To measure how robust an AI model is, practitioners and researchers look at a variety of measurements:

Accuracy
: How many predictions the model gets right.

Error rate
: How many incorrect predictions the model makes.

Sensitivity (recall)
: The model's ability to correctly identify items that have a given condition (true positives). For example, if we are implementing a binary classifier, of all the cases that should be labeled "positive," how many are correctly identified?

Specificity
: The model's ability to correctly identify items that do not have a given condition (true negatives). For example, of all the cases that should be labeled "negative," how many are correctly rejected?

Robustness curves
: Graphs that show how the model's performance changes when we introduce challenges, like more noise, missing information, or unusual inputs.

All of these measurements can help us understand the model's strengths and weaknesses. However, the best way to measure robustness typically depends on the specific problem and requirements of the AI system.

Privacy and Data Governance

The second requirement of trustworthy AI systems is that they must ensure full respect for privacy and personal data protection, in line with Articles 7 and 8 of the Charter of Fundamental Rights of the European Union (*https://oreil.ly/nPDrM*).

Many AI systems, such as recommender systems and systems that provide personalized predictions, require some amount of personally identifiable information (PII). Handling of PII is a subject to regulations within the EU and the US, under the General Data Protection Regulation (GDPR) and the California Consumer Privacy Act (CCPA).

By examining how an AI system collects, stores, processes, and shares personal or sensitive data, *privacy impact assessments* (PIAs) help organizations spot areas where privacy might be at risk and guide them in modifying the system, implementing safeguards, and complying with relevant privacy laws and regulations. PIAs should ideally be conducted early in the design process, to proactively identify, assess, and mitigate potential privacy risks. This is an example of *privacy by design*, an engineering philosophy that involves embedding privacy protections into every phase of an AI system's lifecycle—from data collection and preprocessing to model training, deployment, and maintenance. This ensures that privacy isn't just treated as a legal afterthought or a check-the-box compliance step at the end of the development process, but as a fundamental design principle that helps organizations maintain user trust and meet regulatory requirements.

Privacy by design incorporates privacy considerations into the foundational components of AI systems. For AI engineers, this might involve using techniques such as minimal data collection, deidentification, and anonymization (encryption, differential privacy, other methods to protect sensitive information before it even reaches the model); adapting model architecture choices (for example, using federated learning); and continuous evaluation and monitoring. The related concept of *data governance* ensures that privacy principles are consistently applied, maintained, and improved within a structured organizational framework.

Data governance is a data management function that guarantees the availability, usability, integrity, and security of the data collected and used in an organization. Its key elements are visualized in Figure 1-3.

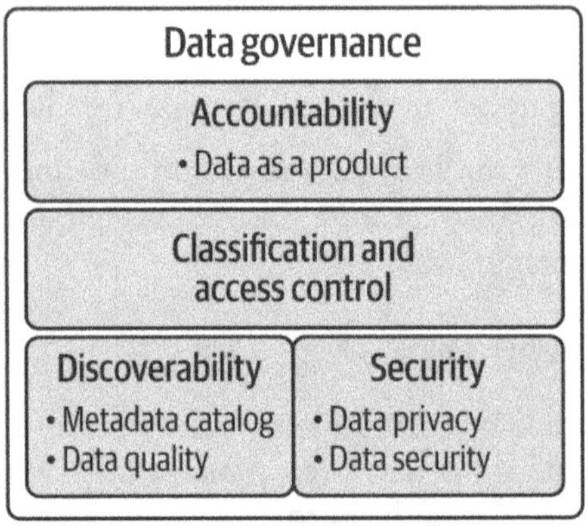

Figure 1-3. Key elements of data governance (adapted from Data Governance: The Definitive Guide *by Evren Eryurek et al. [O'Reilly])*

Data governance has become increasingly important as data volumes have grown, organizations have become more data-driven, and access to data has expanded. The ultimate goal of data governance is to enhance the trustworthiness of data, which is fundamental to trustworthy AI. There are three key aspects to this: discoverability, security, and accountability.

Discoverability refers to the availability of the dataset's metadata, data provenance (lineage), and glossary of domain entities. It's essential for ensuring users and AI systems can easily access the data they need. Data governance establishes procedures that guarantee that the right data is accessed by the appropriate people in the organization and determine what data AI systems can access. *Data quality* is a related concept that is crucial in building trust in data: data should be correct, complete, timely, and integral.

In the context of AI engineering, data *security* means protecting the data used to train, validate, and run models from unauthorized access, theft, tampering, or loss. Together with privacy, data security is an essential aspect of protecting data and ensuring adherence to regulations such as the GDPR (or CCPA).

The third aspect of data governance, *accountability*, involves ensuring that everyone involved with an AI system, from data suppliers to model developers and operators, knows their role, can explain their choices, and can be held responsible for the system working ethically, legally, and safely.

AI development should respect the fundamental right to privacy at all points of the AI application lifecycle, including data collection, processing, and storage and model design, development, and deployment. Privacy issues can arise in various aspects of AI systems, such as when social media platforms using AI to analyze user behaviors and preferences inadvertently expose sensitive information through targeted advertising or data breaches, or when AI is used to enhance the capabilities of surveillance systems, leading to potential overreach in monitoring activities. This can result in a loss of anonymity and freedom, as every action can be watched and recorded. For example, governmental structures using facial recognition technologies in public spaces can track individuals without their consent, potentially leading to misuse of power and privacy violations.

AI systems can also amplify biases present in their training data. When these biases affect how data is collected, processed, or used, they can disproportionately impact the privacy of certain groups. For instance, AI-driven credit scoring models might use biased data that discriminates against certain racial or gender groups, raising concerns about fairness and privacy in relation to financial data.

Example metrics and mechanisms to define and track privacy and data governance include:

Data encryption levels
: These determine the degree of data protection during transmission and at rest.

Access controls
: These are policies and tools that manage who can access or alter data.

Data retention and deletion policies
: These ensure compliance with data minimization principles and regulations.

Transparency

Data, AI models, and software systems that include AI components must be transparent and provide traceability. Regardless of the industry or use case, transparency is the most commonly cited ethical principle (*https://oreil.ly/_pir3*) in existing AI guidelines.

Transparency in AI systems refers to the ability to understand how an AI system works internally and makes decisions. It provides comprehensible explanations about the AI system's components, algorithms, decision-making process, and overall functioning to stakeholders such as users, developers, and regulators. Key dimensions of AI transparency include:

Explainability
: The ability to clearly articulate in human-understandable terms how and why an AI system, encompassing its data sources, model components, and decision-making processes, arrived at a specific output or decision for a given case. This is important for building trust and accountability. As depicted in Figure 1-4, explainable AI (XAI) models might not be the models with the highest accuracy, so depending on the use case requirements, engineers might select an explainable but less accurate AI algorithm. Techniques for XAI are used at every stage of the AI lifecycle, including analyzing data for model development, incorporating interpretability into the system architecture, and producing post-hoc explanations of system behavior.[1]

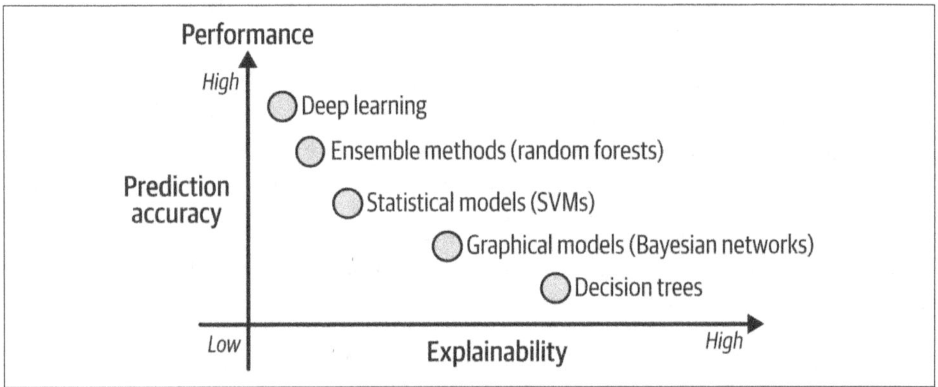

Figure 1-4. Balancing explainability and accuracy is a common challenge in AI systems

Data transparency
: Openness about the training data used to build an AI model, including its sources, characteristics, and potential biases or limitations.

Algorithmic transparency
: Visibility into the AI algorithms and how they process input data to generate outputs or decisions. This includes understanding the features, weights, and logic the model uses.

1 For further reading on this and other topics introduced in this chapter, see the list of references at the end of the chapter.

Governance transparency
: Documenting key decisions made during an AI system's development process, establishing clear protocols and responsibilities, and ensuring organizational oversight. This aspect is particularly relevant to compliance with the EU AI Act.

Communication transparency
: Sharing information about the AI system's purpose, capabilities, and limitations with relevant stakeholders in a timely, clear, and accessible manner.

AI transparency aims to open the "black box" representing the internal operations of AI systems, which are often complex and opaque. This enables humans to understand the inner workings of the systems and audit them for errors or biases, fostering trust in their use.

Examples of metrics to define and track transparency in AI systems include the following:

Explainability index
: How easily the system's decisions can be explained to users. This depends on the availability of explanations throughout the system's lifecycle, the types of explanations provided (e.g., feature importance, counterfactual examples, visual aids), and the scope of those explanations (whether they address global model behavior or local, individual predictions).

Documentation completeness
: Availability and clarity of documentation on the AI system's purpose, functionality, limitations, model training details, and feature engineering process.

Algorithmic auditability
: Ease of auditing AI algorithms for compliance and performance.

Diversity, Non-Discrimination, and Fairness

Discussion about bias and fairness in machine learning has become a hot topic over the past decade. Because data collected in an unequal manner and processed by non-diverse teams could potentially cause harm, incorporating diversity and inclusion throughout the entire AI system lifecycle is a clear requirement for trustworthy AI. This includes accessibility, a user-centric approach that guarantees that the usability of the AI system takes everyone into account—especially people with disabilities.

Inclusive engineering (*https://oreil.ly/n3qlT*) is defined as "the process of ensuring that engineering products and services are accessible and inclusive of all users, and are as free as possible from discrimination and bias, throughout their lifecycle." This approach is crucial in the development of AI systems, extending beyond just technical engineering to encompass broader social considerations.

Potential biases should be identified and addressed at every stage of AI system development. It is vital to establish a well-defined strategy or set of procedures to mitigate bias and promote fairness, both in the collection and use of input data and in the algorithm design. In this book, I focus on the CRISP-ML(Q) (*https://oreil.ly/srSRa*) development process model to specify a fair and effective AI system development strategy. This model requires establishing processes for testing and monitoring for potential biases and detecting non-representativeness in data across all phases of development.

Evaluating the complete end-to-end AI development workflow for fairness is important for building successful AI systems. Improving diversity and representativeness in AI systems is a step toward compliance with the EU AI Act and providing value for all users of those systems. Establishing a robust mechanism for flagging issues related to bias, discrimination, or poor performance—such as through bias detection tools, categorized reporting systems, and clear reporting guidance for affected individuals—helps developers and end users become aware of and address these issues.

An often underestimated and less technical aspect of an organization's data culture is educational and awareness initiatives for bias and fairness in AI. These initiatives are intended to help AI product managers, designers, and engineers become more aware of the possible bias they can inject while designing and developing AI systems.

The EU AI Act ensures that every entity along the AI system's value chain, from producer to deployer, is responsible for providing users with a fair and ethical experience. Several metrics are used to evaluate fairness in AI systems, and technical approaches for fairness improvement and bias mitigation can be applied before modeling (preprocessing), at the point of modeling (in-processing), or after modeling (post-processing), as illustrated in Figure 1-5.

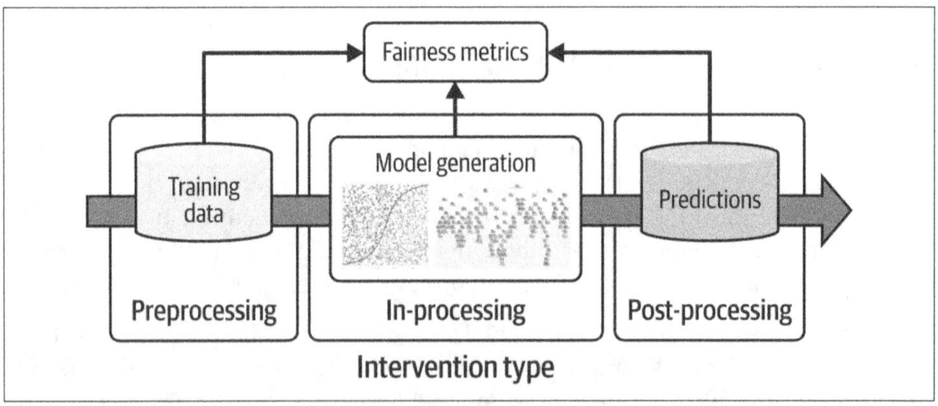

Figure 1-5. Various metrics and approaches can be implemented at different stages of the modeling process to ensure equitable outcomes and reduce bias (source: https://oreil.ly/CGjLK)

Table 1-1 lists some metrics that are commonly used to evaluate fairness and non-discrimination. These metrics quantify potential biases or disparities in the AI model's predictions across different demographic groups.

Table 1-1. Preprocessing, in-processing, and post-processing fairness metrics

Metric category/name	Definition
Preprocessing	
Statistical/demographic parity	Ensures equal probability of being classified with positive labels across groups
Disparate impact	Measures the ratio of positive classification rates between unprivileged and privileged groups
Individual fairness	Ensures similar individuals receive similar treatment
In-processing	
Equal opportunity	Ensures equal true positive rates across different groups
Equalized odds	Requires equal true positive and false positive rates across protected groups
Overall accuracy equality	Compares relative accuracy rates between different groups
Treatment equality	Considers the ratio of false negatives to false positives
Post-processing	
Test fairness/calibration	Ensures equal probability of a positive outcome given a particular score across groups
Well calibration	Requires predicted probabilities to match actual probabilities across groups
Balance for positive/negative class	Ensures equal expected scores for positive and negative classes across groups
Generalized entropy index	Measures individual-level fairness impacts of classification outcomes

Societal and Environmental Well-Being

AI can have positive or negative impacts depending on how it is used. The EU AI Act addresses the societal and environmental implications of trustworthy AI.

AI technology has proven negative impacts on the environment. The primary environmental concerns associated with AI include energy consumption, carbon footprint, e-waste, and indirect environmental impacts. AI and machine learning models, especially large ones, require significant computational power (as visualized in Figure 1-6). The data centers housing these processors thus require vast amounts of energy to run and to cool, which means large-scale AI systems have a significant carbon footprint. To mitigate this concern, efforts are being made to power data centers with renewable energy sources. The production of AI hardware also requires precious metals and rare earth elements, which can be environmentally damaging (in terms of extraction, resource depletion, and recycling challenges). Additionally, hardware quickly becomes obsolete, contributing to electronic waste.

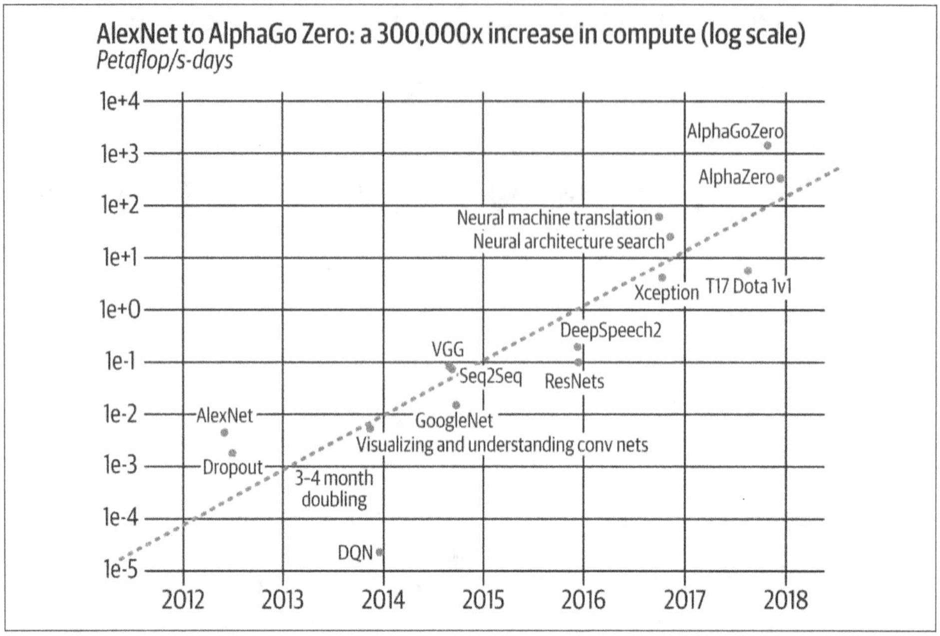

Figure 1-6. The amount of computing resources used to train deep learning models increased 300,000-fold between 2012 and 2018 (source: https://oreil.ly/WJOOw)

Depending on its applications, AI can have indirect effects on the environment as well. For instance, AI-driven automation can lead to increased production capacities and potentially increased resource consumption. Conversely, AI can optimize systems to be more energy-efficient, reduce waste, or enhance resource management, thereby potentially having a positive impact.

As well as model accuracy, the proposed "Green AI" approach (*https://oreil.ly/jGAsk*) considers *efficiency*, measured as the number of floating-point operations (flops) required to generate a result, as a key evaluation criterion. Financial operations (FinOps), a cloud financial management practice that helps organizations efficiently manage their cloud spending, can also be leveraged to address the environmental and financial impacts of AI.

With regard to the societal aspect, AI is changing the way we work in three key ways: by automating tasks, reshaping work processes, and affecting required job skills. Job displacement is an important concern, as AI has the potential to automate many roles—especially those that involve repetitive tasks (*https://oreil.ly/7Pdjg*). At the same time, AI technology has the potential to create new job roles (*https://oreil.ly/zFqNJ*) that demand advanced technological and analytical skills, such as machine learning engineers, data scientists, and AI ethics specialists. Additionally, AI can drive the development of innovative products and services, opening up new career opportunities in emerging sectors like AI-driven digital assistants and smart devices.

A related concern is that the rise of AI is leading to increased job polarization (*https://oreil.ly/hW0gZ*), with demand for high-skilled workers growing and low-skilled positions facing obsolescence. This worsens income inequality and creates challenges for those without access to education and training. As a result, AI in the workplace can lead to increased stress, anxiety, and job insecurity due to the fear of job loss and uncertainty about the future.

AI systems also have the potential to negatively impact society at large through misinformation. AI—particularly generative AI—can produce misinformation and disinformation at scale. This can harm democracy by contributing to misinformation in elections, spreading propaganda, and influencing voter behavior. Tools like ChatGPT, pi.ai, and perplexity.ai can easily create realistic but false content, which can be used to spread misinformation. AI-generated "deepfakes" (convincing but fake videos and images) can be used to manipulate public opinion, and AI-driven content personalization can create "information bubbles" where individuals are exposed only to information that reinforces their existing beliefs, leading to increased polarization and social fragmentation.

The use of AI for surveillance is also an area of concern with regard to societal well-being and privacy. Research has shown that at least 75 countries actively utilize AI technologies for surveillance (see Figure 1-6). This can lead to unauthorized data collection, privacy violations and unauthorized access to sensitive data, and potential misuse of personal information. In addition, use of AI in law enforcement, such as for predictive policing, can result in biased outcomes and discrimination against certain demographic groups.

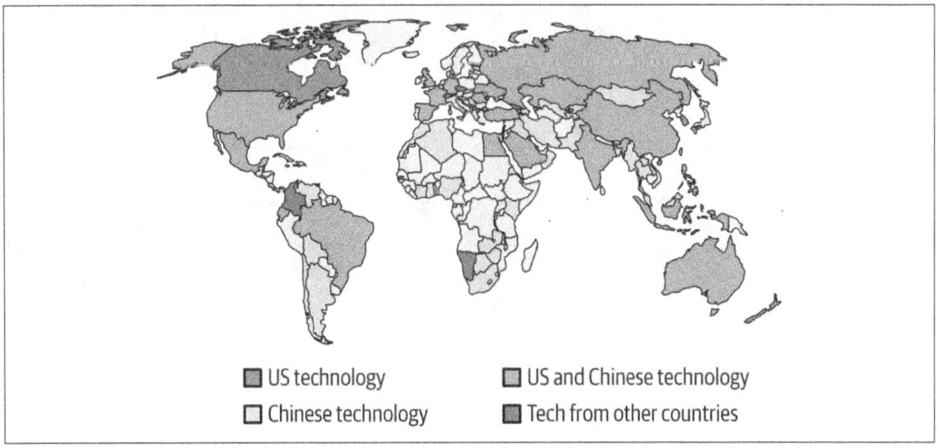

Figure 1-7. AI surveillance technology is being adopted by a larger number of countries and at a faster pace than experts typically believe (source: https://oreil.ly/9_iB7)

Addressing these challenges requires robust ethical guidelines, transparent regulatory frameworks, and ongoing public dialogue to ensure that AI is developed and deployed to support democratic values and societal well-being.

Accountability

AI systems must be developed and operated responsibly. *AI accountability* involves establishing mechanisms for holding the developers and users of AI systems responsible for the impacts of those systems throughout the entire development cycle.

Accountability implies that information about the system's purpose, design, data, and processes is available to internal and external auditors. As an example, we can refer to Google's Responsible Generative AI Toolkit, which covers risk and mitigation techniques to address safety, privacy, fairness, and accountability (see Figure 1-8). This includes maintaining detailed documentation and records of the AI development process, decision making, and outcomes to enable traceability. Logging and recordkeeping are essential for accountability. Additionally, accountability requires that an AI system can explain or justify its decisions. Finally, accountability ensures that there are mechanisms and processes for redress in place to minimize or correct negative impacts or unfair outcomes caused by AI systems. AI systems should provide appropriate opportunities for feedback, relevant explanations, and defined procedures for escalating concerns.

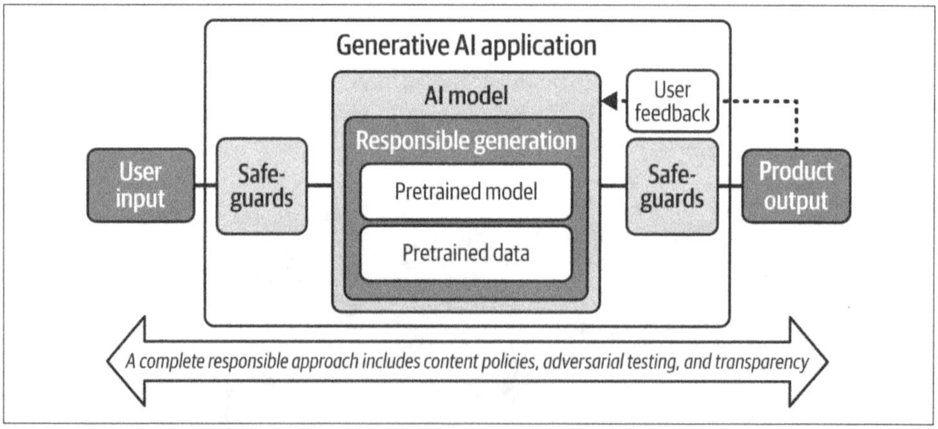

Figure 1-8. Google's Responsible Generative AI Toolkit takes a holistic approach to accountability (source: https://oreil.ly/maEI5)

In the context of trustworthy AI, key mechanisms that should be implemented to create accountability include:

Clear responsibility guidelines and processes
: Establish guidelines and clear responsibilities for various stakeholders involved in the AI system lifecycle, including developers, deployers, and users.

Transparency and explainability
: Maintain detailed documentation of the AI development process, training data, algorithms used, and decision-making criteria to enable traceability. Ensure that AI systems are transparent about their capabilities, limitations, and decision-making processes. Provide clear explanations for decisions made based on the AI predictions.

Human oversight and intervention
: Implement human checks and oversight, especially for high-stakes AI decisions, with the ability to override the AI when needed.

Auditing and evaluation
: Conduct regular internal and third-party audits to identify and eliminate biases, ensuring compliance with regulations and ethical standards. By systematically auditing their AI systems using the CRISP-ML(Q) process model, organizations can assess the systems' quality, reliability, and trustworthiness. The audit depth and focus areas can be tailored based on the risk and criticality of the use case.

Redress and complaint mechanisms
: Establish user-friendly channels for submitting complaints, feedback, or requests for explanations about AI decisions. Provide clear processes for affected individuals to challenge decisions and seek remedy.

Trustworthy AI is the foundational concept behind the legislation of the EU AI Act. You should now have a general understanding of the seven key requirements of trustworthy AI systems. Next, we'll take a look at how the Act itself is structured.

The EU AI Act in a Nutshell

The EU AI Act focuses on promoting human-centered and trustworthy artificial intelligence. Its primary objective is to foster innovation while ensuring a high level of protection for health, safety, and fundamental rights as outlined in the Charter—including democracy, the rule of law, and environmental protection—and mitigating the potential harmful effects of AI systems in use in the European Union. To fully understand the EU AI Act, it is essential to grasp its scope, who it applies to, and the timeline for compliance with the AI system requirements. This section provides a high-level overview of the EU AI Act. I'll explain the detailed requirements for different risk categories later in the book.

Per the General Provisions (*https://oreil.ly/6MMz1*), the Act establishes:

1. "Harmonized rules for the placing on the market, the putting into service, and the use of AI systems in the Union;
2. Prohibitions of certain AI practices;
3. Specific requirements for high-risk AI systems and obligations for operators of such systems;
4. Harmonized transparency rules for certain AI systems;
5. Harmonized rules for the placing on the market of general-purpose AI models;
6. Rules on market monitoring, market surveillance, governance and enforcement;
7. Measures to support innovation, with a particular focus on [small and medium-sized enterprises], including startups."

It is structured into the following main sections:

Chapters
: The Act is divided into 13 chapters covering different aspects, such as general provisions, prohibited AI practices, requirements for high-risk AI systems, governance, etc.

Articles
: Each chapter contains one or more articles laying out the specific rules and obligations. The articles are numbered sequentially throughout the Act and may be grouped into sections within each chapter. For example, Article 6 under Section 1 of Chapter III covers the "Classification Rules for High-Risk AI Systems."

Annexes
: The Act has 13 annexes that provide supplementary information such as lists, definitions, and procedures. You can navigate to a specific Annex by its number or title, e.g., "Annex III" or "High-Risk AI Systems Referred to in Article 6(2)."

Recitals
: The recitals are numbered paragraphs that explain the rationale and context behind the Act's provisions. They can help readers interpret the articles but are not binding.

Definitions

Chapter I, Article 3 of the EU AI Act provides a set of definitions for terms used in the legislation. Perhaps most importantly for the purposes of this book, it defines an *AI system* as:

> A machine-based system that is designed to operate with varying levels of autonomy and that may exhibit adaptiveness after deployment, and that, for explicit or implicit objectives, infers, from the input it receives, how to generate outputs such as predictions, content, recommendations, or decisions that can influence physical or virtual environments.

Note, however, that given the rapid pace and unpredictability of technological and AI development, this definition is not entirely static, and a dynamic regulatory tool has been integrated into the Act to allow it to adapt over time.

The definition covers a wide range of AI techniques and approaches, including:

- Machine learning methods (such as supervised, unsupervised, and semi-supervised machine learning)
- Deep learning methods
- Reinforcement learning
- Logic- and knowledge-based methods (such as logic programming, expert systems, inference and deductive engines, reasoning engines)
- Statistical approaches
- Bayesian methods
- Search and optimization approaches

Pretrained generative models such as BERT, DALL·E, Claude, Mistral, and GPT have become increasingly popular in recent years. They are developed using large-scale self-supervised learning on massive datasets and can be adjusted to various downstream tasks. These are commonly referred to as *general-purpose AI (GPAI) models*, which the Act defines as follows:

> An AI model . . . trained with a large amount of data using self-supervision at scale, that displays significant generality and is capable of competently performing a wide range of distinct tasks regardless of the way the model is placed on the market and that can be integrated into a variety of downstream systems or applications, except AI models that are used for research, development or prototyping activities before they are placed on the market

The EU AI Act aims to ensure that the previously mentioned techniques used in digital and physical products, services, or systems are safe and respect existing laws on fundamental rights and European Union values.

Key Players from Creation to Market Operation

The EU AI Act is a legal framework for developing, distributing, and using AI in the EU. This regulatory framework applies to companies and persons that make, bring in, or distribute AI systems or general-purpose AI models in the EU, even if those entities are located in a country outside the EU. Figure 1-9 visualizes the key players who are affected by the EU AI Act throughout the complete AI system lifecycle.

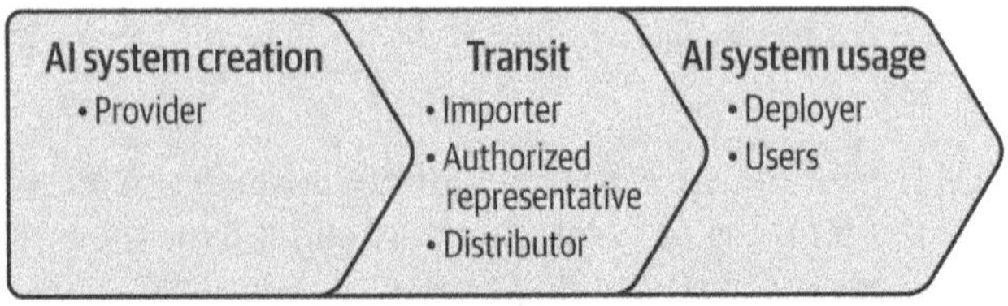

Figure 1-9. Key players

Article 3 defines these roles as follows:

- A *provider* is a natural or legal person (company, organization, or other body) that develops an AI system or GPAI model (or has one developed) and puts it on the market or uses it, whether for payment or for free, under their own name or brand.
- An *importer* is a natural or legal person in the EU who places on the market an AI system bearing the name or trademark of an entity in a non-EU country.
- A *distributor* is a natural or legal person in the supply chain, other than the provider or the importer, that makes an AI system available on the EU market.
- An *authorized representative* is a natural or legal person in the EU who has been given written permission by the provider of an AI system or GPAI model to carry out the responsibilities and procedures outlined in the Act on their behalf.
- A *deployer* is a natural or legal person using an AI system for professional activities.

A *user* is considered to be any natural person or group of persons who use or are otherwise affected by an AI system.

Classification of AI Systems by Risk Levels

Another important aspect of the EU AI Act is its risk-based approach. According to the regulation's classification system, AI systems are categorized into four risk levels:

1. Prohibited
2. High risk
3. Limited risk
4. Minimal risk

It is also important to note that GPAI models are specifically regulated and classified under this Act. In Chapter 7, I will lay out the foundation for understanding the requirements for compliance with the Act for GPAI models, and their relation to the currently popular generative AI.

The EU AI Act prohibits certain AI systems that are considered to pose an unacceptable risk. The bans are aimed at AI systems that could heavily influence or harm people's decision making or infringe upon their rights. Specifically, the Act prohibits AI practices such as using manipulative subliminal techniques, exploiting vulnerabilities based on age, disability, or social circumstances, and making high-stakes assessments based on profiling or predictive traits without sufficient human oversight. The legislation also prohibits the unregulated use of "real-time" biometric identification in public spaces, unless under strict conditions for law enforcement purposes related to significant public safety concerns. (See Chapter II, Article 5 (*https://oreil.ly/0KGOH*), for more information.)

Figure 1-10 illustrates the risk categories and their expected distribution. Roughly 20% of all AI systems are expected to be classified as high risk.

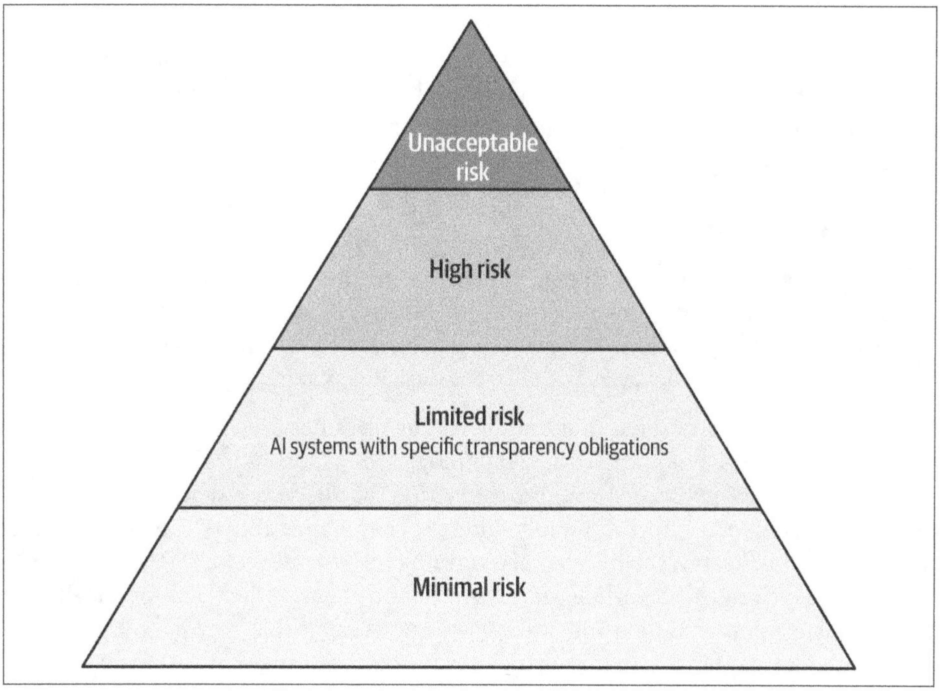

Figure 1-10. AI system risk categories

High-risk AI systems, as defined by the EU AI Act, either are intended to be used as safety components of products or are products themselves (see Chapter III (*https://oreil.ly/_o2pw*)). These AI systems are subject to specific legislation and require third-party conformity assessments. In addition, high-risk AI systems specified in a designated list (Annex III) are subject to stringent compliance requirements due to their potential impact on the health, safety, or fundamental rights of individuals. These include systems in areas such as biometrics, critical infrastructure, education, etc.

Like many products traded on the extended Single Market in the European Economic Area (EEA), AI systems classified as high risk must receive the CE marking (Figure 1-11) to be certified within the EU. This mark indicates that products sold in the EEA have been evaluated to meet stringent safety, health, and environmental protection requirements.

Figure 1-11. The CE mark

Limited-risk AI systems pose lower risks, mostly in the form of manipulation, deception, or impersonation. This category includes systems like chatbots and generative AI systems capable of producing deepfakes. For limited-risk AI systems, the main obligation is transparency—providers must disclose that the output is AI-generated and users must be made aware they are interacting with an AI system. There are also requirements to label deepfakes clearly.

The last category is minimal-risk AI systems. According to the EU AI Act, these are systems that pose little to no risk to people's safety, fundamental rights, or privacy. They include AI applications like video games, spam filters, or simple image editing tools that perform narrow tasks with limited decision-making capabilities.

It is important to understand that the EU AI Act classifies use cases (AI systems and GPAI models) and not the AI/ML technologies or algorithms themselves. Proper classification has an impact on the estimation of the AI system's requirements, because different risk categories imply different governance and MLOps architectural decisions and obligations. However, determining the risk level of an AI system can be challenging as it relies on various factors and involves classifying how the capabilities of a nondeterministic system will affect users and systems that may interact with it in the future. In Chapter 4, I outline a risk classification framework for AI systems.

Note that scientific research and military applications of AI fall outside the scope of the EU AI Act. However, so-called "dual use" technologies—systems that can be used for both civilian and military purposes—may still be subject to the Act if used in civilian contexts.

Enforcement and Implementation

The implementation of the EU AI Act follows a structured timeline. Here are the key milestones and deadlines:

EU AI Act enters into force (August 2024)
: The Act is effective 20 days after it is published in the Official Journal of the EU.

Six months after entry into force (Q4 2024–Q1 2025)
: Prohibitions on unacceptable-risk AI systems are effective.

Nine months after entry into force (Q1 2025)
: Codes of practice for GPAI models must be finalized.

Twelve months after entry into force (Q2–Q3 2025)
: Obligations on providers of GPAI models are effective.

Eighteen months after entry into force (Q4 2025–Q1 2026)
: The Commission implements acts on post-market monitoring for high-risk AI systems.

Twenty-four months after entry into force (Q2–Q3 2026)
: Obligations on high-risk AI systems listed in Annex III become applicable. Member states must have implemented rules on penalties and established AI regulatory sandboxes.

Thirty-six months after entry into force (Q4 2026–Q1 2027)
: Obligations for high-risk AI systems not prescribed in Annex III but subject to existing EU product safety laws are effective.

By the end of 2030
: Obligations for specific AI systems that are components of large-scale EU IT systems in areas like security and justice become applicable.

This timeline, depicted in Figure 1-12, implies that organizations that create high-risk AI systems today have a grace period to prepare their internal processes. They are responsible for complying fully with the provisions of the Act by the end of the grace period (June 2026).

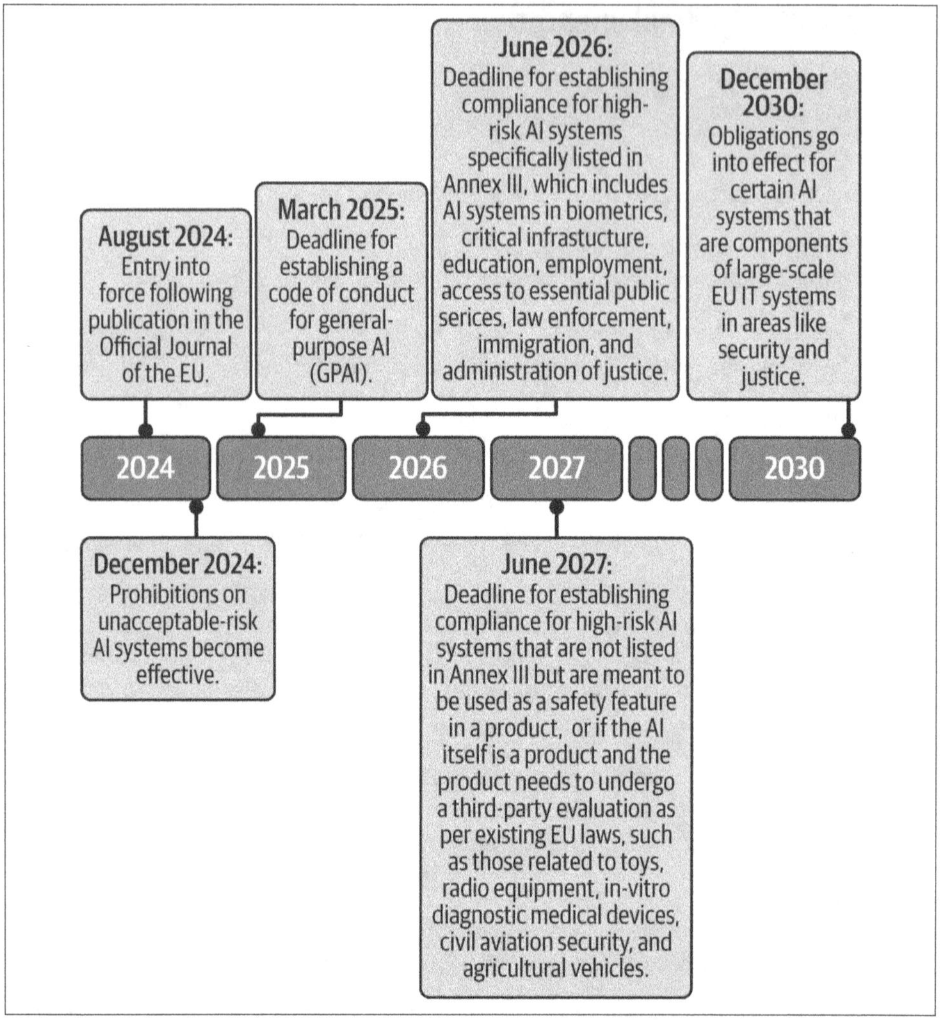

Figure 1-12. Timeline outlining the key milestones and deadlines for the implementation of the EU AI Act

The Full Picture of Compliance

Many organizations using and embedding AI technology into their products are asking the same question: "What does the EU AI Act mean for us?" The Act aims to ensure that all digital and physical products that incorporate AI—whether as a feature or as a core function—are used in a safe and ethical manner, in line with EU fundamental rights. To this end, the Act treats AI systems as regulated products. Like other products in the EU market, AI systems that are considered high risk must be CE marked to indicate compliance, as described earlier, or they are not permitted for use.

Table 1-2 briefly outlines the process steps needed to meet the EU AI Act's requirements for this category of AI systems.

> Again, the author is not a lawyer. This book does not provide legal advice.

Table 1-2. The end-to-end process for EU AI Act compliance

EU AI Act compliance step	Guiding questions
AI system inventory and risk classification	• How many AI systems are in place already or are intended to be put in production? • What risk categories do each of these AI systems belong to? • Do any of them utilize models that are classified as systemic risk GPAI models?
Identification of compliance requirements	• What requirements do we need to fulfill?
Compliance operationalization	• What processes, structures, engineering practices, and roles need to be established to comply with the Act?
Pre-market compliance verification	• What has to be done before placing AI systems on the market and putting them into service? • What internal and external conformity assessments are required for compliance verification? • How do we CE-mark our AI systems? • Where should our AI systems be registered?
Post-market continuous compliance	• What has to be done to ensure compliance after putting the AI systems into service?

Let's take a closer look at these essential steps for providers and deployers of AI systems to ensure conformity with the EU AI Act:

1. *AI system inventory and risk classification*

   Before setting up the technical and organizational processes for achieving compliance, you must determine the required scope of compliance measures. Start with an inventory of all AI systems that are currently in use or in development. Then assign a risk level to each of those systems (I discuss risk classification for AI systems in detail in Chapter 4). Any AI use cases that fall into the prohibited category must be discontinued.

2. *Identification of compliance requirements*

   The compliance measures to implement will depend on the results of the risk classification. It's important to distinguish between obligations for AI systems and for GPAI models used in those systems, which may be subject to transparency obligations or systemic risk requirements. The Act lays out concrete requirements for both categories.

3. *Compliance operationalization*
   Identifying compliance requirements allows you to define the scope of the technical and organizational processes needed for conformity with the EU AI Act. This includes establishing governance structures, engineering practices, and clearly defined roles. The Act outlines specific obligations, such as implementing risk management measures, maintaining technical documentation, ensuring human oversight, and guaranteeing the accuracy, robustness, and security of AI systems. This phase, which is the focus of this book, also involves setting up a quality management system that covers testing, incident reporting, data governance, record retention, and logging.

4. *Pre-market compliance verification*
   The next step is to demonstrate compliance through internal and, where necessary, external conformity assessments. Once these are completed, the AI systems must be CE marked and registered in the EU database. These steps are mandatory before the systems can be placed on the market or put into service.

5. *Post-market continuous compliance*
   The final phase focuses on ensuring that the AI systems continue to meet the requirements of the Act throughout their lifecycle. This involves demonstrating continued adherence to compliance standards, regardless of changes to the system, through continuous monitoring of system performance and addressing any issues that arise to maintain alignment with regulatory requirements.

Penalties for EU AI Act Violation

The EU AI Act introduces significant penalties and fines for companies that violate its rules and requirements. Table 1-3 provides an overview.

Table 1-3. Penalties for violating the terms of EU AI Act

Violation	Penalties
Prohibited AI practices (AI practices listed in Article 5, such as exploiting vulnerabilities, social scoring, real-time biometric identification in public spaces, etc.)	Administrative fines of up to €35 million or 7% of total worldwide annual turnover for the preceding financial year, whichever is higher
Noncompliance with requirements for high-risk AI systems under Article 10	Administrative fines of up to €30 million or 6% of total worldwide annual turnover, whichever is higher
Noncompliance with other obligations (apart from Articles 5 and 10)	Administrative fines of up to €20 million or 4% of total worldwide annual turnover, whichever is higher
Providing incorrect, incomplete, or misleading information to authorities	Administrative fines of up to €10 million or 2% of total worldwide annual turnover, whichever is higher

Existing AI Regulations and Standards

The EU AI Act serves as a comprehensive regulatory model for non-EU nations, underscoring the balance between innovation and trustworthy AI. Its strict regulations on biometric systems and high-risk AI applications set a high standard for AI governance globally. Let's briefly review the existing landscape of AI regulations:

UNESCO AI ethics recommendations
: The Recommendation on the Ethics of Artificial Intelligence (*https://oreil.ly/Qr8eM*), adopted in November 2021 by UNESCO's 193 Member States, provides a framework for ethical AI development. It outlines core values and principles for the ethical development and deployment of AI, including respect for human rights, inclusion and diversity, fairness and non-discrimination, transparency and explainability, accountability, safety and security, and sustainability. The recommendation aims to influence ethical AI practices globally and includes innovative tools and methodologies to translate ethical principles into practice.

US executive order on trustworthy AI
: The Executive Order on the Safe, Secure, and Trustworthy Development and Use of Artificial Intelligence (*https://oreil.ly/zRfHi*), issued in October 2023, emphasizes the potential benefits and risks of AI. It highlights the importance of responsible AI governance to address societal issues and prevent negative consequences such as fraud, bias, and threats to national security. The order stresses the need for collaboration across government, industry, academia, and civil society to ensure the safe and responsible development and application of AI.

China generative AI services law
: The Interim Measures for the Administration of Generative Artificial Intelligence Services (*https://oreil.ly/Axc-r*), jointly issued by the Cyberspace Administration of China (CAC) and six other government agencies in July 2023, signal China's proactive approach to regulating generative AI services (including models and related technologies that produce text, graphics, audio, and video). The regulation applies to all entities offering these services to the general Chinese population. The Interim Measures recognize the potential for foreign investment while also promoting innovation and research. Future artificial intelligence laws are expected to expand the regulation's scope beyond generative AI. Given the potential penalties or shutdowns for noncompliant services operating in China, it is essential to ensure compliance.

National Institute of Standards and Technology (NIST) AI Risk Management Framework
: The NIST Artificial Intelligence Risk Management Framework: Generative Artificial Intelligence Profile (*https://oreil.ly/sISXu*) released in July 2024 identifies 12 key risks unique to or exacerbated by GenAI technologies that organizations

should take care to identify and mitigate. These include risks related to chemical, biological, radiological, or nuclear information, dangerous or violent recommendations, data privacy, environmental impacts, information integrity and security, and intellectual property. The framework proposes over 400 actions organizations can take to manage these risks.

Institute of Electrical and Electronics Engineers Standards Association (IEEE SA) recommended practice
: The IEEE's Recommended Practice for Organizational Governance of Artificial Intelligence (*https://oreil.ly/Pd2qj*) outlines governance criteria for AI development and use within organizations, including safety, transparency, accountability, responsibility, and bias minimization. It also provides steps for implementation, auditing, training, and compliance. The document aims to promote responsible AI practices by integrating internal governance structures with external AI governance instruments.

These laws and frameworks collectively aim to regulate AI in a way that promotes innovation while ensuring safety, transparency, and respect for human rights, similar to the objectives of the EU AI Act.

Conclusion

The EU AI Act focuses on promoting the development and use of human-centered and trustworthy artificial intelligence, to safeguard health, safety, fundamental rights, democracy, the rule of law, and environmental protection within the European Union. In this first chapter, we examined the concept of trustworthiness in AI, which is based on three pillars: lawfulness, ethics, and robustness. I outlined the seven key requirements for trustworthy AI systems, which include human agency and oversight; technical robustness and safety; privacy and data governance; transparency; diversity, non-discrimination, and fairness; societal and environmental well-being; and accountability.

Understanding the Act requires knowledge of its scope, who it applies to, and the established timeline for AI system compliance. The EU AI Act is a comprehensive risk-based legal framework that establishes rules for the development, distribution, and use of AI systems and GPAI models. It applies to businesses and individuals both within and outside the European Union, including providers, importers, distributors, authorized representatives, deployers, and users of AI systems.

The Act classifies AI systems into four categories based on risk and establishes corresponding obligations. It prohibits AI systems that pose unacceptable risks, imposes strict requirements on high-risk systems, and mandates transparency and labeling for limited-risk systems. The Act also lays out a specific set of obligations for GPAI models, with additional rules for models deemed to pose systemic risk. These regulations apply not only to the AI systems themselves but to all organizations involved in their development and deployment across the AI value chain.

Classifying the AI systems in use in your organization and identifying the corresponding compliance requirements will help determine the scope of required data and AI governance measures, as well as the necessary AI engineering practices. In the next chapter, I'll discuss the CRISP-ML(Q) structured AI system development process and MLOps, which provides technical and organizational best practices for AI system operationalization.

Further Reading

Ali, Sajid, Tamer Abuhmed, Shaker El-Sappagh, Khan Muhammad, José M. Alonso-Moral, Roberto Confalonieri, Riccardo Guidotti, et al. "Explainable Artificial Intelligence (XAI): What We Know and What Is Left to Attain Trustworthy Artificial Intelligence." *Information Fusion* 99 (November 2023): 101805. *https://oreil.ly/WERsh*.

Braiek, Houssem Ben, and Foutse Khomh. "Machine Learning Robustness: A Primer." arXiv preprint arXiv:2404.00897, May 2024. *https://oreil.ly/6iJoo*.

Caton, Simon, and Christian Haas. "Fairness in Machine Learning: A Survey." *ACM Computing Surveys* 56, no. 7 (2024): 166. *https://oreil.ly/ykP9I*.

High-Level Expert Group on AI (AI HLEG). *The Assessment List for Trustworthy Artificial Intelligence (ALTAI) for Self-Assessment*. European Commission, July 2020. *https://oreil.ly/QNzCW*.

Li, Bo, Peng Qi, Bo Liu, Shuai Di, Jingen Liu, Jiquan Pei, Jinfeng Yi, and Bowen Zhou. "Trustworthy AI: From Principles to Practices." *ACM Computing Surveys* 55, no. 9 (2023): 177. *https://oreil.ly/sAQ99*.

Malhotra, Tanya. "Top Artificial Intelligence (AI) Governance Laws and Frameworks." *Marktechpost*, May 2, 2024. *https://oreil.ly/OvYAI*.

Monteith, Scott, Tasha Glenn, John R. Geddes, Peter C. Whybrow, Eric Achtyes, and Micheal Bauer. "Artificial Intelligence and Increasing Misinformation." *The British Journal of Psychiatry* 224, no. 2 (2024): 33–35. *https://oreil.ly/KgesS*.

Novelli, Claudio, Mariarosaria Taddeo, and Luciano Floridi. "Accountability in Artificial Intelligence: What It Is and How It Works." *AI & SOCIETY* 39 (2023): 1871–82. *https://oreil.ly/yEJ1b*.

Radclyffe, Charless, Mafalda Ribeiro, and Robert H. Wortham. "The Assessment List for Trustworthy Artificial Intelligence: A Review and Recommendations." *Frontiers in Artificial Intelligence* 6 (2023): 1020592. *https://oreil.ly/bmSIN*.

Reinsel, David, John Gantz, and John Rydning. *Data Age 2025: The Evolution of Data to Life-Critical*. Seagate, April 2017. *https://oreil.ly/PYxM2*.

Repetto, Marco. "Fostering Robust AI: Understanding Its Importance and Navigating the EU Artificial Intelligence Act." CertX, June 12, 2023. *https://oreil.ly/U2WUK*.

Schwartz, Roy, Jesse Dodge, Noah A. Smith, and Oren Etzioni. "Green AI." *Communications of the ACM* 63, no. 12 (2020): 54–63. *https://oreil.ly/S7AJT*.

Studer, Stefan, Thanh Binh Bui, Christian Drescher, Alexander Hanuschkin, Ludwig Winkler, Steven Peters, and Klaus-Robert Mueller. "Towards CRISP-ML(Q): A Machine Learning Process Model with Quality Assurance Methodology." arXiv preprint arXiv:2003.05155, February 2021. *https://oreil.ly/srSRa*.

Turri, Violet. "What Is Explainable AI?" *SEI Blog* (Carnegie Mellon University Software Engineering Institute), January 17, 2022. *https://oreil.ly/pciy_*.

Wu, Carole-Jean, Ramya Raghavendra, Udit Gupta, Bilge Acun, Newsha Ardalani, Kiwan Maeng, Gloria Chang, et al. "Sustainable AI: Environmental Implications, Challenges and Opportunities." arXiv preprint arXiv:2111.00364, January 2022. *https://oreil.ly/vplRJ*.

CHAPTER 2

AI Engineering: A Proactive Compliance Catalyst

AI engineering can support companies in complying with the EU AI Act by promoting appropriate tools and practices. A key part of this is machine learning operations (MLOps), which focuses on the operationalization of ML models. Together, these disciplines provide the technical components and repeatable processes necessary for designing, developing, deploying, and maintaining AI systems in a reliable and compliant way.

Implementing engineering practices such as automation, versioning, testing, reproducibility, deployment, and monitoring helps ensure AI systems meet the EU AI Act's requirements for high-quality, safe, and trustworthy AI. This chapter introduces some practical frameworks that you can use to design and architect compliant AI systems (although these are by no means the only options). Tools like the Machine Learning Canvas and the MLOps Stack Canvas are designed to address key requirements such as risk management, technical documentation, transparency, robustness, and post-market monitoring. We'll also discuss CRISP-ML(Q), a machine learning process model with built-in quality assurance that emphasizes risk assessment, quality assurance, comprehensive documentation, and continuous monitoring throughout the AI lifecycle. The synergy between CRISP-ML(Q) and AI engineering enables organizations to proactively engineer compliance into the AI lifecycle, ensuring that AI systems are developed and deployed in an EU AI Act–compliant manner.

Structuring the AI System Development Process with CRISP-ML(Q)

In this section, we'll explore developing *AI-powered applications*, which are software applications that embed machine learning models as a technological solution for one or several features. We'll focus on CRISP-ML(Q), the Cross-Industry Standard Process for the development of Machine Learning applications with Quality assurance methodology. CRISP-ML(Q) offers a systematic and quality-focused approach for developing AI systems, facilitating compliance with the EU AI Act across various risk levels.

> Appendix A introduces the principles of designing AI-powered applications with an emphasis on aligning AI initiatives with business goals and user needs. As explained in the appendix, the "backward thinking" approach and the Machine Learning Canvas offer practical frameworks for planning and executing AI projects effectively.
>
> The Machine Learning Canvas underlines the importance of a holistic perspective, which incorporates the value proposition, monitoring, and the integration of both prediction and training components within a larger software system. Furthermore, it highlights critical considerations around data management, ethical implications in feature engineering, and the collaborative nature of building successful AI products. See Appendix A for further details.

As described in the paper "Towards CRISP-ML(Q): A Machine Learning Process Model with Quality Assurance Methodology" (*https://oreil.ly/srSRa*), CRISP-ML(Q) builds upon the established CRISP-DM framework (see Figure 2-1). The motivation for extending CRISP-DM was twofold: it focused on data mining rather than ML models deployed over extended periods, and it lacked guidance on quality assurance. CRISP-ML(Q) better meets the needs and challenges of designing and operationalizing machine learning products, with a strong emphasis on quality assurance.

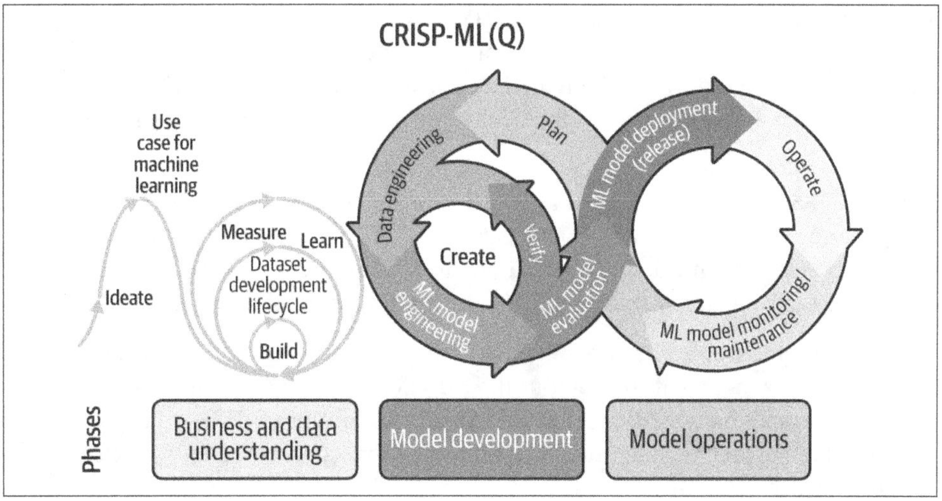

Figure 2-1. The phases of the CRISP-ML(Q) framework

Risk Mitigation, Quality Assurance, and Alignment with the EU AI Act

Working with CRISP-ML(Q) will help you incorporate the requirements of the EU AI Act for high-risk and limited-risk AI systems into your development processes. The framework emphasizes continuous risk assessment throughout the ML development process, from understanding the business needs to deployment and monitoring. This approach aligns with the EU AI Act's requirements for ongoing quality assessment and risk management.

As you learned in Chapter 1, the EU AI Act defines four levels of risk for AI systems: unacceptable, high, limited, and minimal or no risk. CRISP-ML(Q) can accommodate these different classifications by tailoring its quality assurance methodology accordingly. For example, high-risk AI systems will require more extensive testing, documentation, and human oversight than limited- or minimal-risk systems.

For each ML development phase, CRISP-ML(Q) defines specific requirements and constraints to address risks (such as bias, overfitting, or lack of reproducibility) that could impact the success of the ML system. Appropriate quality assurance methods, such as cross-validation and thorough documentation processes, are implemented to mitigate these risks. This supports compliance with the EU AI Act's requirement that providers establish robust risk management systems to identify, assess, and mitigate risks.

CRISP-ML(Q) also mandates that AI systems be thoroughly tested prior to deployment to ensure they perform consistently for their intended purpose and comply with requirements. Testing is carried out against defined metrics and thresholds. This meets the EU AI Act's requirement for pre-market conformity assessments for high-risk AI systems. Additionally, CRISP-ML(Q) incorporates continuous post-deployment monitoring to detect performance degradation or deviations. Serious incidents must be reported. The EU AI Act has similar requirements for market surveillance, human oversight, and incident reporting by providers and users of high-risk AI.

Finally, CRISP-ML(Q) requires that you document the entire ML development process, including the risk management measures. This is important because the EU AI Act introduces technical documentation and transparency obligations to ensure humans are appropriately informed when interacting with AI systems.

In summary, the framework's quality assurance methodology and emphasis on continuous risk management throughout the ML lifecycle are well aligned with the risk-based approach mandated by the EU AI Act. Adopting CRISP-ML(Q) can help organizations proactively identify and mitigate the risks of AI systems to ensure safer and more trustworthy AI.

The Six Phases of CRISP-ML(Q)

As described in the previous section, a key principle of CRISP-ML(Q) is integrating quality assurance practices into each phase of the AI development lifecycle. This includes defining requirements, identifying risks, and applying risk mitigation methods based on established best practices. As a result, CRISP-ML(Q) provides a comprehensive methodology for developing a high-quality, sustainable AI system that meets the defined business objectives and is ready for real-world deployment.

CRISP-ML(Q) defines six key phases in the ML development process:

1. Business and data understanding
2. Data preparation
3. Modeling
4. Evaluation
5. Deployment
6. Monitoring and maintenance

Each phase involves specific tasks and results in specific outputs. Importantly, while CRISP-ML(Q) is often depicted as a sequential process, it's actually iterative and admits several backward trajectories—insights gained in later phases often require revisiting earlier steps.

Let's briefly examine each phase in more detail.

Business and data understanding

The initial phase focuses on defining the ML application's business goals and success criteria. Key tasks include:

- Determine business objectives
- Identify data sources
- Collect initial data
- Describe data
- Explore data
- Verify data quality

Close collaboration between business stakeholders and the data science team is critical to ensure business alignment. The main outputs include the project objectives, success criteria, and an initial assessment of data quality and project feasibility.

Data preparation

After business goals are defined and communicated across the organization, you are ready to prepare the data for modeling. Data preparation tasks include:

- Select data
- Clean data
- Construct data
- Integrate data
- Format data

This phase involves feature engineering, handling missing values, and normalizing data. Outputs include the final dataset(s) for modeling and documentation of how they were constructed.

Model engineering

The core machine learning work happens in this third phase, which is also called the *modeling* phase. Key tasks here include:

- Select modeling techniques
- Generate test design
- Build model
- Assess model

You should build and compare multiple models using appropriate evaluation metrics and cross-validation techniques. Domain knowledge can be incorporated to improve results. This phase concludes by selecting the best-performing model(s).

Model evaluation

Before deploying a model, you must thoroughly evaluate it from both a data science and a business perspective. Model evaluation tasks include:

- Evaluate prediction results
- Review process
- Decide on next steps

The model is tested on independent data to validate its real-world performance. You should also examine the explainability and robustness of the model, and business stakeholders should verify that the model meets the defined success criteria. Outputs are the final model approval and deployment plan.

Model deployment

Deploying the model into the production environment involves tasks such as the following:

- Plan deployment
- Plan monitoring and maintenance
- Produce final report
- Review project

Deployment can range from generating a simple report to persisting the model in the model repository or embedding it into a complex production system. Create monitoring and maintenance plans to ensure the model performs well over time.

Model monitoring and maintenance

ML models can degrade in performance if not proactively monitored and updated. This final phase involves these tasks:

- Monitor the model
- Evaluate the model
- Retrain/update the model as needed

Data inputs, model predictions, and business outcomes are continuously tracked to identify issues. Models are retrained on new data to prevent drift. The ML application is maintained and enhanced based on changing business needs.

CRISP-ML(Q) provides a robust framework for developing machine learning applications. By implementing a systematic process and integrating risk identification with quality assurance, organizations can enhance the success rate and business impact of their ML initiatives while guaranteeing compliance with the EU AI Act.

Understanding MLOps

In this section we'll turn our attention to *MLOps*, a set of processes and technical components designed to ensure AI systems are developed, deployed, and maintained in a continuous and reliable manner. By understanding and implementing MLOps, you establish the technical foundation necessary for complying with the EU AI Act, as many of its requirements depend on MLOps practices.

MLOps practices are not tied to a specific language, framework, platform, or infrastructure. However, deploying ML in production involves various interconnected components. Figure 2-2 shows a canonical architecture for ML systems. In the next section, we'll explore an application- and industry-neutral MLOps Stack Canvas framework that can be used to specify appropriate components.

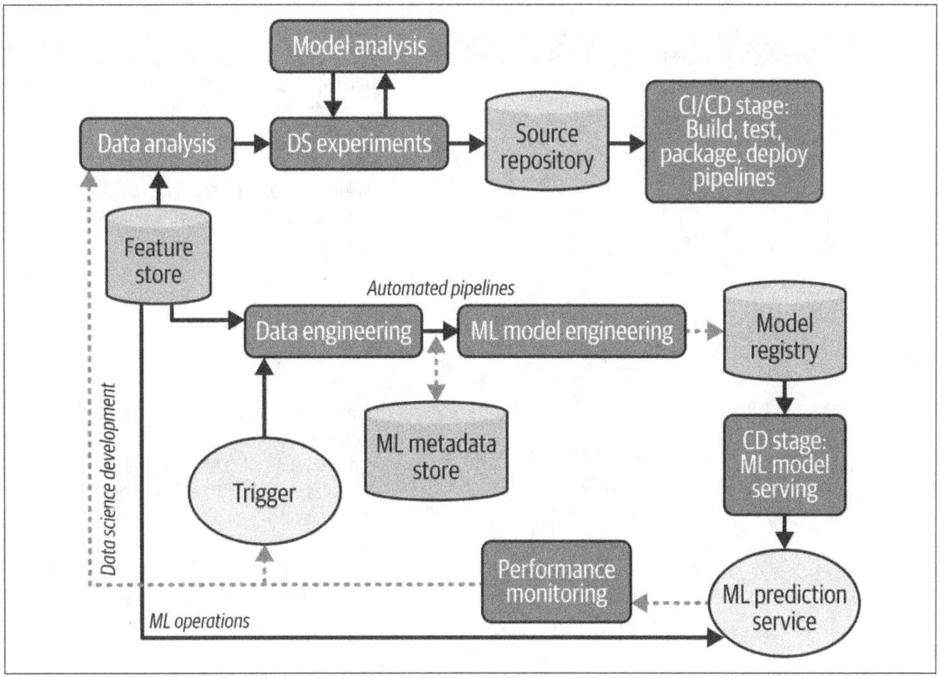

Figure 2-2. A canonical architecture for ML systems

ML/AI technologies are currently widely utilized across various applications. Consequently, software systems often incorporate ML/AI components as standard practice. However, as organizations seek to enhance their products or processes with machine learning, many ML models remain in the experimental phase or fail to move beyond the proof of concept (PoC) stage. To increase your chances of success, when designing ML systems it's essential to clearly define the interface, algorithms, data, infrastructure, and hardware to ensure they meet the specific requirements of the software system.

MLOps has emerged as a discipline aimed at automating the development and deployment of machine learning models. Its primary value lies in optimizing business outcomes by improving the efficiency, reliability, and scalability of ML workflows through a supporting technology stack and infrastructure. MLOps also focuses on automating and streamlining the development lifecycle, facilitating deployment into production for newly developed ML models. To ensure model quality and adaptability, any changes in the code, training data, or model should automatically trigger the build process in the ML development pipeline.

Table 2-1 summarizes the core principles of MLOps: automation, version control, rigorous testing, reproducibility, streamlined deployment, and continuous monitoring. Later in the book, we will explore relevant requirements for the EU AI Act and how the MLOps engineering principles address these requirements.

Table 2-1. MLOps core principles

MLOps principle	Key aspects	Why is it important?
Automation focuses on transitioning experimental ML models into fully operational production systems. The goal is to automate repetitive tasks in the areas of data preparation, model training, evaluation, deployment, and monitoring.	Consider automating: • Data pipelines for data ingestion, cleaning, and feature engineering • Model training and hyperparameter tuning • Testing and validation of models • Deployment of models to production environments • Monitoring and retraining of models • Model auditing	Automation permits increased developer efficiency and productivity and reduces manual errors. It also enables faster iteration and experimentation, making it easier to scale machine learning workflows. Tools like DVC, Airflow, Kubeflow, and MLflow can be used to build automated ML pipelines.
Version control is crucial for tracking and managing changes across the ML lifecycle.	What should be versioned: • Data: Tracking different versions of datasets used for training and evaluation • Code: Version control of ML code, scripts, and notebooks • Models: Versioning trained model artifacts and associated metadata • Configurations: Tracking hyperparameters, environment configurations, etc.	Proper versioning is essential as it allows for reproducibility of experiments and results, enabling you to roll back to previous versions if any issues occur. It also facilitates collaboration between team members and provides the traceability needed for auditing and compliance with industry standards. Tools like Git, DVC, and MLflow can be used to version different ML assets.

MLOps principle	Key aspects	Why is it important?
Thorough *testing* is essential for building robust and reliable ML systems.	Key types of tests include: • Unit tests to test individual components and functions • Integration tests to test interactions between components • Data tests to validate data quality and integrity • Model tests to evaluate performance and behavior (fairness, non-discrimination, bias, robustness)	Automating testing and integrating it into continuous integration/continuous delivery (CI/CD) pipelines helps catch issues early in the development process. The benefits of comprehensive testing include improved model quality and reliability, faster debugging and issue resolution, and increased confidence in model behavior. Tools like pytest, Great Expectations, and Deepchecks can be used for ML testing.
Reproducibility ensures that ML experiments and results can be reliably re-created. This is crucial for debugging, auditing, and scientific rigor.	Engineering processes that guarantee reproducibility include: • Versioning of code, data, and models • Tracking of random seeds and configurations • Documenting the model development, dependencies, and environments • Containerization of ML workflows	The benefits of reproducibility include simplifying debugging and troubleshooting, enabling validation of results by others, and supporting regulatory compliance. When it comes to improving reproducibility in ML experiments, containerization tools like Docker and workflow management and metadata management tools play a significant role.
Automated *deployment* focuses on reliably and efficiently moving ML models from development to production.	Considerations include: • Model packaging and containerization • Deployment strategies (e.g., canary, blue–green) • Scaling and load balancing • Monitoring and logging • Security and access control	Automated deployment practices allow for ML models to be brought to production more quickly, without human intervention, and for model serving to be reliable and scalable. If issues arise, the deployment process should allow for easy rollback. Tools such as Kubernetes, TensorFlow Serving, and cloud ML platforms can help streamline the model deployment process.
Monitoring ensures that ML models perform as expected in production.	Key elements to monitor include: • Model performance metrics • Data drift and concept drift • System health and resource utilization • Prediction latency and throughput • Business validation metrics • AI product health metrics	Effective monitoring enables teams to quickly detect and respond to issues, gain an understanding of model behavior in production, and make data-driven decisions on when to retrain the model. Tools like Prometheus, Grafana, and specialized ML monitoring platforms can be used to implement comprehensive monitoring.

In general, MLOps addresses the challenge of maintaining software products that incorporate ML/AI components in continuous, reliable operation. The specific activities and technical components of MLOps depend on the expected operational lifespan and performance requirements of the system.

Defining Technical Components with the MLOps Stack Canvas

This section outlines a structured approach for defining the infrastructure for an AI project. It uses the MLOps Stack Canvas framework to identify and organize the workflows, architecture, and infrastructure components needed for the MLOps stack.

As you plan for implementation, it's important to ensure that the ML models deliver measurable business value. This involves accounting for the costs associated with the infrastructure components within the MLOps stack and the costs of orchestrating and maintaining the ML system throughout its lifecycle. Key considerations include continuous integration, training, and delivery of ML assets; monitoring to ensure the system meets business objectives; and alerting mechanisms to detect and address model failures.

The ML system should also be designed to ensure reproducibility (through versioning, feature stores, and pipelines), reliability (by minimizing outages and enabling safe failovers), and efficiency (by ensuring model predictions are fast and cost-effective).

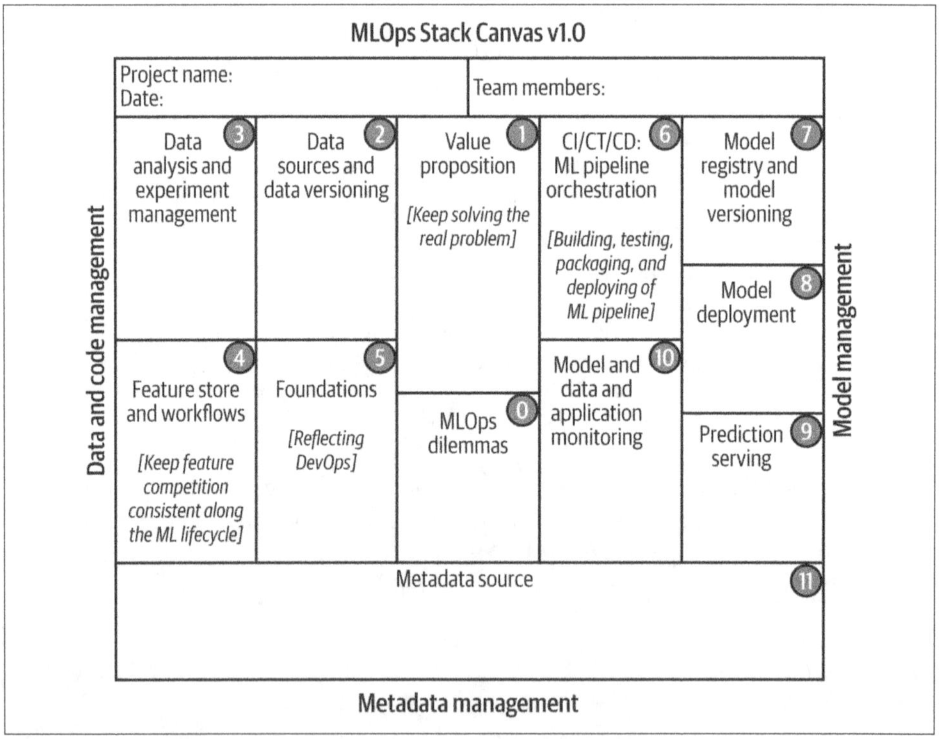

Figure 2-3. The application- and industry-neutral MLOps Stack Canvas framework to specify an architecture and infrastructure stack for ML operations

As shown in Figure 2-3, the MLOps Stack Canvas is structured into three main areas: Data and Code Management, Model Management, and Metadata Management, each with its building blocks. In the following sections, we'll go through the items in each area. Note that the general discussion about building the ML project's infrastructure should include consideration of various organizational aspects of MLOps, such as tooling, platforms, and required skills. Issues that are identified should be noted in the MLOps Dilemmas section of the canvas.

Value Proposition

We'll start with the Value Proposition (item 1 on the MLOps Stack Canvas). The framework emphasizes the value proposition as a critical element behind the motivation for building the MLOps architecture because it aims to create awareness about the pain points being addressed. Here's an example value proposition for a hypothetical "MLOps Platform":

> **For** data science and machine learning teams
> **who** need to efficiently build, train, and deploy ML models at scale.
> **The MLOps Platform** is an end-to-end machine learning platform
> **that** enables teams to rapidly develop and operationalize ML solutions to drive business value.
> **Unlike** other ML platforms that require complex setup and lack key features such as observability and monitoring
> **our MLOps platform** provides a fully managed, intuitive interface with automated workflows, built-in experiment tracking, powerful AutoML capabilities, and seamless deployment to accelerate the ML lifecycle from prototype to production.

This allows you to identify key elements such as:

Target customers
: Data science and ML teams

Need
: Efficiently building and deploying ML models at scale

Product name and category
: MLOps Platform, an end-to-end machine learning platform

Key benefit
: Rapidly develop and operationalize ML to drive business value

Competition
: Other ML platforms that are complex and lack features such as observability and monitoring

Differentiation

Fully managed, intuitive, automated, with experiment tracking, AutoML, and seamless deployment to accelerate the full ML lifecycle

Identifying the right target customers and their needs is essential for building a right-sized MLOps platform without unnecessary technical complexity.

Answering the following questions will help you confidently articulate your value proposition:

- What are we trying to do for the end user(s)?
- What is the problem?
- Why is this an important problem?
- Who is our persona? (ML engineer, data scientist, operation/business user)
- Who owns the model(s) in production?

You can learn more about crafting value propositions in Appendix A.

Data and Code Management

The Data and Code Management block of the MLOps Stack Canvas consists of technical components required for managing data and code—two essential elements of every ML system. Let's examine the next building blocks of the canvas, namely, Data Sources and Data Versioning, Data Analysis and Experiment Management, Feature Store and Workflows, and Foundations.

Data Sources and Data Versioning

Data is the backbone of any machine learning system. After articulating the business problem in the Value Proposition, the next step is Data Sources and Data Versioning. The goal here is to estimate the cost of data acquisition, storage, and processing during the business and data understanding and data preparation phases of the CRISP-ML(Q) framework. Dataset development and further processing for ML algorithms may be costly. Data versioning is essential for analyzing model performance with new data and may be a regulatory requirement.

Here are some considerations for the Data Sources and Data Versioning building block:

- Is data versioning optional or mandatory? For example, is it a regulatory requirement?
- What data sources are available (e.g., owned, public, purchased)?
- Where is that data stored (e.g., in a data lake or data warehouse)?

- Is manual labeling required? Do we have human resources for it?
- How do we version data for each trained model?
- What tooling is available for data pipelines/workflows?

You might also use the Data Landscape Canvas (*https://oreil.ly/hsXsZ*) to inventory your organization's available, accessible, and required data sources for the ML project.

Data Analysis and Experiment Management

According to the CRISP-ML(Q) framework, the project's initial phase includes running experiments and implementing a proof of concept. The Data Analysis and Experiment Management block focuses on the applicability of ML technology for specific business goals and data preparation. Here, you need to answer the following questions regarding tooling:

- What programming language will you use for analysis (e.g., R, Python, Scala, Julia, SQL)?
- What ML-specific and business evaluation metrics need to be computed?
- What metadata about ML experiments is collected, for reproducibility (datasets, hyperparameters, etc.)?
- What ML framework expertise is available on the team?

Feature Store and Workflows

Feature engineering is the process of transforming raw input data into features, a numerical representation suitable for machine learning algorithms. The feature store is a technical component in the MLOps stack used for managing, reproducing, discovering, and reusing features across ML projects and data science teams. It separates feature engineering from ML model development and speeds up the process. However, as this is an advanced component, using a feature store may add complexity, so you need to consider whether it's appropriate for the project at hand. Here are some questions to ask:

- Is a feature store optional or mandatory? Do we have a data governance process that requires feature engineering to be reproducible?
- How are features computed (workflows) during the training and prediction phases?
- What are the infrastructure requirements for feature engineering?
- Should we buy or make the feature store?
- What databases are involved in feature storage?
- Do we design APIs for feature engineering?

Foundations (Reflecting DevOps)

DevOps is a set of practices and tools that integrates software development and IT operations to automate, streamline, and accelerate the building, testing, and deployment of software applications with a focus on reliability and scalability.

In the next step in the MLOps Stack Canvas, you'll take stock of the available DevOps infrastructure and promote awareness of current DevOps principles within the ML project. This helps in extrapolating DevOps best practices to MLOps activities. If there are gaps in traditional DevOps practices, it's essential to address them before moving on to more complex activities such as model and data versioning, continuous model training, or implementing a feature store.

Follow the guidelines in the DORA "Accelerate State of DevOps Report" (*https://oreil.ly/YzySM*) and execute a self-assessment of your software delivery performance by answering the following questions:

- How do we maintain the code? What source version control system is used?
- How do we monitor the system performance?
- Do we need versioning for notebooks?
- Is a trunk-based development approach used?
- What is the CI/CD pipeline for the codebase? What tools are used for it?
- Do we track metrics such as deployment frequency, lead time for changes, mean time to restore, and change failure rate?

Adhering to DevOps principles directly influences the performance of software delivery. MLOps is built on top of DevOps, so establishing a stable DevOps culture for software projects is essential for the success of ML projects.

Model Management

Model management encompasses a set of practices, processes, and tools used to efficiently track, version, deploy, and monitor machine learning models throughout their lifecycle, guaranteeing consistency, reproducibility, and scalability while meeting business requirements. The building blocks in this area of the MLOps Stack Canvas include CI/CD/CT: ML Pipeline Orchestration, Model Registry and Model Versioning, Model Deployment, Prediction Serving, and Model, Data, and Application Monitoring.

CI/CT/CD: ML Pipeline Orchestration

You reviewed the existing CI/CD pipelines for software delivery in the previous block. In this block, you'll examine the CI/CD routine for ML model release. You'll also introduce continuous training (CT). While continuous integration involves the building, testing, and packaging of data and model pipelines, continuous training focuses on automatically retraining ML models. You'll use the pipeline pattern, which involves steps such as data verification, feature and data selection, data cleaning, feature engineering, and model training.

A pipeline is structured as a directed acyclic graph (DAG) representing the overall workflow. This is a common way to represent dependencies and execution order. Depending on the maturity level, you can automate the data and model training pipeline workflows to operationalize the model. You should trigger data preparation and model training pipelines whenever new data is available or when the source code for a pipeline has changed.

In this block of the MLOps Stack Canvas, you should clarify the processes and the toolchain for CI/CT in the CRISP-ML(Q) model engineering phase by answering the following questions:

- How often are models expected to be retrained? What is the trigger for this (scheduled, event-based, or ad hoc)?
- Where does this happen (locally or in the cloud)?
- What is the formalized workflow for an ML pipeline? What tech stack is used?
- Is distributed model training required? Do we have the necessary infrastructure for distributed training?
- What is the workflow for the CI pipeline? What tools are used?
- What are the nonfunctional requirements for the ML model (efficiency, fairness, robustness, interpretability, etc.)? How are they tested? Are these tests integrated into the CI/CT workflow?

Model Registry and Model Versioning

The next section in the MLOps Stack Canvas is concerned with the ML model registry and versioning component, which is a crucial element of the model evaluation phase in the CRISP-ML(Q) process. The machine learning model, along with the data and the software code, is an essential asset. As with code versioning in traditional software engineering, establishing a model and data versioning practice is the foundation for reproducibility in machine learning.

Depending on your use case, a change in code or data might require retraining the model. Models may also need to be updated due to "model decay," where the model's performance declines over time with new data. In regulated industries like healthcare, finance, and the military, all ML models should be versioned and thoroughly documented. It's also important to ensure backward compatibility by being able to roll back to previously built models. By tracking multiple versions of the ML model, it is possible to implement different deployment strategies, such as "canary" or "shadow" deployment (methods used to gradually roll out changes in a controlled manner to mitigate risk while evaluating the performance of the newly trained model).

In this section of the MLOps Stack Canvas, you should answer the following questions:

- Is using a model registry and model versioning optional or mandatory? A model registry might be required if you have multiple models in production and need to track them all. Model versioning might be necessary if you have a requirement for reproducibility.
- Where should new ML models be stored and tracked?
- What versioning standards are used (e.g., semantic versioning)?

Note that implementing versioning and an ML model registry may be more appropriate in the later stages of ML projects.

Model Deployment

After training and evaluating the model, you'll move on to the next phase of the CRISP-ML(Q) process and deploy the machine learning model. Deploying an ML model means making it available in the target environment to receive prediction requests. In this section of the MLOps Stack Canvas, you'll define your model exposure strategies and the infrastructure aspects of continuous deployment (the automatic deployment of ML models into the target environment based on predetermined evaluation metrics) by addressing the following questions:

- What is the delivery format for the model?
- What is the expected time for changes (time from commit to production)?
- What is the target environment to serve predictions?
- What is our model release policy? Is A/B testing or multi-armed bandits testing required (e.g., for measuring the effectiveness of the new model on business metrics and deciding what model should be promoted in the production environment)?
- What is our deployment strategy? For example, is shadow or canary deployment required?

Prediction Serving

This section of the MLOps Stack Canvas covers the process of applying a machine learning model to new input data, commonly referred to as model serving. There are two primary serving modes: online and batch. ML models can be deployed using five different patterns: Model-as-a-Service, Model-as-a-Dependency, Precompute, Model-on-Demand, and Hybrid Serving. Each pattern requires different infrastructure settings. For example, Model-as-a-Service involves distributing the model as a service for input requests via a REST API and uses an on-demand mode for prediction responses. On the other hand, the Precompute pattern uses the batch prediction mode, with model predictions precomputed and stored in a relational database.

To identify the environment for model serving, you should answer the following questions:

- What is the serving mode (batch or online)?
- Is distributed model serving required?
- Is multi-model prediction serving required?
- Is pre-assertion for input data implemented?
- What fallback method for an inadequate model output (post-assertion) is implemented? (Do we have a heuristic benchmark?)
- Do we need ML inference accelerators (like special hardware such as Tensor Processing Units)?
- What is the expected target volume of predictions per month (or hour/day)?

Model, Data, and Application Monitoring

Once the ML model is put into operation, it must be monitored continuously to ensure that its quality is maintained and it continues to deliver accurate results. This section of the MLOps Stack Canvas addresses the monitoring aspect of operating the ML system in production. It corresponds to the sixth stage of the CRISP-ML(Q) process, model deployment and monitoring. Here are some questions to answer:

- Is continuous monitoring optional or mandatory? For instance, do you need to assess the effectiveness of your model during prediction serving? Do you need to monitor your model for performance degradation and trigger an alert if it starts performing badly? Is model retraining automatically triggered by specific events, such as data drift or concept drift?
- What ML metrics are collected?
- What domain-specific metrics are collected?
- How is the model performance decay detected?
- How is the data skew detected?
- What operational aspects need to be monitored (e.g., model prediction latency, CPU/RAM usage)?
- What is the alerting strategy (e.g., thresholds)?
- What triggers model retraining? Is it ad hoc, event-based, or scheduled?

Metadata Management

Metadata management for machine learning systems is a holistic process of collecting, organizing, storing, and utilizing data about the various components and stages of the ML lifecycle. This includes tracking information related to datasets, models, experiments, deployments, and performance metrics to ensure reproducibility, comparability, and traceability throughout the ML pipeline (see Figure 2-4).

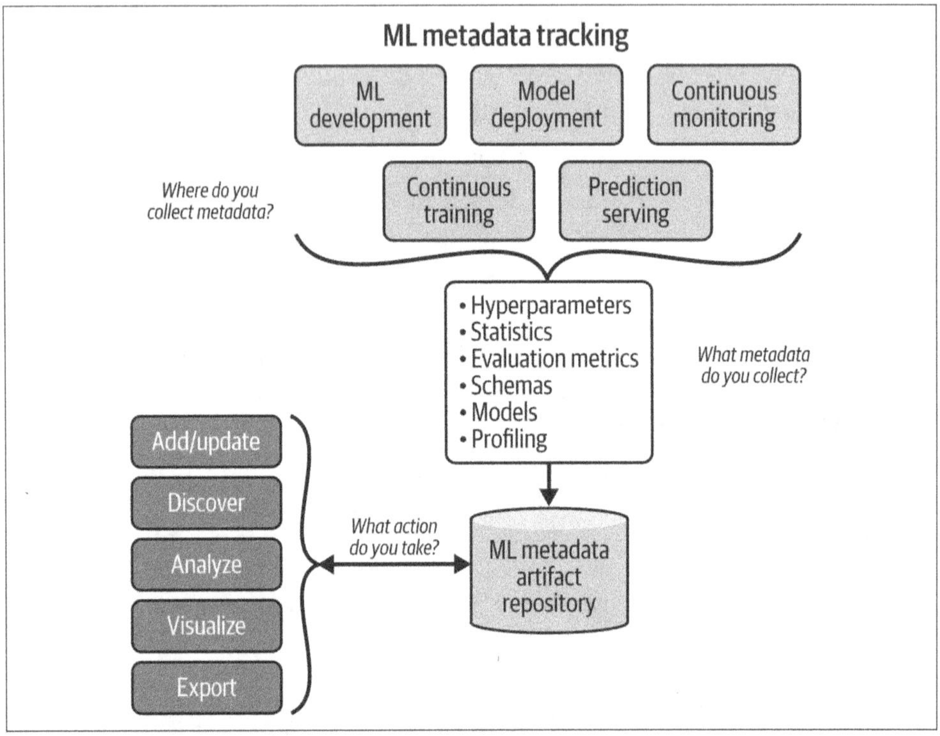

Figure 2-4. Metadata management

The *metadata store* is a cross-cutting component that supports all elements of the MLOps infrastructure stack. Implementing an ML model governance process—which may be necessary, depending on your organization and regulatory requirements—relies heavily on metadata, making a metadata store an essential component.

In the last block of the MLOps Stack Canvas, you'll answer the following questions:

- What kind of metadata related to the code, data, and model management needs to be collected (e.g., the pipeline run ID, trigger, performed steps, start/end timestamps, train/test dataset split, hyperparameters, model object, various statistics, etc.)?

- Are any ML governance processes included in the MLOps lifecycle? What metadata will be required?
- What is the documentation strategy? Do we treat documentation as a code?
- What operational metrics need to be collected (e.g., time to restore, change fail percentage)?

Additional Considerations of MLOps

An MLOps platform comprises self-service APIs, tools, services, knowledge, and support organized as a product (for more on this concept, see the Team Topologies video "WTF Is Platform as Product?" (*https://oreil.ly/2IZ7x*)). Platforms are designed to enable multiple autonomous delivery teams to release product features more quickly, with decreased dependencies and coordination between teams. There are also organizational aspects of AI engineering to consider as part of the broader discussion about constructing the infrastructure for AI projects. For example:

Tooling
: Should we purchase, use existing open source, or develop in-house tools for each of the MLOps components? What are the risks, trade-offs, and impacts of each decision?

Platforms
: Should we standardize on a single MLOps platform or create a hybrid solution? What are the risks, trade-offs, and impacts of this decision?[1]

Skills
: What is the cost associated with either hiring or training our own machine learning engineering talent?

Using the MLOps Stack Canvas helps you identify the workflows, architecture, and infrastructure components for your AI project and develop a good cost estimation for your AI project in every phase.

CRISP-ML(Q) and MLOps

MLOps and CRISP-ML(Q) are complementary approaches that can work together synergistically to support and improve the development and deployment of machine learning models. While CRISP-ML(Q) provides a structured process framework, MLOps offers technical and organizational best practices for implementing and operationalizing ML projects. Figure 2-5 illustrates the synergy between the two.

1 Thoughtworks provides an excellent guide (*https://oreil.ly/nE93Z*) for understanding the MLOps platform landscape.

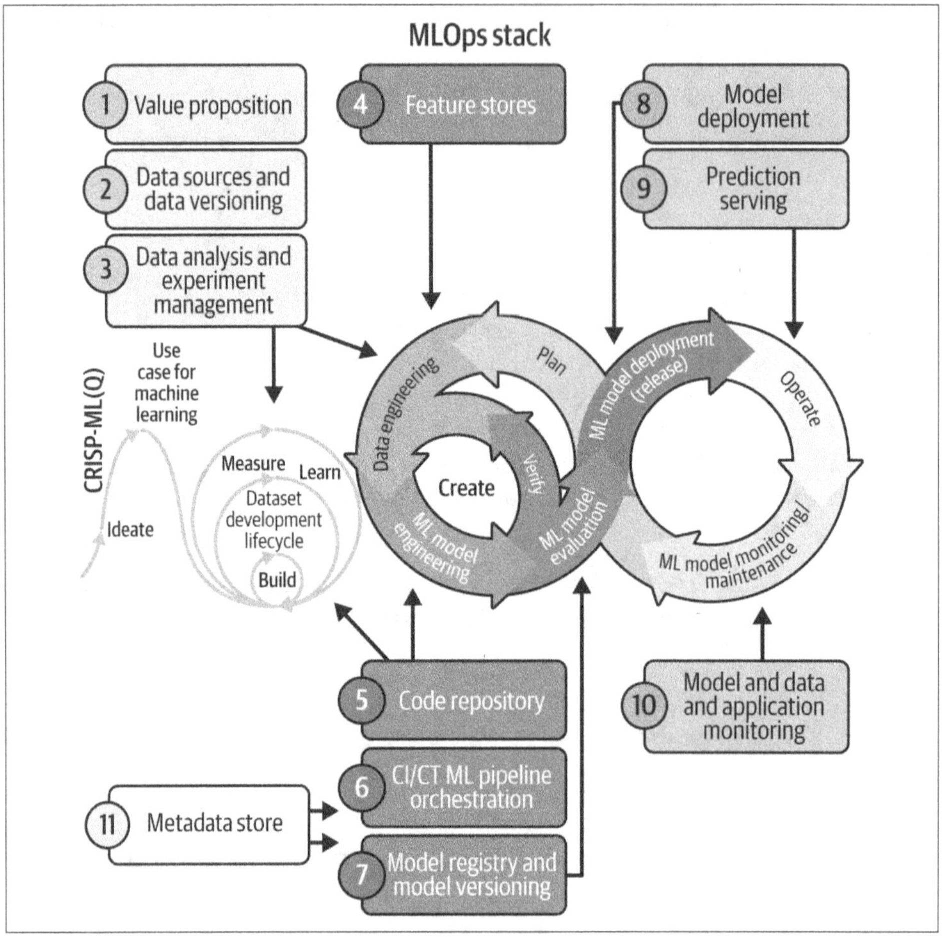

Figure 2-5. MLOps and CRISP-ML(Q) synergy

These two approaches can be integrated to bind the ML development process with technical implementation. In particular, CRISP-ML(Q) suggests a high-level, structured process for machine learning projects, dividing the development workflow into six main phases: business and data understanding, data preparation, modeling, evaluation, deployment, and monitoring and maintenance. MLOps provides the technical infrastructure and best practices to implement these phases effectively. For example, during the data engineering phase of CRISP-ML(Q), MLOps practices can be applied to automate data pipelines, ensure data versioning, and maintain data quality.

The main strength of CRISP-ML(Q), and what makes it a suitable ML process model for EU AI Act implementation, is its integration of quality assurance and risk awareness throughout the machine learning lifecycle. MLOps complements this by providing tools and practices for continuous integration, continuous delivery, and automated testing, which are essential for maintaining quality in production environments.

ML development is, by nature, iterative, and both CRISP-ML(Q) and MLOps support this. CRISP-ML(Q) provides a framework for iterating through the phases of ML development, while MLOps offers technical solutions for rapid experimentation, version control, and automated retraining of ML models. Furthermore, MLOps facilitates model retraining by incorporating practices such as continuous monitoring, logging, and automated model updates. Research by DORA (*https://oreil.ly/YzySM*) shows that employing continuous delivery (and hence MLOps) practices can significantly improve organizations' technical and business performance. By enabling teams to consistently deliver value and adapt to changes in market demands more effectively, MLOps practices not only lower the risks of deployment and production failures but also reduce time to feedback, decrease cognitive load, and lessen the general stress associated with operating models in production.

Being quality-driven, CRISP-ML(Q) emphasizes the importance of documenting business decisions, data, the ML model development process, and the models and experiments themselves. MLOps complements this approach by providing version control for code, data, and models, thereby ensuring the reproducibility of results. It also introduces technical components, such as metadata, model, and feature stores, to support these functions.

CRISP-ML(Q)'s iterative nature aligns well with the emphasis of MLOps on continuous improvement. MLOps practices can be used to implement the feedback loops suggested by CRISP-ML(Q), allowing for ongoing refinement of models and processes. MLOps also offers technical solutions for scaling ML operations, including automated model training, evaluation, and deployment pipelines.

In practice, organizations can use CRISP-ML(Q) as a high-level framework for structuring their machine learning projects, while applying MLOps best practices and tools within each phase. This combination ensures that projects follow a well-defined process while benefiting from modern, efficient, and scalable technical implementations.

Conclusion

This chapter introduced CRISP-ML(Q) and MLOps and showed how this pairing provides a robust framework for addressing EU AI Act compliance requirements: CRISP-ML(Q) provides the process blueprint, while MLOps supplies the tools and practices needed to operationalize that process in a compliant manner. Together, they enable organizations to proactively embed EU AI Act compliance into the ML lifecycle, from data collection to monitoring, rather than treating it as an afterthought.

In the following chapter, to complete the compliance engineering picture, you will learn about data governance, a framework of policies, processes, and responsibilities that ensures the quality, security, compliance, and ethical use of data throughout the AI development lifecycle. You will also see how AI governance ensures that AI systems are developed, deployed, and monitored in a responsible, ethical, secure, and compliant manner.

CHAPTER 3

Data and AI Governance and AI Engineering

The first chapter of this book introduced the EU AI Act and laid the foundation for understanding trustworthy AI as its primary motivation. We then explored the engineering aspects of the ML development process and examined the synergy between the CRISP-ML(Q) lifecycle model and the technical components of MLOps, highlighting how this integration supports the development of trustworthy AI through structured processes, transparency, and reproducibility. Here, we will focus on compliance from an organizational perspective, considering the interplay between data and AI governance, risk management, and conformity with the EU AI Act.

The Importance of Data and AI Governance in the EU AI Act Era

Let's start with three notable real-world examples that illustrate how poor data governance and AI governance practices have led to significant failures of AI products:

IBM Watson for Oncology
: The development of Watson for Oncology (launched in 2016) faced significant criticism due to the system recommending unsafe and incorrect cancer treatments (*https://oreil.ly/iCQ0B*). This was attributed to incomplete and biased training data that included only a small number of synthetic cancer cases rather than real clinical data, resulting in flawed recommendations and limited clinical relevance. Internal documents and customer feedback highlighted a lack of transparency, systemic issues, and dissatisfaction with the product's recommendations. This case emphasizes the critical need for high-quality, accurate, and relevant data in AI training.

Amazon's AI recruiting tool

In 2018, Amazon developed an experimental AI recruiting tool to automate candidate screening. However, the system was found to exhibit bias against women (*https://oreil.ly/L2cEr*), due to the AI model being trained on 10 years' worth of resumes that had come overwhelmingly from male candidates. This led to it downgrading resumes containing the word "women's" and penalizing candidates from all-women's colleges. This result highlighted the lack of sufficient auditing of the training data and model for demographic bias and led to Amazon scrapping the tool entirely. This case underscores the need for careful data screening and debiasing in AI applications.

iTutor Group's AI recruiting tool

In 2023, iTutor Group used AI-powered recruiting software that automatically rejected female applicants aged 55 and older and male applicants aged 60 and older. The system's screening criteria were based on age, leading to discriminatory practices. As a result, the US Equal Employment Opportunity Commission (EEOC) filed a suit against iTutor Group, which the company settled (*https://oreil.ly/66rkj*) by agreeing to pay $365,000 and implement new anti-discrimination policies. This case highlights the need for oversight and bias prevention in AI recruiting tools.

These and other famous AI disasters (*https://oreil.ly/l3E9Y*) illustrate the critical need for rigorous data governance practices, including ensuring data quality, representativeness, and transparency. Thorough data quality assessments, robust data protection measures, and ethical considerations in AI development and deployment are essential. Comprehensive bias testing across diverse populations is particularly important in sensitive areas such as healthcare and education, and ongoing monitoring and auditing of AI systems in production are necessary to identify and address issues early.

Data and AI governance play a vital role in the age of the EU AI Act. Organizations must have robust data and AI governance frameworks in place to meet the Act's strict requirements related to data quality, documentation, transparency, human oversight, and risk management. Moreover, effective governance is essential for identifying, assessing, and mitigating the risks associated with AI systems, which can pose threats to fundamental rights, safety, and the environment if not properly managed.

Strong data and AI governance promote responsible and ethical AI development, in line with the EU AI Act's aim to foster the development of trustworthy AI that upholds EU values and principles. This approach enables organizations to innovate with AI while safeguarding privacy and other fundamental rights.

Transparency and explainability in AI systems are not just technical challenges but legal and ethical requirements. The examples mentioned here underscore the critical need for rigorous data governance practices, including ensuring data quality, representativeness, transparency, and ethical considerations in AI development and deployment. Next, we'll take a closer look at what those practices entail.

Overview of Data Governance

At the heart of the EU AI Act lies a motivation to create AI systems that are not just powerful but trustworthy. Data governance is a pretty dry topic to describe, so I recommend you start by reviewing the metaphorical framework in the following sidebar to make the abstract concepts more tangible.

Data Governance: Managing the Ingredients

I'll use a metaphor to explain data governance: imagine a vast kitchen in a high-end restaurant, where data represents the ingredients and AI is the collection of sophisticated cooking utensils and equipment.

Metaphorically speaking, data governance is like running the kitchen's ingredient management system:

- *Sourcing* involves ensuring that data comes from reliable sources, much like ensuring that ingredients come from trustworthy suppliers.
- *Storage* entails organizing and storing data properly to maintain its quality and prevent any contamination, similar to how ingredients in the kitchen are stored to maintain freshness.
- *Labeling* means clearly marking data with details such as contents, expiration dates, and usage guidelines, just as ingredients are labeled for easy identification.
- *Access control and data privacy* are about determining who can access which data and for what purposes, similar to how access to ingredients is controlled in a kitchen.
- *Quality checks* involve regularly inspecting data to maintain high standards, much like inspecting ingredients to ensure their quality.

The goal is to ensure that every dish (data-driven decision or product) starts with the best possible ingredients.

Data Governance Defined

As we saw in Chapter 1, data governance is a data management function that guarantees the availability, usability, integrity, and security of the data collected and used in an organization. While the core principles of data governance remain consistent across industries, the specific focus and implementation can vary based on industry needs and regulatory requirements. For instance, data governance in healthcare encompasses "the overall administration, through clearly defined procedures and plans, that assures the availability, integrity, security, and usability of the structured and unstructured data available to an organization while ensuring compliance with regulations such as HIPAA."[1] Here, the focus is on ensuring patient data privacy and security and maintaining compliance with healthcare regulations (e.g., HIPAA).

On the other hand, data governance in banking involves "establishing policies, procedures, and controls for data quality, privacy, and security; implementing data management technologies and systems; and ensuring that data across the organization is consistent, accessible, and properly used."[2] Here, the focus is on ensuring data accuracy for risk assessment and management, complying with financial regulations (e.g., Basel III, the Dodd-Frank Act), and protecting sensitive financial information.

The Data Engineering Lifecycle and Data Governance

One way to understand the data governance framework is to apply governance concepts across each stage of the typical data engineering lifecycle, as depicted in Figure 3-1.

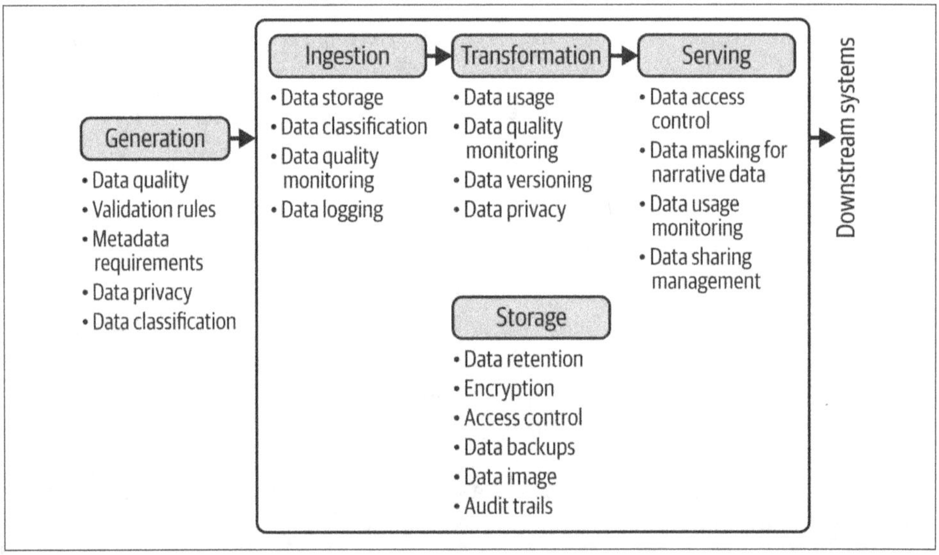

Figure 3-1. The data governance process across the stages of the data engineering lifecycle (adapted from Fundamentals of Data Engineering *by Joe Reis and Matt Housley [O'Reilly])*

1 OvalEdge Team, "The Importance of Data Governance in Healthcare," OvalEdge, March 22, 2023, *https://oreil.ly/dXnvR*.

2 Yuriy Voloshynskyy, "Data Governance in Banking and Finance: A Complete Guide," N-iX, March 27, 2024, *https://oreil.ly/dHAXj*.

The data engineering lifecycle comprises the following stages: data generation, storage, ingestion, transformation, and serving. Let's take a closer look at how governance applies to each of those stages.

Data generation

At the start of the data engineering lifecycle, data is created or collected from various source systems (applications, databases, Internet of Things devices, etc.). In the data generation stage, data governance processes focus on establishing data quality standards and validation rules.

Usually, at this point you define metadata requirements and implement data collection policies compliant with privacy regulations. Additionally, within the organization, data ownership is defined and corresponding roles are assigned. For example, an organization can implement automated data quality checks at the point of data creation, ensuring that customer data adheres to predefined formats and completeness criteria.

Ingestion

In the next phase, data is moved from the source systems into centralized storage or processing systems. Data governance processes focus on data lineage tracking, implementing data classification, and tagging. An important part of data governance is monitoring data quality during ingestion and maintaining audit logs of data movement. Often, organizations automatically tag incoming data with source information and sensitivity levels. This enables easier tracking and management of data throughout its lifecycle.

Transformation

During the transformation stage of the data engineering lifecycle, raw data is cleaned, normalized, aggregated, and converted into formats suitable for analysis. At this point, data governance ensures that data quality rules are enforced. You should maintain data lineage throughout all transformations and apply version control to data models.

Imagine a retail company processing customer purchase data. Here, data governance tasks might include data quality (error) checks, such as verifying that email formats are valid and there are no duplicate entries, and data cleaning procedures such as removing inconsistencies in product names. All extract–transform–load (ETL) processes should be documented, and changes to the customer data model should go through a formal approval process. In addition, it's essential to ensure compliance with data privacy regulations during transformations.

Storage

Next, the transformed data is stored in systems such as data lakes, data warehouses, or other cloud-based storage solutions. At this stage, data governance involves defining data retention policies, implementing access controls and encryption, and ensuring proper data backups. Maintaining data lineage and audit trails is also essential for accountability and traceability.

For instance, organizations may implement role-based access controls and encrypt sensitive data at rest to protect personal information in compliance with the GDPR. Scheduling regular data backups and disaster recovery tests are also common practices to ensure data resilience and availability.

Serving

In the final stage of the data engineering lifecycle, serving, processed data and insights are made available to end users, applications, or external partners for consumption and analysis. Data governance requires that organizations control access to data based on user roles and permissions and implement data masking for sensitive information. Monitoring data usage, access patterns, and compliance with data sharing agreements is also essential. Many organizations implement self-service data portals that allow users to access datasets appropriate to their roles or use cases, with sensitive information automatically masked, redacted, or anonymized based on predefined governance rules.

Organizations can ensure data quality, security, and compliance by applying these governance processes across the data engineering lifecycle. This approach to data governance helps AI engineers understand the importance of maintaining data integrity and security throughout the entire data pipeline.

Integrating Data Governance into MLOps

As you learned in Chapter 2, the MLOps Stack Canvas provides a comprehensive blueprint for designing the end-to-end technical infrastructure needed to develop, deploy, and maintain machine learning applications in a robust, scalable, and governed manner. It facilitates cost estimation, planning, and decision making for operationalizing machine learning across the entire lifecycle. By extending the MLOps Stack Canvas with data governance considerations (which you will do here), you can ensure that data is managed responsibly and complies with relevant regulations throughout the ML lifecycle. This holistic approach to MLOps and data governance enables organizations to build trustworthy, compliant, and sustainable ML systems.

Let's take a look at how we can incorporate data governance into each of the MLOps Stack Canvas's components.

Value Proposition

When you formulate a general value proposition for the MLOps platform you're building, be sure to include data governance goals and compliance requirements in the value proposition. Consider how data governance enhances the overall value of the ML project.

A useful way to track the success of data governance integration into the AI lifecycle is to define and track particular metrics, such as:

Policy compliance rate
: The percentage of data management activities that comply with established policies and standards.

Regulatory compliance
: The percentage of data processes and policies that comply with relevant regulations.

Audit compliance rate
: The success rate of internal and external audits in terms of compliance with data governance policies.

Incident response time
: The average time taken to respond to data governance–related incidents or issues.

Data audit results
: The number of audit findings related to data governance and the severity of these findings.

Training and certification levels
: The number of employees who have completed data governance training and certifications.

Cost of poor data quality
: The financial impact of data quality issues, including costs associated with correcting errors.

Useful metrics to consider to track data usage, quality, and security include:

Data accessibility
: The ease with which authorized users can access the data they need. Collect feedback from users on the ease of accessing and using the data.

Data usage frequency
: The number of times datasets are accessed or used within a specific period.

Data accuracy
: The percentage of data entries that are correct.

Data completeness
: The percentage of missing values or incomplete data entries.

Data consistency
: The percentage of data that is uniform and consistent across different databases.

Data timeliness
: The time it takes for data to be updated and available for use.

Data validity
: The percentage of data entries that meet the specified format, type, or range.

Number of data breaches
: The count of security incidents involving unauthorized access to data.

Time to detect and mitigate security threats
: The average time to detect and address data security threats.

Data Sources and Data Versioning

In addition to the standard tasks for the Data Sources and Data Versioning component in the MLOps Stack Canvas, you should also implement the following governance-related tasks:

- Identify, catalog, and classify data sources based on sensitivity, privacy, and regulatory requirements. Define roles and responsibilities for data access (e.g., data owners, stewards, consumers).
- Establish data access controls and permissions based on data classification, such as personally identifiable information (PII), protected health information (PHI), and payment card industry (PCI) data.
- Establish a data taxonomy and metadata schema for consistent data organization and labeling.
- Implement data lineage to track data origin and transformations and ensure data provenance, including information about data sources, ownership, and quality, to enable traceability and reproducibility.
- Establish sustainable data documentation processes to document data origin, transformations, and dependencies throughout the data lifecycle.
- Ensure data versioning aligns with data retention policies and compliance needs.

To implement data lineage and provenance, you can utilize tools to capture and visualize data flows and dependencies automatically. Examples include OpenLineage, Apache Atlas, Cloudera Navigator, and Talend Data Fabric.

To implement data version control to track and manage changes to datasets over time, you can use a tool like DVC, Pachyderm, lakeFS, or Delta Lake.

For implementing data privacy and compliance solutions to ensure adherence to regulations (e.g., GDPR, HIPAA), tools such as Privitar, OneTrust, BigID, and Informatica can be helpful.

Data quality and validation frameworks to ensure data accuracy, completeness, and consistency include Apache Griffin, Deequ, Great Expectations, and Monte Carlo.

Data Analysis and Experiment Management

Incorporating data governance into the Data Analysis and Experiment Management component of the MLOps Stack Canvas involves the following steps:

- Enforce data privacy and security measures during analysis and experimentation.
- Define strict access controls for data and experimental artifacts, and implement privacy controls (such as redaction, pseudonymization, or anonymization) for sensitive data used in experiments. Use role-based access control systems to ensure only authorized personnel can access sensitive data and critical experiment configurations.
- For reproducibility and compliance, maintain audit trails of data usage in experiments. Use version control systems not only for code, but also for experiment configurations and datasets. All changes should be logged with user information, timestamps, and descriptions to provide a clear and complete audit trail.
- Continuously monitor experiments and data handling practices to ensure compliance with internal policies and external regulations (e.g., GDPR, HIPAA). This might involve automated checks or periodic reviews.

You can use experiment tracking and management platforms like MLflow, Weights & Biases, or Neptune.ai to manage and govern metadata—including data lineage, versioning, and governance information—and artifacts. These tools (and others, such as TensorBoard) also support logging and visualizing metrics, hyperparameters, and outcomes. They help streamline the experimentation process and guarantee that all metadata is captured systematically.

Feature Store and Workflows

When extending the Feature Store and Workflows component of the MLOps Stack Canvas to include data governance, several key processes and tools should be implemented to support compliance, reproducibility, and proper management of features:

- Secure and govern the feature store by cataloging features with metadata such as creation date, creator, and usage rights. Thoroughly document feature engineering workflows to ensure compliance with data privacy regulations.
- Establish policies and guidelines for feature creation, storage, and usage to comply with data protection regulations (e.g., GDPR, HIPAA).
- Implement access controls and authentication for the feature store. Define policies for granting, reviewing, and revoking access to features based on user roles and responsibilities.
- Maintain feature lineage and track data sources, transformations, and feature dependencies for auditing and reproducibility. For feature provenance, include the creation date, version, and owner.
- Establish data retention policies for features that align with regulatory requirements. For data minimization purposes, create and store only features that are necessary.
- Document all features, providing clear descriptions and justifications for each.

Some feature store platforms have built-in governance capabilities such as access control, versioning, and lineage tracking. Examples include Feast, Hopsworks, AWS SageMaker Feature Store, and Google Cloud Vertex AI Feature Store. You can implement data lineage and provenance to capture and visualize feature dependencies and transformations using tools like OpenLineage, Apache Atlas, Cloudera Navigator, or Talend Data Fabric.

Foundations (Reflecting DevOps)

Organizations can embed data governance throughout the development and deployment lifecycle by integrating appropriate processes and tools into the DevOps Foundations component of the MLOps Stack Canvas. Consider the following best practices:

- Integrate data governance policies and processes into DevOps practices by adding data governance checks and automated compliance checks for data handling to CI/CD pipelines.
- Implement data security measures, such as data masking, encryption, tokenization, and other minimization controls, to enforce data security and privacy in CI/CD pipelines.

- Protect sensitive data throughout the build, test, and deployment processes.
- Establish secure data handling practices and access controls within the CI/CD workflow.
- Automate data quality checks and validations as part of your DevOps workflows, incorporating data quality gates in CI/CD pipelines to maintain integrity and consistency.
- Set up automated data profiling and anomaly detection mechanisms to identify data quality issues. Include data profiling reports as artifacts in CI/CD pipelines for easy access and review.

CI/CT/CD: ML Pipeline Orchestration

Here are some steps you can take to maintain data integrity, compliance, and reliability throughout the ML pipeline when incorporating data governance into the CI/CT/CD component of the MLOps Stack Canvas:

- Integrate data validation and quality checks into ML pipelines.
- Automate data bias and fairness assessments during model training.
- Implement data drift detection and alerting within the CI/CD workflow. Establish baseline data distributions and monitor for significant deviations over time, triggering automated alerts and notifications when data drift exceeds predefined thresholds.
- Define metrics and thresholds to evaluate the fairness and representativeness of the training data (e.g., demographic parity, equal opportunity, disparate impact).
- Automate bias detection and mitigation techniques to ensure models are trained on unbiased data.

To evaluate and mitigate bias in training data, you can use tools such as IBM AI Fairness 360 or Google's What-If Tool. Tools to implement data drift detection and monitoring platforms to identify and alert on data drift in the ML pipeline include Evidently AI, Arthur AI, and Fiddler AI. You can also utilize MLOps platforms that have built-in data governance features, such as MLflow on Databricks, Kubeflow, AWS SageMaker, or the Google Cloud AI Platform.

Model Registry and Model Versioning

Extending the Model Registry and Model Versioning component of the MLOps Stack Canvas to include data governance requires the implementation of proper management, versioning, and governance practices for ML models (we'll look at AI model governance later in this chapter). Here are some best practices:

- Maintain a centralized model registry with governance metadata (e.g., data used, compliance checks).
- Implement access controls and permissions for the model registry.
- Ensure the model registry includes data lineage and provenance information. Implement a process for tracking model lineage, including data sources, hyperparameters, training artifacts, and who trained the ML models.
- Establish a model versioning strategy aligned with the data versioning and governance policies.
- Maintain a comprehensive version history of models in the registry, along with the associated governance metadata.

Integrating data governance and model management practices fosters transparency, accountability, and trust in the ML models deployed in production environments. To capture and visualize the relationships between models, data, and other artifacts, you can use data lineage and provenance tools such as OpenLineage, Datakin, Pachyderm, and Marquez. To track and monitor model governance activities and maintain audit trails, use tools like Apache Ranger, Privacera, Immuta, or Informatica.

Model Deployment

Incorporating data governance into model deployment involves deploying models in a controlled environment where performance can be monitored against criteria such as fairness and privacy impact. Consider the following activities to integrate data governance into your model deployment practices:

- Implement staged deployment practices like canary releases to evaluate compliance in production settings.
- Use data privacy and anonymization platforms to protect sensitive data during model inference and deployment.
- Track and audit data usage throughout the deployment process.
- Automate data compliance checks as part of the deployment workflow.

Model governance and orchestration frameworks such as Kubeflow, MLflow, Apache Airflow, and Seldon Core can be used to manage and automate the deployment process in compliance with data governance policies.

Prediction Serving

Integrating data governance into the Prediction Serving component involves controlling how models are served while ensuring compliance with data protection regulations. To achieve this, you should:

- Validate that production data meets governance standards (input data validation).
- Implement measures to protect sensitive predictions (output data protection).
- Encrypt prediction inputs and outputs both in transit and at rest.
- Enforce data access controls and authentication for prediction requests.
- Monitor and audit data usage during prediction serving for compliance.
- Establish data retention policies for input data and predictions.
- Establish a process for protecting sensitive data during prediction serving.
- Use data masking, anonymization, tokenization, and data minimization techniques to safeguard PII or other sensitive data.
- Audit and log prediction requests and responses.
- Capture metadata such as timestamp, input data, and prediction results for each prediction request.
- Store audit logs securely and make them accessible for compliance and monitoring purposes.
- Continuously monitor prediction quality and fairness.
- Implement mechanisms to detect and alert on any deviations in prediction quality, performance, or fairness metrics and regularly assess the prediction serving system for potential biases or discriminatory outcomes.

Data privacy and protection tools such as HashiCorp Vault, AWS Key Management Service (KMS), Azure Key Vault, and Google Cloud Data Loss Prevention (DLP) can be used to safeguard sensitive data during prediction serving. To capture and store prediction request and response metadata, you can use auditing and logging frameworks such as Elastic Stack, Splunk, Fluentd, AWS CloudTrail, or Google Cloud Audit Logs. For tracking prediction quality, performance, and fairness metrics, consider tools such as Prometheus, Grafana, Datadog, New Relic, AWS CloudWatch, or Google Cloud Monitoring.

Model, Data, and Application Monitoring

To incorporate data governance into the ML model, data, and system monitoring part of the MLOps Stack Canvas, extend your monitoring capabilities to include governance metrics such as data quality, model drift, and compliance with data usage policies. The following tasks are recommended:

- Monitor data quality, bias, and drift in production ML systems.
- Set up alerts and notifications for data governance violations and anomalies.

- Continuously audit data usage and access to ensure compliance with relevant regulations. Establish processes for investigating and remediating governance issues.
- Track operational metrics (e.g., latency, throughput, resource utilization) alongside governance-specific metrics defined in the value proposition.
- Establish governance policies and thresholds for acceptable operational performance.
- Implement alerts and escalation procedures for operational issues that affect model availability, reliability, or compliance.

This monitoring component should aggregate and unify all relevant metrics, thresholds, and alerts from the other parts of the MLOps Stack Canvas to provide a comprehensive view of system health and governance compliance.

Operational monitoring and alerting tools such as Prometheus, Grafana, Datadog, New Relic, and Elastic Stack can be used to track system performance, resource utilization, and availability. Platforms like PagerDuty, OpsGenie, Splunk On-Call, and xMatters help organizations respond to ML system issues and compliance breaches quickly. These tools reduce incident response times and improve overall system reliability.

Metadata Management

Metadata management for AI system compliance engineering is such a large and important topic that it deserves a separate book. The Metadata Management section of the MLOps Stack Canvas spans the entire AI system lifecycle, capturing information about datasets, models, experiments, deployments, and more to support ML governance, reproducibility, and comparability.

Integrating data governance into metadata management requires developing a unified strategy that provides greater visibility into data lineage, model history, and EU AI Act compliance. You will need to:

- Establish a metadata schema and taxonomy to standardize data labeling and organization. Include fields such as model purpose, data sources, performance metrics, compliance checks, and approval status.
- Capture and store governance-related metadata (e.g., data and model lineage and provenance, compliance checks, and access logs).
- Consistently capture and maintain governance and ML metadata to create a comprehensive audit trail for every model version. Use that metadata to support compliance reporting and lifecycle tracking.

- Document and catalog metadata associated with datasets, features, models, and experiments. Experiment metadata should include data lineage, versioning, and governance information.
- Enable metadata integration and interoperability across tools and lifecycle stages. Develop processes to harmonize metadata across ML development, deployment, and monitoring systems, facilitating traceability and regulatory alignment.

There are various tools and platforms available to support metadata management across the ML lifecycle. These include:

- Metadata management platforms that capture, store, and govern metadata across ML systems, such as Alation, Collibra, Informatica Enterprise Data Catalog, and Apache Atlas
- Data lineage and provenance tools to track and visualize the flow and dependencies of data and metadata, such as OpenLineage, Datakin, Nexla, and Octopai
- Centralized metadata catalogs or repositories that enable discovery, search, and access to ML system metadata, such as Amundsen, DataHub, Metacat, and Datum
- Compliance and audit tools to enforce governance policies and assess the adherence of metadata to standards, such as Collibra Governance, Informatica Axon, and Apache Ranger
- APIs and integration frameworks to support interoperability and data exchange between ML tools and platforms, such as OpenMetadata, Egeria, and Apache Kafka

By deeply embedding data governance into each component of the MLOps Stack Canvas, you guarantee that data governance is not an afterthought but a fundamental aspect of the machine learning lifecycle. This approach not only helps you meet regulatory requirements but also builds trust with stakeholders by promoting the ethical use of data and models.

Data governance is tightly linked to AI governance, and understanding this relationship is especially important in the context of the EU AI Act. AI systems are only as good and as safe as the data they are trained on. Weak data governance will cause AI governance to fall short. We'll turn our attention to this critical topic next.

Overview of AI Governance

The introduction of the EU AI Act has caused enterprises to increasingly prioritize AI governance. To explain what this entails, let's return to the earlier metaphor of a high-end restaurant kitchen, where data represents the ingredients and AI is the collection of sophisticated cooking utensils and equipment.

AI Governance: Managing the Kitchen Equipment

AI governance is similar to managing the kitchen's specialized cooking equipment:

- *Safety protocols* establish guidelines for using powerful tools like the AI-powered sous chef robot or smart ovens.
- *Training* ensures that all staff know how to properly use and maintain the AI equipment.
- *Maintenance* mandates regular check-ups and updates to keep the AI tools functioning correctly and safely.
- *Output monitoring* is like taste-testing dishes prepared by AI to guarantee quality and consistency.
- *Ethical considerations* ensure that AI tools are used fairly.

The aim is to use advanced AI instruments to enhance the kitchen's capabilities while maintaining control, safety, and the human touch in cooking.

Together, data governance and AI governance help create a well-run kitchen that consistently produces excellent meals (outcomes) in an ethical and efficient manner. They help balance innovation with responsibility, ensuring that the restaurant (organization) maintains its reputation and meets all health and safety standards.

AI Governance Defined

The objective of AI governance is to establish and maintain a framework that ensures AI systems are developed, deployed, and used responsibly, ethically, and in alignment with organizational goals and values. AI governance covers various aspects, including AI algorithms, decision making based on AI predictions, security, and data privacy. It operates as an ecosystem within the enterprise, involving people, processes, and policies.

AI governance is a key responsibility of the company's leadership and oversight bodies such as AI ethics boards. These individuals are accountable for defining policies and guidelines, implementing AI risk management processes, and establishing monitoring and auditing mechanisms. Other stakeholders include AI and data science teams, legal and compliance teams, business unit leaders, risk management teams, external advisors and auditors, and customers and end users.

A strong AI governance framework includes AI training and awareness programs to provide guardrails and guidance for AI development and use across the organization. AI governance policies may cover ethical AI principles, AI risk assessment and mitigation, data governance and privacy protection, model development and deployment standards, transparency and explainability requirements, AI model monitoring and evaluation processes, and ML-centric incident response procedures. As this suggests, robust data governance provides the foundation for effective AI governance.

The AI System Lifecycle and AI Governance

Ensuring AI systems are developed and used responsibly, ethically, and in alignment with organization goals and values requires a holistic approach involving people, processes, and technologies. Organizations can integrate AI governance checkpoints throughout the entire AI system development lifecycle to create ethical, transparent, fair, and accountable AI systems. The key is to make AI governance an integral part of the development process rather than an afterthought. Table 3-1 shows how the AI governance principles outlined earlier map to the corresponding phases of the CRISP-ML(Q) framework discussed in Chapter 2.

Table 3-1. Integrating AI governance into each phase of CRISP-ML(Q)

CRISP-ML(Q) phase	AI governance principles	Relevance to the EU AI Act
Business and data understanding	Human-centered design: Ensure the AI project aligns with human needs and values. Involve stakeholders from various departments to validate the AI project's goals.	The EU AI Act promotes human-centric and trustworthy AI (Article 1). Ensuring alignment with human needs during this phase contributes to achieving this objective.
	Ethical and responsible AI practices: Conduct an ethical impact assessment to identify potential risks and harms.	The Act prohibits certain harmful AI practices (Article 5) and outlines specific requirements for high-risk AI systems (Article 6). Conducting an ethical impact assessment aligns with its risk-based approach.
	Privacy and data security: Implement data governance practices during data collection and verification.	Article 10 mandates data quality and governance for high-risk AI systems. Establishing robust data governance practices in this phase is crucial for compliance.
	Fairness and inclusiveness: When defining success criteria, include metrics for fairness and inclusiveness. Examine the data for potential biases that could lead to unfair outcomes.	Article 10 also requires addressing potential biases in data for high-risk systems. Incorporating fairness metrics in this phase helps ensure compliance and mitigate potential discrimination.
	Accountability: Define clear roles and responsibilities for the AI project.	The EU AI Act demands accountability by requiring providers to demonstrate compliance with its requirements. Defining clear roles in this phase supports establishing accountability throughout the AI system lifecycle.

CRISP-ML(Q) phase	AI governance principles	Relevance to the EU AI Act
Data preparation	Privacy and data security: Implement robust data protection measures during data cleaning and transformation. Where necessary, apply data anonymization or pseudonymization techniques. Ensure that data handling complies with relevant privacy regulations.	Article 10 requires data governance for high-risk AI, while Article 27 concerns GDPR compliance. Article 59 provides provisions for further processing of personal data under specific conditions, which may be relevant in this phase.
	Fairness and inclusiveness: Address class imbalances and potential biases in the data.	Article 10 mandates addressing potential biases in data for high-risk AI systems. This phase offers a critical opportunity to mitigate bias and ensure fairness.
	Reproducibility: Document all data preparation steps and use version control for datasets.	Article 11 mandates the provision of technical documentation to support reproducibility and enable the traceability of data preparation steps.
	Transparency and explainability: Keep detailed records of any data transformations or feature engineering steps.	Article 13 emphasizes transparency and explainability for high-risk AI systems. Maintaining detailed records in this phase supports fulfilling these requirements.
Modeling	Safety, security, and dependability: Choose modeling techniques appropriate for the application's level of risk and implement safeguards against potential vulnerabilities.	The Act requires a risk management system (Article 9) and specific provisions for the accuracy, robustness, and cybersecurity of high-risk AI systems (Article 15). Implementing safeguards in this phase is crucial for achieving compliance.
	Fairness and inclusiveness: Monitor and mitigate any biases that emerge during the modeling process. Use fairness-aware machine learning techniques if necessary.	Articles 10 and 50 highlight the importance of addressing bias and promoting fairness. Monitoring and mitigating bias during model engineering is essential for compliance.
	Transparency and explainability: Implement model documentation practices (e.g., model cards and dataset sheets).	Article 13 mandates transparency and explainability for high-risk AI systems. Implementing documentation practices in this phase contributes to fulfilling these requirements.
	Reproducibility: Ensure that the modeling process is fully documented and reproducible. This includes recording random seeds, hyperparameters, and model architectures.	Article 11 sets requirements for technical documentation, supporting reproducibility and allowing for auditing and verification of the modeling process.
	Robustness: Develop models that are robust to variations in input data and potential adversarial attacks.	Robustness is a key requirement for high-risk AI systems under Article 15. Developing robust models in this phase is essential for compliance.

CRISP-ML(Q) phase	AI governance principles	Relevance to the EU AI Act
Evaluation	Human-centered design and oversight: Involve domain experts in interpreting model results and assessing potential impacts.	Human oversight is a crucial aspect of the EU AI Act, particularly for high-risk systems (Articles 14 and 26). Involving domain experts in this phase aligns with this principle.
	Fairness and inclusiveness: Conduct thorough testing for fairness across different subgroups.	Focusing on fairness and inclusiveness is essential for identifying, assessing, and mitigating risks associated with AI systems. This is relevant to Articles 10 and 50, highlighting the importance of addressing bias and promoting fairness.
	Transparency and explainability: Use model interpretation techniques to understand and communicate how the model arrives at its decisions.	Transparency and explainability are central to the Act, with Article 13 focusing on high-risk systems and Article 86 providing a right to explanation for individuals affected by AI decisions. Using interpretation techniques in this phase supports compliance.
	Robustness: Perform extensive testing of the model's performance under various conditions, including edge cases and potential adversarial scenarios.	Robustness is a key requirement for high-risk AI systems under Article 15. Comprehensive testing in this phase helps ensure the model's resilience and compliance.
	Accountability and redress: Establish clear criteria for model performance and define processes for handling cases where the model fails to meet these criteria.	Article 20 addresses corrective actions. Establishing criteria and processes for redress in this phase contributes to meeting these obligations.
Deployment	Human oversight: Establish human-in-the-loop processes for high-stakes decisions. Design the deployment process to allow for human oversight and intervention when necessary.	Articles 14 and 26 mandate human oversight, particularly for high-risk systems. Implementing human-in-the-loop processes during deployment is essential for compliance.
	Safety, security, and dependability: Implement safeguards to protect the deployed model from tampering or unauthorized access.	Article 15 addresses security and robustness. Implementing safeguards during deployment ensures ongoing compliance.
	Transparency and explainability: Provide clear documentation on how the model should be used, including its limitations and potential biases.	Transparency is crucial under the EU AI Act. Providing clear documentation during deployment contributes to meeting this requirement.
	Accountability and redress: Log model inputs/outputs for auditing purposes. Establish clear lines of responsibility for the model's outputs and decisions. Set up mechanisms for users to challenge or appeal decisions made by the AI system.	The Act requires recordkeeping (Article 12), places obligations on providers (Article 16), outlines corrective actions (Article 20), and grants a right to appeal AI decisions (Article 85).

CRISP-ML(Q) phase	AI governance principles	Relevance to the EU AI Act
Monitoring and maintenance	Human oversight: Regularly review model performance and decisions with human experts.	Human oversight is a continuous requirement for high-risk systems. Regular reviews with experts contribute to fulfilling this obligation.
	Safety and dependability: Monitor for data/concept drift and model performance degradation. Continuously evaluate the model's performance and security, updating as necessary to address any emerging vulnerabilities.	The EU AI Act mandates risk management (Article 9) and robustness and security (Article 15). Continuous monitoring and updates align with these requirements.
	Fairness and inclusiveness: Track fairness metrics in production. Regularly check for any emerging biases or unfair outcomes as the model operates on new data.	Articles 10 and 50 emphasize addressing bias. Monitoring fairness metrics in this phase helps ensure ongoing compliance.
	Accountability and redress: Establish processes for addressing and correcting model errors or biases. Implement a feedback loop to incorporate lessons learned from the model's real-world performance into future iterations.	Continuously improving the model within ethical boundaries may be guided by codes of practice (Article 56).

The integration of AI governance and MLOps is discussed in Appendix C.

To further demonstrate why data and AI governance are interleaved and should be considered holistically, let's consider an example. Suppose an EU-based company develops an AI model for job candidate screening (a high-risk AI use case under the EU AI Act). Without data governance, it may unknowingly train the model on biased data (e.g., historical hiring patterns favoring one gender), leading to discriminatory decisions. Without AI governance, it may deploy the model without proper transparency, testing, or monitoring. This would result in noncompliance with the EU AI Act, risking fines, reputational damage, and harm to individuals.

However, if both data and AI governance are integrated:

- The dataset will be assessed for fairness, diversity, and quality.
- The model will be explainable, monitored, and thoroughly documented.
- The organization will be able to demonstrate compliance and maintain trust.

Emerging Trends in Data and AI Governance

The evolving landscape of data and AI governance highlights the need for more advanced, automated, and ethical approaches to managing and using data and AI technologies. Organizations that adapt to these trends will likely gain a competitive advantage in leveraging their data assets while ensuring compliance and security. Let's look at the five most notable trends in data and AI governance:

Focus on ethics, trust, and enhanced data privacy
: There's a growing emphasis on building trust in AI systems through ethical practices. This includes addressing concerns about fairness, bias, privacy, and the potential misuse of AI technologies. In the age of generative AI, organizations are increasingly developing and implementing ethical frameworks for AI governance to address issues such as large language model hallucinations and to implement corresponding safety guardrails. These frameworks address issues of bias, fairness, and transparency in AI systems and ensure adherence to the organization's own ethical values and industry-specific standards.

  In addition, amid growing privacy concerns—especially around AI—companies are placing more focus on data privacy measures. This includes strengthening data protection policies and increasing transparency about data usage.

Adoption of AI in data management and proactive compliance automation
: AI and ML technologies are being integrated into data governance processes to automate data governance tasks, enhance data quality, and provide predictive analytics. This trend enables more efficient data processing and improved scalability in data management. Furthermore, AI is increasingly used to automate and improve compliance processes, including risk forecasting, regulatory change management, and real-time monitoring.

Focus on data lineage and provenance in AI
: With the rise of generative AI, there's an increased emphasis on tracing data lineage throughout AI models. This trend is crucial for error detection, analysis, and ensuring regulatory compliance in AI applications. I expect proactive data and AI governance frameworks to emerge based on data lineage and active metadata.

Shift left data and AI governance
: Companies are prioritizing a "shift left" approach, implementing data governance and security measures early in the data collection and processing stages. This proactive approach simplifies data security, improves data quality, and addresses issues early on.

Decentralized data governance
: There's currently a shift toward more decentralized governance structures. This allows for greater autonomy and agility within domain teams while maintaining overall organizational standards. With the growing emphasis on "data as a product" thinking and data contracts, many companies are adopting this approach to data governance.

Conclusion

This chapter discussed the data and AI governance processes required for compliance with the EU AI Act. The Act emphasizes the importance of robust data and AI governance frameworks. Data governance ensures high-quality, representative data for training AI models, which is crucial for both regulatory compliance and the development of trustworthy AI systems. AI governance frameworks provide the oversight and controls needed to align AI development with business strategy, regulatory requirements, and ethical principles. Both data and AI governance are essential for managing the risks associated with AI use, which is central to business strategy, compliance, and trustworthiness. Transparency and accountability, core principles of governance, are not only required by the EU AI Act but are fundamental to trustworthy AI.

In the next chapter, I will outline the classification framework for AI system risk. For high-risk and limited-risk AI systems, planning AI engineering processes to ensure compliance with the EU AI Act is critical. When integrating ethical and compliance aspects into the AI system development process, it's also vital to structure team topologies to include dedicated ethics, compliance, and governance roles.

CHAPTER 4
AI System Assessment and Tailoring AI Engineering for Different Risk Levels

In this chapter, the main learning objective is to understand how to practically classify different AI system risk levels and how to design AI engineering processes for each risk level (see Figure 4-1 for a visual of the steps to take to move toward compliance with the EU AI Act). We'll explore the EU AI Act's risk classification framework and the obligation mapping phase. For high-risk and limited-risk AI systems, careful planning of data governance, AI governance, and MLOps processes is essential to ensure compliance with the Act.

Figure 4-1. This chapter focuses on creating the AI system landscape in an organization and classifying the risk types. See Chapter 1 for an explanation of the end-to-end process steps toward EU AI Act compliance.

This chapter will help you answer the following questions:

- How many AI systems are currently in place or intended to be put into production?
- What risk categories do those AI systems belong to?
- How can clarity be established about the role of the provider or deployer of each AI model?

In discussions about the EU AI Act, people frequently use terms such as "AI compliance," "AI governance," and "risk management." While closely related and complementary, these are distinct concepts. Let's begin by clarifying what each one means.

AI Compliance, Governance, and Risk Management

We explored AI compliance and governance in the previous chapters. As a reminder, *AI compliance* focuses on adhering to legal, regulatory, and policy standards, ensuring ethical behavior, and promoting transparency through rigorous processes, metrics, and stakeholder engagement. *AI governance* establishes a framework for ethical and responsible AI development, emphasizing transparency, stakeholder engagement, and balancing innovation with ethical considerations. *AI risk management* involves identifying and addressing risks associated with AI systems, focusing on robust assessment practices, effective mitigation strategies, and promoting a culture of awareness and proactive action.

AI Risk

NIST (*https://oreil.ly/PcOcW*) describes risk in the context of AI systems as a function of the negative impact, or magnitude of harm, that would arise if a certain circumstance or event occurs, and the likelihood of its occurrence. That negative impact or harm can be experienced by individuals, groups, communities, organizations, society, the environment, or the planet.

Here are some well-known examples that illustrate the diverse range of risks associated with AI, spanning ethical, social, economic, and technical domains:

Algorithmic bias
: AI systems can perpetuate or strengthen existing societal biases, leading to unfair treatment of certain groups. For example, facial recognition systems have shown higher error rates for women and people of color.

Privacy violations and social manipulation

AI systems that process large amounts of personal data can pose risks to individual privacy. For instance, AI algorithms used by social media platforms can be exploited to influence user behavior and opinions, potentially impacting democratic processes. The Cambridge Analytica scandal, where personal data from millions of Facebook users was harvested and used for targeted political advertising, is a prominent example.

Deepfakes

AI-generated videos or audio recordings can be used to spread misinformation or manipulate public opinion.

Autonomous weapons

The development of AI-powered weapons that can operate without human control raises ethical concerns and the risk of unintended harm.

AI-enabled cyberattacks

AI can be used to enhance the scale of cyberattacks, making them more difficult to detect and defend against.

Lack of transparency

The opaque nature of some AI algorithms and models can make it difficult to understand or explain their decision-making processes, which is problematic in high-stakes domains like healthcare and criminal justice.

Environmental impact

The energy consumed to train and operate large AI models contributes to carbon emissions and raises environmental concerns.

Safety risks in critical systems

AI failures in critical infrastructure or systems—such as healthcare, power grids, or transportation—can have severe consequences.

Intellectual property issues

AI-generated content raises questions about copyright and ownership, potentially infringing on intellectual property rights.

Autonomous vehicle accidents

While designed to improve safety, self-driving cars have been involved in accidents, highlighting the challenges of integrating AI into complex real-world environments.

Table 4-1 compares and contrasts AI compliance, governance, and risk management frameworks along a number of dimensions, including objectives, people and processes involved, engineering considerations, cultural practices, and more.

Table 4-1. Comparison of AI compliance, governance, and risk management in the context of the EU AI Act

	AI compliance	AI governance	AI risk management
Objective	Ensure AI systems adhere to the requirements and obligations set forth in the EU AI Act, including risk management, data governance, human oversight, transparency, accuracy, robustness, and cybersecurity.	Establish a framework for overseeing AI development, deployment, and use in alignment with the EU AI Act, organizational values, and ethical principles.	Identify, assess, and mitigate risks associated with AI systems throughout their lifecycle, in compliance with the EU AI Act's risk-based approach.
People	Compliance officers, legal teams, data protection officers, AI ethics committees	AI ethics board, chief AI officer, AI ethics officer, cross-functional AI steering committee, AI project managers	Risk management teams, data scientists, AI engineers, cybersecurity experts
Processes	• Implement risk assessment procedures to categorize AI systems. • Establish documentation practices for high-risk AI systems. • Develop incident reporting and management protocols. • Create processes for conformity assessments and CE marking.	• Develop AI policies and guidelines aligned with the EU AI Act. • Implement review and approval processes for high-risk AI systems. • Establish mechanisms for ongoing monitoring and auditing of AI systems. • Create escalation procedures for AI-related issues and decisions.	• Perform regular AI risk assessments. • Conduct scenario planning for AI failures. • Ensure continuous monitoring of AI system performance. • Create incident response and recovery plans. • Define processes for regular risk reporting and review.
Metrics and KPIs	• Number of compliance violations • Time to address compliance issues • Percentage of AI projects passing compliance checks • Percentage of AI systems with proper documentation • Frequency of compliance audits	• Number of AI projects reviewed and approved by the governance committee • Percentage of AI systems adhering to established governance policies • Frequency and outcomes of AI system audits • Number of ethical reviews conducted	• Number of risks identified, assessed, and mitigated • Reduction in AI-related incidents over time • Time to resolve identified risks • Percentage of high-risk AI systems with completed risk assessments
Stakeholder engagement	• Internal: Collaboration between legal, technical, and operational teams • External: Interaction with regulators, compliance bodies, and industry standards organizations	• Internal: Cross-department collaboration, inclusive decision-making processes • External: Engagement with external advisors, industry forums, and regulatory bodies	• Risk communication to executive leadership • Collaboration with customers to align on risk tolerances • Engagement with insurers on AI-related coverage • Collaboration with industry partners on risk management best practices

	AI compliance	AI governance	AI risk management
Engineering practices	• Implement privacy-by-design and security-by-design principles. • Develop testing procedures for bias detection and mitigation. • Establish version control for data, code, and AI models. • Conduct regular code reviews, ensuring adherence to ethical guidelines and traceability.	• Implement standardized AI development methodologies. • Establish governance checkpoints at key stages of the AI lifecycle. • Integrate code review practices that specifically include governance considerations. • Incorporate governance requirements into DevOps practices.	• Integrate risk considerations into AI architecture design. • Implement robust testing procedures for AI systems, including adversarial testing. • Develop failsafe mechanisms and ensure graceful degradation for high-risk AI systems. • Establish monitoring systems for early risk detection in deployed AI systems.
Technology and infrastructure	• Compliance management software • Automated auditing tools • Explainable AI • Data protection technologies • Secure data storage • Robust logging systems • Compliance tracking systems	• AI model registries • Centralized AI governance platform • Data lineage tracking system • AI performance monitoring tools • Ethical AI framework	• AI risk monitoring and alerting systems • Simulation environments for risk testing • Automated risk assessment tools • Secure sandboxing for AI testing • Secure data environments • Resilient system architectures
Training and education	• Regular compliance training for AI developers • Workshops on emerging AI regulations • Certification programs for AI compliance	• Governance training for all employees involved in AI projects • Specialized courses on AI ethics and responsible AI development • Workshops on interpreting and applying EU AI Act requirements	• Risk management training specific to AI technologies • Educating developers on identifying and mitigating AI-specific risks
Change management	• Develop a roadmap for transitioning existing AI systems to comply with the Act. • Establish clear communication channels about compliance updates. • Create feedback mechanisms to continuously improve compliance processes.	• Develop a communication strategy for rolling out new governance policies. • Create transition plans for adapting existing AI systems to new governance requirements. • Establish feedback loops to continuously refine governance practices.	• Develop strategies for integrating risk management into existing AI workflows. • Make regular updates to risk management policies. • Communicate with stakeholders about risk status.

	AI compliance	AI governance	AI risk management
Cultural considerations	• Foster a culture of ethical AI development and responsible innovation. • Promote transparency and accountability in AI decision-making processes. • Facilitate cross-functional collaboration to address compliance challenges.	• Foster a culture of responsible AI innovation and ethical decision making. • Encourage open discussions about AI risks and governance challenges. • Recognize and reward adherence to AI governance principles.	• Foster a culture of proactive risk identification and mitigation. • Enable open reporting of potential risks without fear (create a "safe space"). • Promote a balanced approach to innovation and risk management.

AI compliance, governance, and risk management are closely interrelated. Compliance is primarily reactive in nature, establishing the baseline requirements for governance, while effective governance is proactive, guiding the responsible development and use of AI. Risk management complements and informs compliance and governance efforts by identifying and addressing potential threats in a timely manner. When implemented holistically and embedded into daily operations, these three pillars provide essential support for compliance with the EU AI Act.

Creating an AI System Inventory

To navigate the EU AI Act and understand its impact on your organization, you should first get an overview of your existing AI systems and potential AI use cases to assess whether they are subject to the legislation.

Note that AI use cases developed as internal research projects are generally excluded from compliance obligations.

Later in this chapter, I will outline the different maturity levels of AI projects and specify when the EU AI Act's requirements must be fulfilled. For now, please note that the Act impacts AI systems based on their risk level and intended use, rather than their development stage.

As described in Chapter 1, the EU AI Act applies to:

- Providers placing AI systems on the EU market or putting them into service
- Users of AI systems located within the EU
- Providers and users outside the EU, if the AI system's output is used within the EU

To help you in your inventory efforts, I recommend creating an *AI system inventory* by following these steps:

1. Identify AI applications across all departments.
2. Include both custom-developed and third-party AI solutions.
3. Document key details like department, purpose, data used, deployment status, and risk category.

> As a reminder, Article 3 of the EU AI Act defines an AI system as "a machine-based system that is designed to operate with varying levels of autonomy and that may exhibit adaptiveness after deployment, and that, for explicit or implicit objectives, infers, from the input it receives, how to generate outputs such as predictions, content, recommendations, or decisions that can influence physical or virtual environments."

You'll want to create a comprehensive inventory template to catalog all AI systems used or developed within your organization, capturing key attributes for each system. Figure 4-2 shows an example of what this might look like.

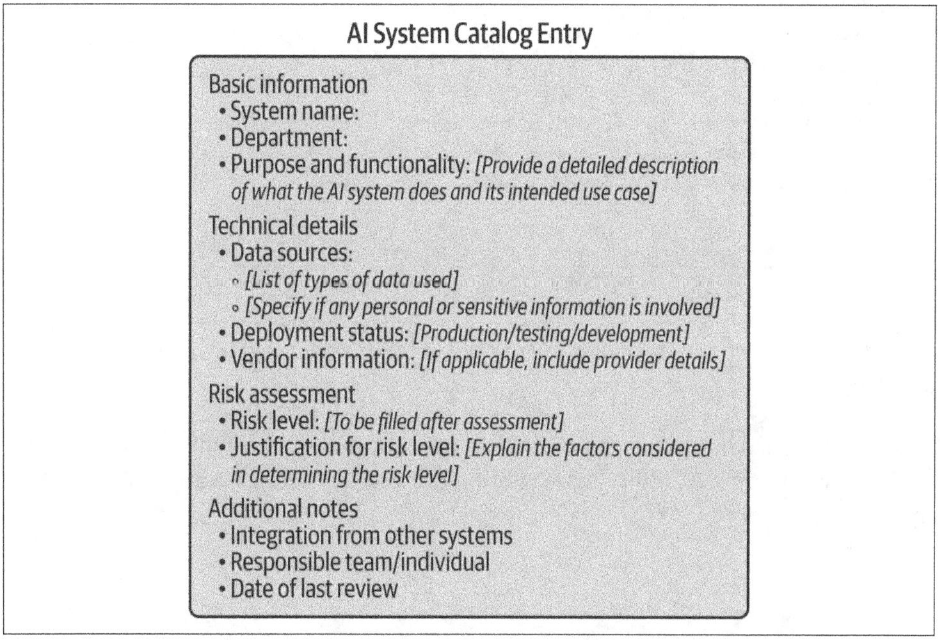

Figure 4-2. An AI system catalog entry should contain basic identifying information, technical details, a risk assessment, and additional relevant notes

Depending on your organization's needs, you can create this template using tools like Microsoft Excel, Google Sheets (as shown in Figure 4-3), Airtable, or more sophisticated database management systems. Knowledge management platforms such as Confluence or Notion can also be helpful for creating a catalog of AI systems, as can specialized AI governance tools like watsonx.ai, Dataiku, or Domino Data Lab.

Field	Description	Smart Price Prediction	Personalized Recommendations
Basic Information			
System Name	Name of the AI system	Smart Price Predictor	Personalized Recommender Engine
Department	Department responsible for the system	Revenue Management	Marketing & Sales
Purpose & Functionality		Predicts future pricing trends to optimize room rates for bookings	Recommends accommodation and travel options to users based on past behavior
Technical Details			
Data Sources	Types of data used by the system	-Historical booking data -Market trends -Competitor pricing	- User search history - Booking preferences - User reviews
Personal/Sensitive Information	Does the system handle any personal or sensitive data?	No	Yes (booking preferences)
Deployment Status	Current stage of the system	Production	Testing
Vendor Information	Information about the vendor (if applicable)	N/A (developed in-house)	N/A (developed in-house)
Risk Assessment			
Risk Level	(To be filled after assessment)	Medium	Low
Justification for Risk Level	Explain the factors considered for risk	Potential impact on revenue if predictions are inaccurate	Privacy concerns with user data
Additional Notes			
Integration with Other Systems		Revenue Management System	Booking Platform, User Profiles
Responsible Team/Individual	Team or person managing the system	Data Science Team	Marketing & Development Team
Date of Last Review	Date of the latest review on the system	2024-08-21	2024-07-15

Figure 4-3. An example of a catalog of existing AI systems for a hypothetical ecommerce company

After creating a complete and detailed inventory of the organization's AI systems, the next question you'll want to answer is whether the EU AI Act is applicable to those systems.

Applicability of the EU AI Act

The EU AI Act's applicability to a given AI system depends on several factors, including whether the system falls within the Act's the scope and definition of AI, whether it has already been placed on the market or put into service, and the timing of the Act's entry into force and application.

> The relevant articles of the EU AI Act are:
>
> - Article 2: Scope (*https://oreil.ly/eBlrf*)
> - Article 3: Definitions (*https://oreil.ly/ogId3*) and Recital 12 (*https://oreil.ly/5h0Su*)
> - Article 111: AI Systems Already Placed on the Market or put into Service and General-Purpose AI Models Already Placed on the Market (*https://oreil.ly/d8_kg*)
> - Article 113: Entry into Force and Application (*https://oreil.ly/s_NYt*)

Complying with the EU AI Act involves a complex process flow with many conditions, as pictured in Figure 4-4. After clarifying whether the Act is applicable to a particular system, you'll need to establish your organization's role (such as provider or deployer) and classify the system's risk level. These two factors determine the specific set of obligations your organization must fulfill.

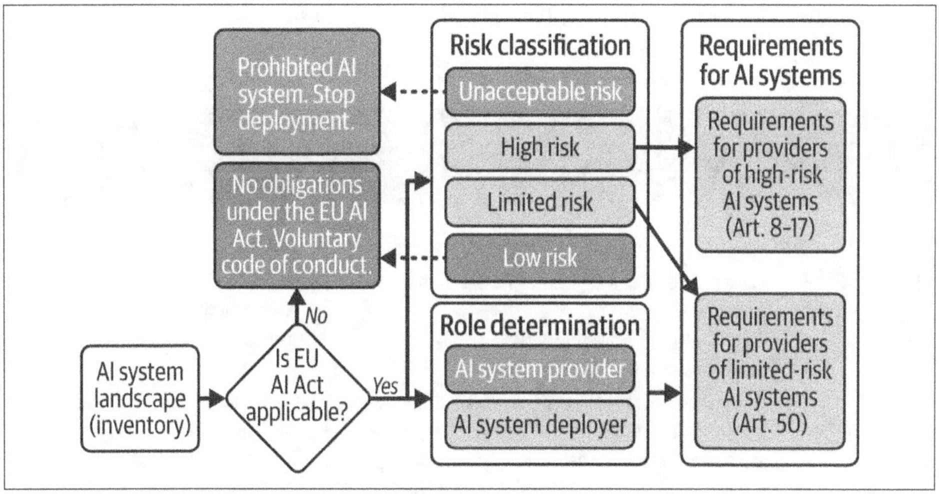

Figure 4-4. The process of determining the EU AI Act's applicability to AI systems and their risk classification (adapted from https://oreil.ly/LUZWC [CC BY 4.0], courtesy of the appliedAI Institute for Europe gGmbH)

We'll look at the processes for determining applicability, risk level, and organizational role in more detail later in this chapter. First, let's examine the use cases that are *prohibited* by the EU AI Act.

Unacceptable Risk—Prohibited AI Practices

Human values such as privacy, integrity, social justice, transparency, and diversity are at the core of EU law, and with the growing adoption of AI technologies, they are becoming increasingly important in software and AI development. To ensure the safety of AI, it's more effective to regulate its applications rather than the technology itself.

Technology itself is neither inherently good nor bad, but it can be used in benevolent or harmful ways. To underscore this idea, Table 4-2 gives some examples of useful and harmful applications of the same technologies. This is important because AI technology is general-purpose, and developers—such as those who release open-weight and open source foundation models—can't fully control how others might use it. To give a specific example, fake reviews were a problem on many websites even before the widespread adoption of generative AI, requiring companies to devote significant resources to detecting and removing them. Traditional fake reviews often used similar language, making them easier to spot. However, the ability of GenAI tools to automatically rephrase or rewrite text has made detecting fake reviews increasingly challenging. In a case like this, the solution is not to limit the use of the technology itself; instead, when AI is used in a harmful way, it is that specific application that should be addressed and, if necessary, restricted or halted.

Table 4-2. Useful and harmful applications of general-purpose technologies

General-purpose technology	Applications	
	Useful	**Harmful**
Nuclear technology	• Electricity generation • Large-scale desalination plants to produce fresh water from seawater • Medical imaging (X-rays, CT scans) • Cancer treatments like radiation therapy	• Nuclear weapons • Nuclear waste (as a byproduct) • Nuclear facilities (potential for reactor meltdowns and radioactive contamination)
Artificial intelligence	• Automating repetitive tasks and streamlining processes • Analyzing vast amounts of data to provide insights for more informed business decisions • Enabling personalized recommendations and experiences	• Autonomous weapons systems • Spreading misinformation or manipulating public opinion • Political deepfakes

Prohibited AI Use Cases

The EU AI Act aims to protect fundamental rights, democracy, and the rule of law by banning AI applications that are incompatible with core EU values and rights. In general, the Act prohibits AI systems from:

- Using subliminal, manipulative, or deceptive techniques to misinterpret behavior and prevent informed decision making, causing significant harm
- Exploiting vulnerabilities related to age, disability, or socioeconomic circumstances to distort behavior, causing significant harm
- Utilizing biometric categorization systems to infer sensitive attributes such as race, political opinions, religious beliefs, and sexual orientation
- Conducting social scoring (i.e., evaluating individuals based on social behavior or personal traits), which can lead to discriminative treatment
- Creating or expanding facial recognition databases through untargeted scraping of facial images from the internet or CCTV footage
- Inferring emotions in workplaces or educational institutions, except for medical or safety reasons

All prohibited AI systems were required to have been removed from the EU market by February 2025, six months after the Act entered into force (please refer to Chapter 1 for details on the implementation timeline). It is important to correctly identify and classify these systems to ensure they are removed from operation, in accordance with the regulation.

Let's take a closer look at the some of the specific types of AI systems that are prohibited:

Systems that manipulate people through subliminal techniques
: These are systems that use hidden tricks, like sounds or images, to influence people without them realizing it—for example, an AI system that plays barely audible music in a store to influence people to buy more things.

Systems that use facial recognition to categorize people based on sensitive characteristics
: This means systems that use facial recognition technology to sort people into groups based on their race, religion, sexual orientation, or other personal characteristics. Such systems are prohibited to protect people from being discriminated against based on these characteristics.

Social scoring systems

These are systems that create a score for a person based on their online behavior or other personal information. This score could then be used to deny people jobs, housing, or other opportunities. (See "Deep Dive: Social Scoring" on page 86 for an example of social scoring.)

Law enforcement facial recognition in public places (except for specific cases)

This means that police and other law enforcement agencies cannot normally use facial recognition technology to scan people in public places. There are some exceptions, though, such as when they are looking for missing people, trying to prevent terrorism, or trying to catch criminals.

AI systems that predict criminality

These are systems that use artificial intelligence to try to guess whether someone is likely to commit a crime in the future. This is not allowed because it could lead to people being punished for something they haven't done.

Systems that build facial recognition databases without people's permission

This means that companies and organizations cannot collect large databases of people's faces without their permission. This is to protect people's privacy.

Emotion recognition systems at work or school (except for special cases)

These are systems that use artificial intelligence to try to guess what emotions people are feeling. This is generally not allowed in workplaces or schools, but there are some exceptions. For example, an AI system might be allowed to do this if it is being used to help people with autism learn to understand emotions.

> Chapter II, Article 5 of the EU AI Act (*https://oreil.ly/I-18Z*) contains 19 recitals—numbers 3 and 28–45—that you can consult to more deeply understand the prohibited AI use cases.

Deep Dive: Social Scoring

Some forms of social scoring are already present in our daily lives. For example, financial institutions may use credit scoring systems that consider past financial behavior and social media data. Similarly, some insurance companies adjust rates based on data collected from fitness trackers. According to the EU AI Act, Recital 31 (*https://oreil.ly/cWYg4*), social scoring systems are prohibited due to the following key concerns:

Discriminatory outcomes

Social scoring systems may lead to discriminatory results and the exclusion of certain groups.

Violation of fundamental rights
: These systems can violate the rights to dignity, non-discrimination, equality, and justice. There are also concerns about AI tools that compromise user privacy by collecting sensitive data without consent.

Unfair evaluation
: Social scoring systems evaluate or classify individuals based on multiple data points related to their social behavior across various contexts or on known, inferred, or predicted personal characteristics over time. The scoring mechanisms often lack transparency, fairness, and accountability.

Harmful treatment
: The social scores obtained from these systems can result in negative treatment of individuals or groups in social contexts unrelated to where the data was initially generated or collected.

Extreme consequences
: Social scoring can lead to harmful treatment that is unjustified relative to the gravity of a person's social behavior.

Broad impact
: These systems can affect individuals' access to services, employment, or other opportunities.

The EU AI Act aims to mitigate these risks by prohibiting social scoring AI systems. This ban applies to public and private actors using AI for social scoring.

Determining EU AI Act Obligations

To determine your obligations under the EU AI Act, you need to take two fundamental steps when assessing your AI systems:

1. Determine whether the Act applies to any AI systems in your inventory and clarify the scope of your obligations by answering the following questions:
   - Do they meet the Act's definition of an "AI system"? (For more on this, see the following sidebar.)
   - If so, are they within the scope of the Act based on their intended use and risk classification? Those systems with low risk are exempt.
   - Are they considered high risk?
   - Do transparency obligations apply?
2. Identify your organization's role with respect to each system. Is it acting as a provider or deployer?

How to Determine Whether a System Qualifies as an AI System Under the EU AI Act

To determine whether an AI system meets the Act's definition, consider the following questions:

1. *Is it a machine-based (computational) system?* The system must be implemented in software and run on hardware (e.g., computers, sensors, robots).
2. *Is it designed to operate with some level of autonomy?* Does it make decisions or perform actions *without constant human direction* (even if partially supervised)?
3. *Does it produce outputs based on input data?* For example, does it generate *predictions, recommendations, decisions, or content* by processing data?
4. *Are the outputs generated through inference (not just fixed rules)?* Does it use *statistical, logical, symbolic, or machine learning techniques* to infer a result from data?
5. *Is it designed to achieve an explicit or implicit objective?* Does it aim to solve a task, meet a goal, or optimize an outcome (e.g., classify images, suggest content)?
6. *Can its outputs influence a physical or virtual environment?* Can it impact the real world or a digital system (e.g., control a robot, change what a user sees)?
7. *Optional but relevant: Can it adapt after deployment?* Does it have the ability to *learn or change behavior over time* based on its experience? (Note: This is not required, but strengthens the case.)

If you answered "yes" to questions 1 through 6, then the system qualifies as an AI system under the EU AI Act. If you answered "no" to any of the first three or four questions, it's likely not considered an AI system under the Act.

Once you've identified which of your AI systems meet the Act's definition, the next step is to classify their risk level. Your exact obligations will vary depending on this classification.

Framework for Classification of AI Systems by Risk Levels

Having already discussed the unacceptable risk category, here we will consider the remaining three categories: high risk, limited risk, and minimal risk. Let's start by reviewing the criteria that determine whether a system is classified as high risk.

High risk

The classification rules for high-risk AI systems, outlined in Article 6 of the EU AI Act (*https://oreil.ly/AyOj1*), aim to identify systems that may pose significant risks to health, safety, or fundamental rights. The classification takes into account both the AI system's intended purpose and the specific context and conditions under which it is used. Key considerations include:

- AI systems are classified as high risk whether they are placed on the market or put into service as standalone products or as components of other products. For AI systems used as safety components of products, the classification aligns with the EU's New Legislative Framework, ensuring consistency with broader product safety regulation.
- AI systems intended to be used as safety components of products covered by EU harmonization legislation (*https://oreil.ly/d5LQd*) are automatically classified as high risk.
- AI systems listed in Annex III (*https://oreil.ly/9-WO8*) are classified as high risk. These include systems intended for use in the areas of:
  - Biometric identification and categorization of natural persons (e.g., AI systems for remote biometric identification in publicly accessible spaces)
  - Management and operation of critical infrastructure (e.g., AI systems used as safety components in the supply of water, gas, heating, or electricity)
  - Education and vocational training (e.g., AI systems used to evaluate students or assess educational institutions)
  - Employment, workers management, and access to self-employment (e.g., AI systems used for recruitment, promotion, and termination decisions)
  - Access to and enjoyment of key private services and public services and benefits (e.g., AI systems used to evaluate creditworthiness or establish credit scores)
  - Law enforcement (e.g., AI systems used by law enforcement to predict crimes or assess recidivism risk)
  - Migration, asylum, and border control management (e.g., AI systems used to process asylum, visa, and residence permit applications)
  - Administration of justice and democratic processes (e.g., AI systems used in judicial proceedings to assist judges)

Certain systems are exempted from high-risk classification even if they might otherwise qualify. These include:

- AI systems used for purely accessory purposes (e.g., performing a narrowly procedural task, improving the result of a previously completed human activity, or performing a preparatory task)
- AI systems used exclusively for scientific research and development
- AI systems used for military applications

EU AI Act high-risk system questionnaire. Classifying AI applications as high risk means they are subject to stricter requirements under the EU AI Act related to risk management procedures, data governance measures, technical documentation, recordkeeping, transparency, human oversight, accuracy, and cybersecurity controls.

Reading and interpreting the EU AI Act can be daunting. To help with determining whether an AI system qualifies as high risk under the Act, I have prepared a straightforward questionnaire, divided into four main sections:

1. Application area
2. Specific use cases
3. Impact assessment
4. Technical characteristics

The questionnaire is presented in Table 4-3. Start with section 1 and work through each section in turn. The more affirmative answers you have, especially in sections 1 and 2, the more likely it is that your AI system is considered high risk.

> Classifying an AI system with confidence can be challenging. In its white paper "AI Act: Risk Classification of AI Systems from a Practical Perspective" (*https://oreil.ly/a_oMu*), the applied AI Institute examined more than 100 AI systems from different enterprise functions (marketing, production, purchasing, etc.) and determined that 18% were in the high-risk class, 42% were low risk, and for the remaining 40% it was unclear whether they fell into the high-risk class or not. The percentage of high-risk systems in this sample thus could be anywhere between 18% and 58%.
>
> The study identified several ambiguities in defining criteria across different areas as the main causes of unclear risk classifications for AI systems. For example, in many cases it is not clear whether a system is functioning as a "safety component."

Table 4-3. EU AI Act high-risk system questionnaire

Question	Yes	No
1. Application area		
Is the AI system intended to be used in any of the following areas?		
• Biometric identification and categorization of natural persons	[ ]	[ ]
• Critical infrastructure (e.g., transport, energy, water supply)	[ ]	[ ]
• Education or vocational training	[ ]	[ ]
• Employment, worker management, or access to self-employment	[ ]	[ ]
• Access to and enjoyment of essential private services and public services and benefits	[ ]	[ ]

Question	Yes	No
• Law enforcement	[ ]	[ ]
• Migration, asylum, and border control management	[ ]	[ ]
• Administration of justice and democratic processes	[ ]	[ ]
If you checked any box in section 1, proceed to section 2. If not, your system is likely not considered high risk.		
2. Specific use cases		
Within the selected area(s), does your AI system fall under any of these specific use cases?		
• AI systems used as safety components of products	[ ]	[ ]
• AI systems for management or operation of critical infrastructure	[ ]	[ ]
• AI systems for determining access to educational institutions or assigning persons to such institutions	[ ]	[ ]
• AI systems for recruitment, evaluation, promotion, or termination of work-related contractual relationships	[ ]	[ ]
• AI systems for evaluating creditworthiness or establishing credit scores	[ ]	[ ]
• AI systems for dispatching emergency first response services	[ ]	[ ]
• AI systems for law enforcement purposes (e.g., predicting crimes, profiling individuals)	[ ]	[ ]
• AI systems for migration, asylum, and border control management (e.g., verifying travel documents)	[ ]	[ ]
• AI systems to assist judicial authorities in researching and interpreting facts and the law	[ ]	[ ]
If you checked any box in section 2, your AI system is likely considered high risk. If not, proceed to section 3.		
3. Impact assessment		
Does your AI system have the potential to:		
• Cause significant harm to the health, safety, or fundamental rights of individuals?	[ ]	[ ]
• Have a significant impact on the lives of a large number of EU residents?	[ ]	[ ]
• Be difficult for individuals to opt out of or avoid?	[ ]	[ ]
Is the AI system intended to be used in a manner that could result in:		
• Discrimination against protected groups?	[ ]	[ ]
• Manipulation of human behavior?	[ ]	[ ]
• Exploitation of vulnerabilities of specific groups?	[ ]	[ ]
If you checked any box in section 3, your AI system may be considered high risk, depending on the context and potential impact.		
4. Technical characteristics		
Does your AI system:	[ ]	[ ]
• Use large datasets for training or operation?	[ ]	[ ]
• Employ complex algorithms or machine learning techniques?	[ ]	[ ]
• Have a high degree of autonomy in decision making?	[ ]	[ ]
• Operate in a manner that is not fully transparent or explainable?	[ ]	[ ]
If you checked multiple boxes in section 4, combined with affirmative answers in previous sections, your system is more likely to be considered high risk.		

Interpretation guide. If you have affirmative answers in sections 1 and 2, or in section 1 combined with multiple affirmative answers in sections 3 and 4, your AI system is likely to be considered high risk under the EU AI Act. However, the final determination may depend on the specific context, implementation, and potential impact of your system.

> It's important to note that the European Commission can adjust Annex III and add new high-risk AI systems as technology evolves, following the criteria outlined in Article 7 (*https://oreil.ly/ipd1a*). This allows the regulation to remain responsive to emerging AI applications and risks.
>
> For a definitive assessment, it is recommended to consult legal experts and stay up-to-date on the latest guidance from EU authorities.

Limited risk (transparency obligations)

To be clear, the EU AI Act does not formally define a category of "limited-risk" AI systems. Instead, it focuses on three main categories: prohibited AI practices under the unacceptable risk category (Article 5), high-risk AI systems (Article 6), and AI systems with specific transparency obligations (Article 50).

However, for clarity, I use the term "limited risk" to refer to AI systems that are not explicitly prohibited or high risk but are still subject to the transparency obligations laid out in Article 50 (*https://oreil.ly/cc73j*). This includes:

1. AI systems that are intended to interact with natural persons
2. Emotion recognition systems and biometric categorization systems
3. AI systems that generate or manipulate image, audio, text, or video content (including deepfakes)

As for high-risk systems, I have created a questionnaire that you can use to determine whether your AI system has specific transparency obligations. I'll discuss what those obligations are in Chapter 6.

EU AI Act limited-risk system questionnaire. Answer the questions in Table 4-4 to help determine if your AI system might be classified as a limited-risk system under the EU AI Act.

Table 4-4. EU AI Act limited-risk system questionnaire

Question	Yes	No
1. Is your AI system intended to interact with humans?	[ ]	[ ]
2. Does your AI system fall into any of these categories?		
• Chatbots	[ ]	[ ]
• Emotion recognition systems	[ ]	[ ]
• Biometric categorization systems	[ ]	[ ]
• AI systems used to generate or manipulate image, audio, or video content ("deepfakes")	[ ]	[ ]
3. Is your AI system specifically excluded from the limited-risk category for any of the following reasons?		
• It's classified as a high-risk AI system under the EU AI Act.	[ ]	[ ]
• It's used for general-purpose AI without a clearly defined intended purpose.	[ ]	[ ]
• It's used for a prohibited AI practice (e.g., social scoring, certain types of biometric identification).	[ ]	[ ]
4. Does your AI system have the potential to influence human behavior or decision making?	[ ]	[ ]
5. Is your AI system designed to be transparent about its AI nature?	[ ]	[ ]
6. Can users easily understand that they are interacting with an AI system?	[ ]	[ ]
7. Does your system provide clear disclaimers about its limitations and potential risks?	[ ]	[ ]
8. For systems that generate synthetic content (or manipulate image, audio, or video content), do you have measures in place to ensure the AI-generated content is clearly labeled as such?	[ ]	[ ]
9. For biometric categorization or emotion recognition systems, do you inform users about the system's purpose, functionality, and limitations?	[ ]	[ ]
10. Do you have processes in place to handle user complaints or concerns about the AI system?	[ ]	[ ]

Interpretation guide. You may interpret your answers as follows:

- If you answered "Yes" to question 1 and to any item in question 2, your system will likely be considered a limited-risk AI system.
- If you answered "Yes" to any item in question 3, your system is likely not a limited-risk system (it may be high risk or prohibited).
- Questions 4–10 relate to transparency and user protection requirements for limited-risk systems. Answering "No" to any of these may indicate areas where your system needs improvement to comply with the EU AI Act's requirements.

> Please note that this questionnaire is intended as a general guide. For a definitive assessment, it is recommended to consult legal experts and stay up-to-date on the latest guidance from EU authorities.

Low risk

Even though the EU AI Act focuses more heavily on high-risk AI systems, it is still important address "low-risk" AI systems, as most AI currently in use across the EU falls into this category and some of these systems (such as chatbots and emotion recognition tools) may still be subject to transparency requirements.

The Act does not explicitly define a "low-risk" category. However, by process of elimination, low-risk AI systems can be understood to be those that:

1. Do not involve practices prohibited under Article 5
2. Are not classified as high risk under Article 6
3. Are not subject to transparency obligations under the terms outlined in Article 50

These systems generally pose minimal risks to fundamental rights or public safety and are typically used for administrative or operational purposes rather than for making decisions with serious consequences.

Some examples of low-risk AI systems include:

- Spam filters (AI systems that help to identify and filter unwanted emails)
- Recommendation systems (AI systems that suggest products, movies, or other content based on user preferences)
- Chatbots that provide customer service (AI systems that can answer simple questions and provide basic assistance)
- AI-powered games (AI systems that can generate challenges or adapt to player behavior)

Since the EU AI Act primarily focuses on regulating high-risk AI systems and prohibiting certain AI practices, no specific obligations are defined for low-risk AI systems as a distinct category.

Note that the classification of an AI system can depend on its specific context and intended use. Even a seemingly low-risk AI system could become high risk if used in a way that could harm individuals or society.

For example, consider facial recognition technology, which can be used for purposes ranging from unlocking personal devices to surveillance:

- Unlocking personal devices is considered minimal risk as it involves a consenting individual using the technology privately and poses little to no risk to broader society.
- Surveillance by law enforcement, on the other hand, is classified as high risk due to its potential implications for fundamental rights and freedoms, such as privacy infringements and the risk of misidentification.

If you'd like more information about this complex topic, check out "Navigating the EU AI Act Maze Using a Decision-Tree Approach" (*https://oreil.ly/Zmit2*) by Himly Hanif et al.

Deployer or Provider

As mentioned earlier, an organization's obligations under the EU AI Act depend on two key factors: the AI system's risk category and whether it acts as a deployer or provider of the system. Let's review the definitions of those two roles.

Under the terms of the EU AI Act, a *provider* is any individual, company, public authority, agency, or other body that:

1. Develops an AI system or model, or has it developed by others
2. Places the system or model on the market or puts it into service, either for a fee or free of charge
3. Does so under their own name or trademark

Examples of providers include a tech company like Google that develops and releases large language models such as Gemini and a startup that develops an AI algorithm for predicting stock market trends and offers it as a service.

The EU AI Act defines a *deployer* as any individual, company, public authority, agency, or other body that:

1. Uses an AI system under their authority or control
2. Does so in a professional or business context (personal, non-professional use is excluded)

This definition applies regardless of whether the deployer is located within the EU or not, as long as the AI system's output is used within the EU.

Examples of deployers include a hospital using an AI system for medical diagnosis or treatment planning, a company using an AI-powered recruitment tool to screen job applicants, or a bank utilizing an AI system for credit scoring or loan approval.

An important distinction is that providers develop, place on the market, or put into service AI systems under their own name or trademark, whereas deployers use AI systems within their professional activities but do not develop or market the systems themselves. A company that develops an AI system for its own use can act as both a provider and a deployer. Additionally, a deployer may become a provider if they substantially modify an AI system or use it for purposes not intended by the original provider.

In Table 4-5, I provide a practical framework to help determine your organization's role and to identify all the relevant players who may act as deployers or providers of an AI system. The first step is to analyze every party involved in the machine learning lifecycle, using the CRISP-ML(Q) phases as a guide. For each actor, outline their specific activities, identify their location, and determine who sets or redefines the intended purpose of the AI system. Also consider the individuals or groups affected by its use. Based on this information, you can accurately assign the appropriate role to each identified organization.

Table 4-5. Analysis of the organizations involved in the machine learning (ML) lifecycle

CRISP-ML(Q) phase	Who is implementing and executing this phase?	What is being done?	Where is the organization located?
Business and data understanding			
Data preparation			
Development			
Evaluation			
Deployment			
Monitoring and maintenance			

Now that you've determined whether the Act applies to your AI systems and clarified your organization's role in relation to each system, you're ready to identify the regulatory implications.

Integrating EU AI Act Engineering Throughout the AI Development Lifecycle

Beyond the requirements and obligations mentioned in the previous sections, the EU AI Act (along with other regulations on AI systems) introduces additional compliance considerations, particularly regarding transparency, risk management, and data governance. It is crucial to incorporate AI engineering efforts into every phase of the AI product lifecycle, especially when developing high-risk AI systems. As pictured in Figure 4-5, the level of engineering engagement and compliance effort tends to increase as a project progresses from ideation and proof of concept to the minimum viable product (MVP) stage, affecting development time, costs, and risk management. By integrating these efforts early in the development process—i.e., adopting a "shift-left" philosophy—teams can reduce risks and ensure that the final product is both technically robust and compliant with evolving AI regulations.

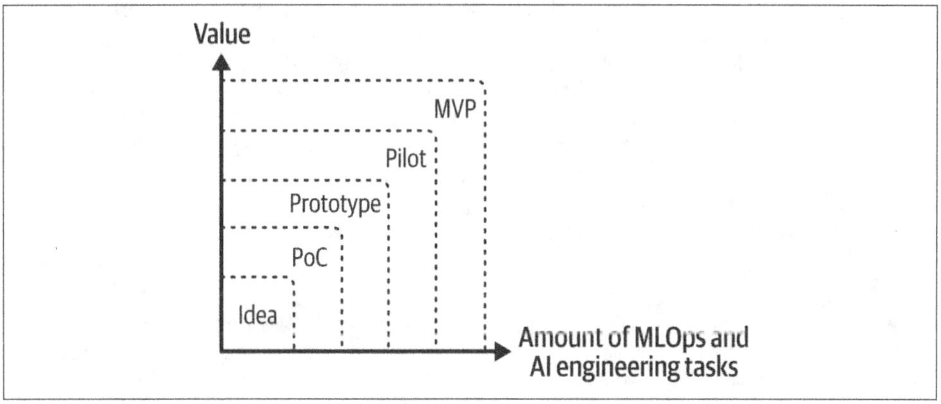

Figure 4-5. The usual delivery sequence and relationship between PoC, prototype, pilot, and MVP

Table 4-6 provides an overview of the different stages of AI development, illustrating the progression from initial idea to a market-ready product. In addition to core criteria such as scope, cost, and expected development time, it highlights relevant AI engineering tasks (both general and those specifically aimed at meeting EU AI Act compliance requirements).

Table 4-6. AI development stages and relevant AI engineering tasks

	Ideation	PoC	Prototype	Pilot	MVP
Purpose	Generate and explore innovative AI ideas.	Validate technical feasibility and potential value.	Create a working model to demonstrate core functionalities.	Test the AI solution in a real-world environment.	Launch a basic version to gather user feedback and validate market fit.
Scope of AI product	Broad, exploring multiple possibilities	Narrow, focused on key technical challenges	Limited, but includes core features and user interactions	Broader than prototype, but still limited to specific use cases or user groups	Includes essential features to solve the core problem
User involvement	Limited, mainly internal stakeholders	Minimal, possibly some expert users	Limited, typically internal testers or focus groups	Moderate, involving a select group of real users	Significant, engaging early adopters and gathering extensive feedback
Dev. time (typical)	Days to weeks	Weeks to a couple of months	1–3 months	3–6 months	6–12 months
Cost	Low	Low to medium	Medium	Medium to high	High
Risk	Very low	Low	Medium	Medium to high	High
AI eng. tasks (general)	• Define initial data requirements. • Sketch basic model architectures. • Outline potential deployment scenarios.	• Set up basic development environment. • Perform initial data collection and preprocessing. • Develop simple model(s). • Perform basic model evaluation.	• Implement data pipelines. • Develop more complex models. • Set up basic model versioning. • Implement basic model serving.	• Refine data pipelines. • Implement model monitoring. • Set up CI/CD for model deployment. • Implement basic A/B testing.	• Optimize data and model pipelines. • Implement advanced monitoring and alerting. • Set up automated retraining. • Implement advanced A/B testing and experimentation.
AI eng. tasks for EU AI Act compliance	• Conduct initial risk assessment. • Identify potential high-risk AI systems.	• Draft preliminary documentation of system architecture. • Define an initial data governance strategy.	• Implement basic data quality measures. • Design initial logging mechanisms. • Draft preliminary technical documentation.	• Implement more robust data governance. • Enhance logging and traceability. • Develop initial risk management system. • Begin human oversight implementation.	• Implement comprehensive data governance. • Establish full logging and traceability. • Implement a complete risk management system. • Finalize human oversight mechanisms. • Prepare for conformity assessment.

	Ideation	PoC	Prototype	Pilot	MVP
Outcomes	• List of potential AI solutions • Initial assessment of feasibility and value	• Technical validation report • Go/no-go decision for further development	• Working AI model • User interface mockups • Initial user feedback	• Performance metrics in real-world conditions • User adoption and satisfaction data • Identified areas for improvement	• Functional AI product • Initial user base • Comprehensive feedback for future iterations • Market validation

The introduction of the EU AI Act has had various implications with regard to AI system development:

1. AI engineering and compliance tasks become more complex as the project progresses from ideation to MVP. As the system matures, the need for robust MLOps processes and governance increases. Many AI engineering tasks, such as implementing robust data pipelines and model monitoring, directly contribute to meeting EU AI Act compliance requirements by ensuring data quality and system reliability.
2. Data governance becomes increasingly important in later stages, helping to ensure data quality and regulatory compliance.
3. Human oversight mechanisms become more sophisticated in later stages, in line with the EU AI Act's requirement for oversight of high-risk AI systems.
4. Risk assessment and management transition from high-level considerations in the early stages to comprehensive, continuous, and automated processes in the later stages.
5. As the project progresses, there's a greater emphasis on automating processes and ensuring scalability, particularly within MLOps tasks.
6. At the MVP stage, the focus shifts toward preparing for audits and conformity assessments, reflecting the regulatory requirements for high-risk AI systems under the EU AI Act.

Emerging Roles in Organizations for EU AI Act Compliance

As mentioned previously, the operationalization of EU AI Act compliance happens on two levels: the organizational level and the AI system level. I focus on the former in Appendix D, but I want to briefly touch on the topic here as well.

With the rapid adoption of AI, several new roles are emerging within organizations to help ensure compliance with the EU AI Act. Some of these roles should be incorporated into machine learning teams to ensure that ethical and compliance aspects are fully integrated into the AI development process. Adopting a Team Topologies perspective provides a concrete framework for meeting the Act's compliance requirements, ensuring that proper data governance is embedded throughout the ML development lifecycle. For further discussion of emerging roles and the implications of EU AI Act compliance for ML teams, see Appendix D.

Conclusion

The chapter explored the initial steps of creating an AI system landscape and classifying AI systems in the context of achieving compliance with the EU AI Act. To determine the specific requirements for your organization, you will need to identify the AI systems that are currently deployed and intended to be put into production and classify each of them based on risk level. You'll also need to determine whether the organization is acting as a provider or deployer of these AI systems, because the obligations differ depending on the role.

In the next chapter, I will cover the requirements for high-risk AI systems as outlined by the EU AI Act and how to implement them. Key topics will include the need for high-quality datasets, comprehensive documentation and recordkeeping, transparency, robustness and accuracy, security, risk management systems, human oversight, addressing ethical concerns and bias mitigation, monitoring in production, premarket compliance verification, and maintaining continuous compliance for high-risk AI systems.

CHAPTER 5
AI Engineering for High-Risk AI Systems

This chapter explores the comprehensive requirements for high-risk AI systems and how to meet them proactively by implementing AI engineering practices to ensure compliance with the EU AI Act (see Figure 5-1 for a visual of the steps to take to move toward compliance). In the previous chapter, I introduced the foundational steps for compliance: creating an inventory of current and planned AI systems, identifying the risk category of each, and determining whether your organization acts as a provider or deployer of these systems. These steps are essential for understanding which systems fall under the high-risk category and what compliance obligations need to be addressed.

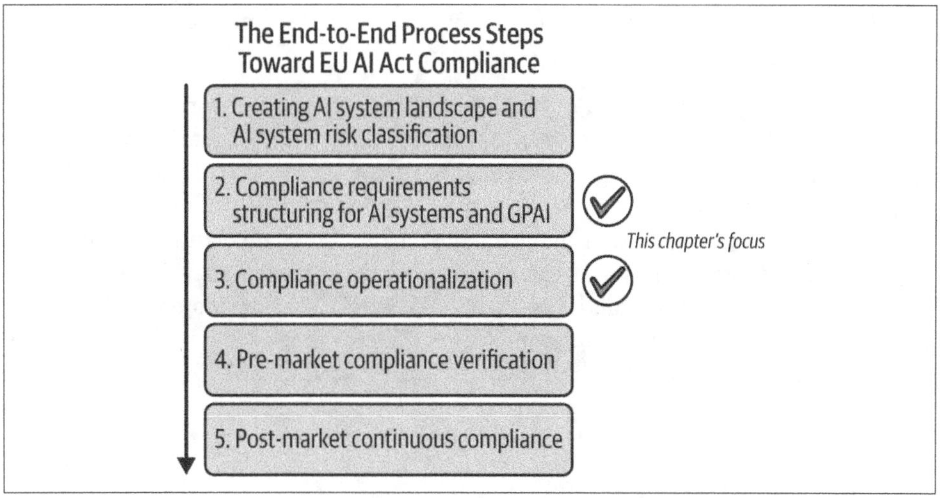

Figure 5-1. This chapter focuses on the requirements for high-risk AI systems and the operationalization of compliance for such systems. See Chapter 1 for an explanation of the end-to-end process steps toward EU AI Act compliance.

Two guiding questions to consider in this chapter are:

- To comply with the EU AI Act, what requirements must high-risk AI systems fulfill?
- What processes, structures, and AI engineering practices need to be established to comply with the EU AI Act?

Let's start by exploring the requirements for high-risk AI systems, translating them into AI engineering practices, and defining the notion of AI engineering for the EU AI Act in this way.

> As mentioned previously, the author is not a lawyer, and this book does not provide legal advice. The intersection of law and artificial intelligence is a complex subject that requires expertise beyond the scope of AI, data science, and machine learning. Legal considerations surrounding AI systems can be complex and far-reaching. If you have any legal concerns related to the AI systems you are working on, seek professional legal advice from qualified experts in the field.

AI Engineering for the EU AI Act

The EU AI Act regulates the development, deployment, and use of AI systems within the European Union. It aims to promote trustworthy AI by mitigating risks and protecting fundamental rights. As depicted in Figure 5-2, Articles 9–15 provide requirements for providers of high-risk AI systems. However, these articles do not provide technical guidance for implementing compliance.

This chapter suggests a method for technical implementation of compliance with the EU AI Act by aligning the Act's articles with the quality model for safety-critical AI systems outlined in the paper "Navigating the EU AI Act: A Methodological Approach to Compliance for Safety-Critical Products" (*https://oreil.ly/2J89P*) by Jessica Kelly et al., presented at the 2024 IEEE Conference on Artificial Intelligence (CAI). The authors propose an expanded product quality model for AI systems, drawing from established standards such as ISO/IEC 25059. This enhanced model includes additional attributes relevant to the EU AI Act, such as ethical integrity, human oversight, and fairness.

Part of Chapter III: High-Risk AI System

Section 2: Requirements for High-Risk AI Systems

← PREVIOUS NEXT →

Articles in this Chapter

Article 8: Compliance with the Requirements

Article 9: Risk Management System

Article 10: Data and Data Governance

Article 11: Technical Documentation

Article 12: Record-Keeping

Article 13: Transparency and Provision of Information to Deployers

Article 14: Human Oversight

Article 15: Accuracy, Robustness and Cybersecurity

Figure 5-2. EU AI Act Requirements for High-Risk AI Systems (source: https://oreil.ly/7h6xE)

Mapping EU AI Act requirements to quality attributes for AI systems is a helpful approach for several reasons, including:

Operationalization of regulatory requirements
: The EU AI Act provides high-level regulatory guidelines, which can be abstract and challenging to implement directly. By mapping these requirements to specific quality attributes, we create a more concrete, actionable framework for compliance. This helps translate legal language into technical specifications that engineers and data scientists can work with.

Integration with existing practices
: Quality attributes are well-established software and systems engineering concepts. Mapping EU AI Act requirements to these attributes facilitates the integration of regulatory compliance into existing development processes and quality assurance practices. This allows organizations to leverage familiar tools, methodologies, and metrics.

Alignment with standards
: Many quality attributes are defined by international standards (e.g., ISO/IEC 25010). Mapping EU AI Act requirements to these attributes helps align regulatory compliance with established standards, potentially simplifying overall compliance efforts.

In short, the mapping of EU AI Act articles to the quality attributes provides technical guidance for achieving compliance. Figure 5-3 provides a high-level overview of this mapping.

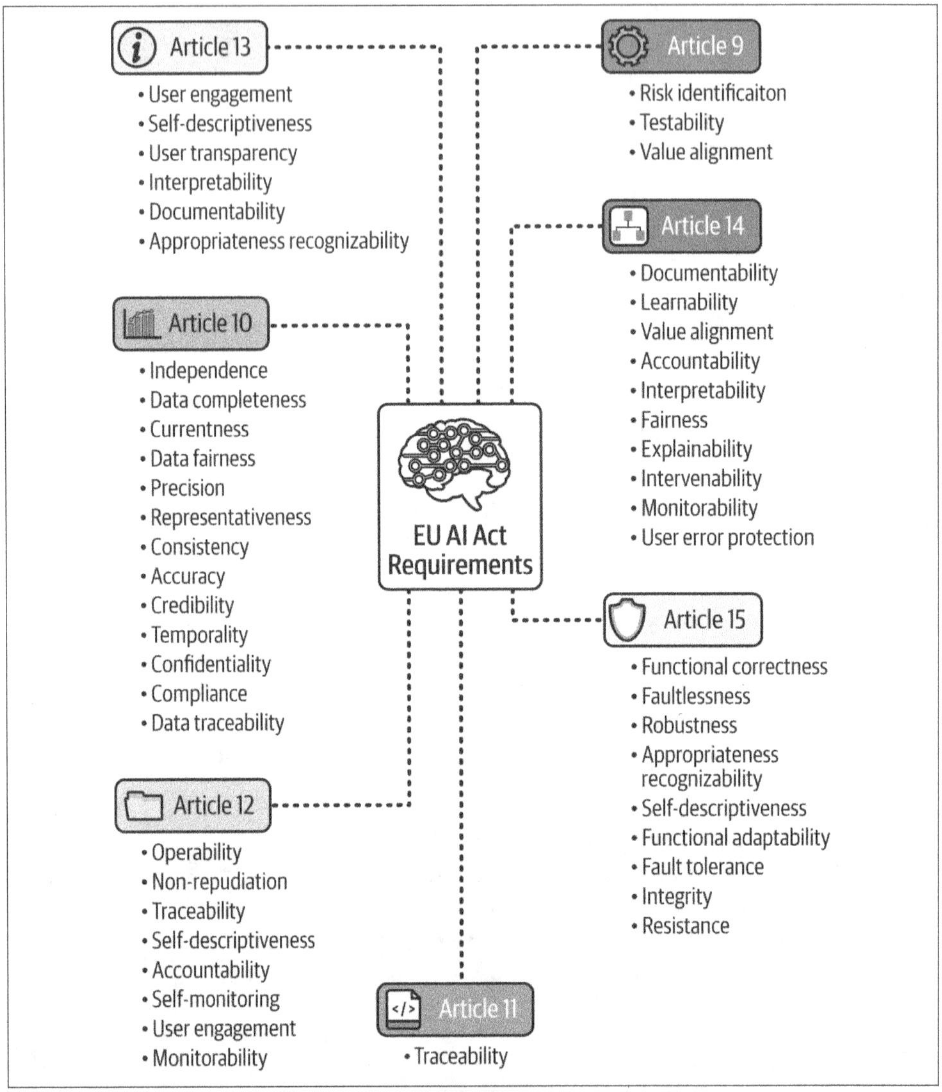

Figure 5-3. Mapping of EU AI Act requirements to quality attributes for AI systems

Goals

Before we discuss the method, let's explore what AI engineering for the EU AI Act involves. This multidisciplinary field focuses on designing, developing, deploying, and maintaining artificial intelligence systems in full compliance with the requirements of the Act. It combines expertise in AI technology, software engineering, data science, law, and ethics in order to achieve the following goals:

- Implement technical measures ensuring compliance with the Act's requirements, including risk assessment, transparency, human oversight, and robustness.
- Develop methodologies for continuous monitoring and auditing of AI systems throughout their lifecycle.
- Create documentation and traceability mechanisms to demonstrate compliance and facilitate regulatory inspections.
- Integrate privacy-enhancing technologies and data governance practices aligned with EU data protection laws.
- Design user interfaces and operational protocols that enable effective human oversight and intervention.
- Collaborate with legal and policy experts to interpret and apply evolving AI regulations across diverse application domains.

Alignment with CRISP-ML(Q) Phases

To establish effective engineering processes, we'll align the quality attributes of safety-critical (i.e., high-risk) AI systems with the phases of the CRISP-ML(Q) development process model introduced in Chapter 2.

A core principle of CRISP-ML(Q) is the integration of quality assurance practices into each phase of the machine learning lifecycle. This includes defining system requirements, identifying potential risks, and applying risk mitigation strategies based on established best practices. As such, this model provides a suitable framework for integrating the quality attributes essential to safety-critical AI systems. As discussed previously, these attributes can be mapped directly to regulatory requirements such as those defined in the EU AI Act. Addressing them throughout the development lifecycle supports *continuous compliance*, rather than treating compliance as a one-time task.

As you already know, CRISP-ML(Q) defines six key phases in the ML development process: business and data understanding, data preparation, modeling, evaluation, deployment, and monitoring and maintenance. It's an iterative framework, where each phase consists of specific tasks (such as dataset cleaning or model training) and outputs (such as datasets or model artifacts). Many quality attributes relate directly to potential risks. By considering these attributes in each development phase, you can identify and address risks early, when changes are less costly and more feasible to implement. In this chapter, I align the CRISP-ML(Q) phases with the quality attributes linked to EU AI Act requirements to establish AI engineering best practices that support robust implementation and sustained compliance.

AI Engineering Practices for Achieving Compliance

The requirements for providers of high-risk AI systems are distributed across several articles in the EU AI Act. For your convenience, I've included them here as condensed action points:

- Establish a risk management system that spans the entire AI system lifecycle.
- Ensure strong data governance by validating and testing datasets to guarantee their relevance, representativeness, and accuracy in relation to the system's intended purpose.
- Create comprehensive technical documentation to demonstrate compliance and provide authorities with the necessary information for assessment.
- Enable automatic logging capabilities in the AI system to track serious incidents and substantial modifications throughout its lifecycle.
- Provide detailed instructions for downstream deployers to support compliance.
- Incorporate human oversight mechanisms into the system's design for downstream deployers.
- Ensure the system meets standards for accuracy, robustness, and cybersecurity.
- Establish a quality management system to support and maintain compliance. The requirements for this system are laid out in Article 17 (*https://oreil.ly/zAKkT*).

In the remainder of this chapter we will explore Articles 9–15 of the EU AI Act, which lay out the requirements for providers of high-risk AI systems, and see how these legal requirements translate into actionable AI engineering practices.

Article 9: Risk Management System

Article 9

Article 9 of the EU AI Act (*https://oreil.ly/an4z8*) introduces a foundational requirement for high-risk AI systems: the establishment of a risk management system. This system is intended to ensure that AI technologies are developed and deployed responsibly, with close attention paid to identifying, assessing, and mitigating potential risks.

As shown in Figure 5-4, key points of Article 9 include:

Continuous process
: Risk management is a continuous, iterative process that spans the entire lifecycle of the AI system.

Systematic approach
: It calls for systematic and proactive identification, assessment, and mitigation of risks associated with high-risk AI systems.

Risk categories
: The article outlines various risk categories, including risks to health, safety, and fundamental rights, and potential discriminatory impacts.

Testing procedures
: It mandates establishing appropriate testing procedures to identify and analyze potential risks.

Risk mitigation
: Developers must implement suitable risk management measures, prioritizing elimination or reduction of risks through proper design and development.

Remaining risk communication
: Any remaining risks must be clearly communicated to users.

Regular review
: The risk management process should be regularly reviewed and updated, especially when significant changes occur in the AI system or its usage context.

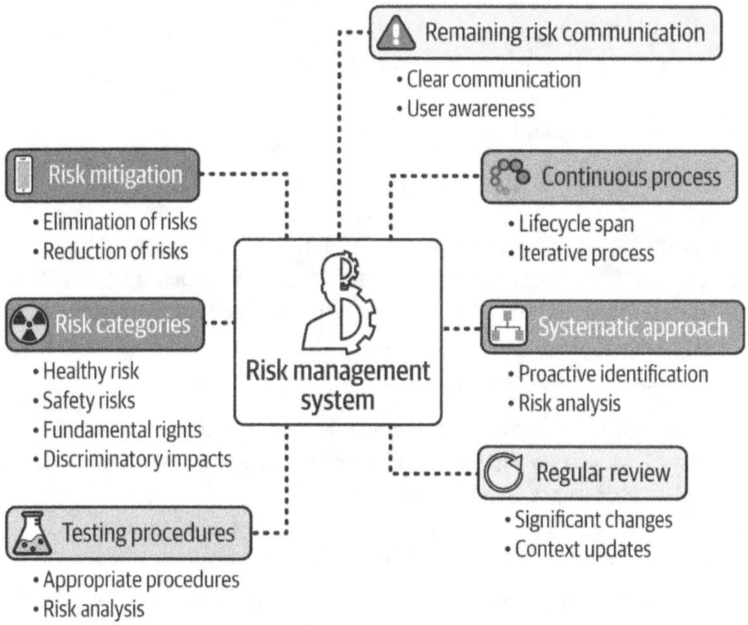

Figure 5-4. Key points of Article 9 of the EU AI Act

To meet the requirements of Article 9 and ensure that high-risk AI systems are developed responsibly, organizations need to implement AI engineering processes that address three quality attributes throughout the AI system lifecycle. As identified by the paper I referenced earlier, "Navigating the EU AI Act: A Methodological Approach to Compliance for Safety-Critical Products" (*https://oreil.ly/2J89P*) by Jessica Kelly et al., these are:

Risk identification
: This involves proactively recognizing potential issues that could arise from the AI system's development, deployment, and operation. Implementing robust risk identification processes ensures that risks are managed before they become critical problems.

Testability
: This ensures that the AI system can be thoroughly evaluated for performance, reliability, and safety before deployment.

Value alignment
: This ensures that the AI system's objectives and behaviors are consistent with human values, ethical principles, and societal norms.

Let's see how we can translate these quality attributes into AI engineering practices. I'll use the CRISP-ML(Q) phases as a framework to tackle the complexity of the end-to-end process, considering each phase separately.

1. Business and data understanding

The initial phase of the AI project focuses on establishing clear business goals and defining success criteria to ensure the application delivers business value. This involves pinpointing the specific objectives of the AI solution, identifying relevant data sources, and assembling an initial dataset. Practically speaking, conducting an AI system risk assessment during this phase involves three steps: identifying potential risks, assessing the impact and likelihood of those risks, and assigning appropriate mitigation strategies to responsible parties.

Consider conducting workshops with stakeholders to identify possible risks. You might also want to use established AI risk frameworks, such as the IEEE AI Ethics Guidelines. Questions to ask include:

- What could go wrong with the data (e.g., bias, privacy breaches)?
- What operational risks could occur (e.g., concept drift, service downtime, poor model performance)?
- What regulatory risks are relevant (e.g., GDPR or EU AI Act noncompliance)?

Failure Mode and Effects Analysis. As part of a proactive risk management strategy, you should conduct *Failure Mode and Effects Analysis* (FMEA) tailored to AI systems. This systematic process used to identify, assess, and mitigate risks associated with potential failure points in a system is especially valuable in safety-critical environments. It enables teams to anticipate and prioritize risks before they impact users or system performance. Incorporating FMEA into your continuous delivery pipelines and model monitoring workflows during the later stages of CRISP-ML(Q) supports ongoing compliance and minimizes operational risk.

Conducting FMEA for AI systems involves the following steps:

1. *Identify potential failure modes.*
   Consider AI-specific failures such as data quality issues (e.g., missing values, outliers), model underfitting or overfitting, concept drift or data drift, adversarial attacks, bias in predictions, explainability failures, performance degradation over time, resource constraints (e.g., memory, computation time), and integration failures with other systems.

2. *Determine potential effects.*
   For each failure mode, identify potential consequences, such as incorrect predictions leading to poor decision making, biased outcomes affecting specific groups, privacy breaches, financial losses, reputational damage, and regulatory noncompliance.

3. *Identify potential causes.*
   For each failure mode, determine possible root causes, such as insufficient or biased training data, poor feature selection, suboptimal hyperparameter tuning, inadequate model architecture, errors in data preprocessing, use of personal data without appropriate consent, and changes in the deployment environment.

4. *Assess current controls.*
   Evaluate existing measures to prevent or detect each failure mode. These might include data validation checks, model performance monitoring, automated testing procedures, human-in-the-loop oversight, and explainability techniques.

Create a template to use for FMEA. Table 5-1 shows an example of what this might look like and the kind of information it might contain.

Table 5-1. Example FMEA specific to an AI system for proactive risk management in alignment with Article 9 of the EU AI Act

Failure mode	Failure cause	Failure effect	S	O	D	RPN	Mitigation plan	Owner
Data bias	Poor data sampling	Biased predictions	9	8	5	360	Use fairness audits	Data team
Model overfitting	Model complexity	Poor generalization in production	7	6	7	294	Conduct regular retraining	ML team
Model drift	Evolving user behavior	Decreasing prediction quality	8	7	6	336	Monitor metrics	MLOps team

Let's walk through each of the columns:

- The *failure modes* are the way in which the ML models that are part of the AI system could fail.
- The *failure causes* are the root causes that might lead to the failures.
- The *failure effects* are the consequences of the failures.
- The *severity* (*S*) can be assigned on a scale from 1 to 10, where 1 = minimal impact and 10 = catastrophic failure.
- The *frequency of occurrence* (*O*) can be assigned on a scale from 1 to 10, where 1 = unlikely and 10 = very frequent.
- The *detection rate* (*D*) can be assigned on a scale from 1 to 10, where 1 = easily detectable and 10 = hard to detect.
- The *risk priority number* (*RPN*) is equal to $S * O * D$; a higher RPN means a higher priority for mitigation.
- The *mitigation plan* is the strategy and concrete steps to mitigate the identified risk.
- The *owner* is the team accountable for mitigating the identified risk.

You can use tools like Jira, Confluence, Google Sheets, or Excel for tracking FMEA.

Testability and value alignment. In addition to risk identification and mitigation, it's essential to establish clear, measurable objectives and key performance indicators (KPIs) that the AI system must meet. This includes creating a comprehensive plan outlining how each component and the system as a whole will be tested.

It's also important to clearly outline the ethical guidelines and principles that the AI system must adhere to, such as fairness and transparency. One practical tool that you can use for this is the Values Canvas (*https://oreil.ly/c79Xu*), a template for developing ethical AI strategies and documenting existing ethics efforts.

Be sure to involve internal and external stakeholders in these processes, to understand their values, expectations, and needs. Internal stakeholders may include data scientists, MLOps engineers, legal teams, product managers, and executives, while external stakeholders can include regulators, customers, partners, and auditors. To categorize and prioritize stakeholders based on their level of influence and interest in the AI system, use the Power–Interest Grid (*https://oreil.ly/CGtNw*).

2. Data preparation

When conducting risk identification, it's vital to assess the quality of the data being used. This includes identifying risks related to data quality, such as missing values, inconsistencies, and potential biases. Typical MLOps practices involve automating data validation and profiling using frameworks like Great Expectations or Deequ that can automatically detect issues like these.

Data quality pipelines should also incorporate unit tests to monitor drift and data integrity in real time. Make sure to write unit tests for the data extraction, transformation, and loading (ETL) processes in the data pipelines to ensure any issues with data handling are caught early. To ensure effective testability, implement scripts to automatically validate the integrity and quality of the data.

Regarding value alignment, when curating data, it's important to ensure that the dataset represents the necessary diversity to prevent biased outcomes. MLOps practices should integrate ethical checks, such as ensuring that no discriminatory proxies are used in feature engineering. To implement ethical checks, integrate tools like SHAP, Fairlearn, Great Expectations, and EvidentlyAI into your MLOps pipelines.

For example, the data pipeline might look like this:

1. Data ingestion
2. Quality checks (Great Expectations)
3. Correlation analysis for proxy detection

Additionally, privacy preservation techniques such as data minimization or anonymization via advanced techniques like differential privacy should be applied to align with ethical standards.

3. Modeling

Risk identification in the modeling phase involves evaluating the risks associated with different modeling approaches, such as overfitting and underfitting.

To incorporate testability into your model code, consider using automated testing frameworks such as pytest for unit tests. Implementing cross-validation techniques can help ensure that your model generalizes well across different datasets and scenarios.

With regard to value alignment, it's important to select algorithms that align with ethical considerations—for example, you should use interpretable models for high-stakes decisions. Additionally, metrics should be incorporated into the model to assess and address biases in model predictions. Collaborate with stakeholders to determine the values you want to uphold (e.g., fairness, robustness, interpretability) and define specific metrics, such as:

Fairness
: Demographic parity, equal opportunity

Robustness
: Tolerance to noisy inputs, resilience to adversarial examples

Integrating relevant tools into the pipeline can help ensure continuous alignment with ethical values throughout the product lifecycle and compliance with the requirements of the EU AI Act. Here are some recommendations:

- MLOps tools: MLflow, Airflow, DVC, Kubeflow, TensorFlow Extended (TFX)
- Fairness tools: Fairlearn, AI Fairness 360
- Monitoring tools: EvidentlyAI for drift detection

4. Evaluation

Next, let's consider how the quality attributes that Article 9 maps to can be implemented in the evaluation phase of the CRISP-ML(Q) model.

Risk identification. Performing model interpretability analysis during the evaluation phase helps identify unexpected or undesirable model behaviors. You can use tools like SHAP (SHapley Additive exPlanations), LIME (Local Interpretable Model-agnostic Explanations), or InterpretML to generate explanations.

When analyzing the results, look for features that are unexpectedly high in importance and counterintuitive feature interactions. Check for proxy variables that might inadvertently introduce bias. Document your findings in a structured report detailing unexpected behaviors and their potential impacts, hypotheses for the causes of these behaviors, and proposed mitigations. Also include key features influencing the model in this report.

To further uncover risks and ensure testability, conduct adversarial testing using libraries such as the Adversarial Robustness Toolbox (ART), PyRIT, or CleverHans. Tailor your approach to the model type, deployment mode, and model exposure strategy.

Relevant types of adversarial attacks might include:

- Evasion attacks (e.g., Fast Gradient Sign Method, Carlini & Wagner)
- Poisoning attacks (e.g., label flipping, backdoor insertion)
- Model extraction attacks

Document your findings regarding the model's vulnerability to different types of attacks and classify them based on severity and likelihood. You can use this not only for recordkeeping but as a "thinking tool" to develop mitigation strategies such as adversarial training or input preprocessing.

Testability. AI systems are always embedded in larger software systems, which are often legacy systems with complex interdependencies. Therefore, comprehensive test suites are needed to ensure that the AI components integrate reliably and function as expected. These should include:

- *Unit tests* to validate individual components of the ML pipeline (e.g., data preprocessing, feature engineering)
- *Integration tests* to ensure that the AI system component interacts correctly with other parts of the system
- *System tests* to evaluate the AI system in a production-like environment (including performance testing, load testing, and error handling)
- *A/B testing* in controlled environments to validate performance, demonstrate the business impact of changes to the model, enable incremental rollouts, and detect issues early

From a compliance perspective, A/B testing can help verify that a new model maintains or improves fairness metrics across different user groups in a real-world setting. It aids in demonstrating due diligence in model deployment, which is crucial for regulatory compliance under the EU AI Act.

Value alignment. Be sure to evaluate model performance against ethical guidelines defined earlier, such as fairness, transparency, privacy, and accountability, by using libraries like Fairlearn or AI Fairness 360 to implement fairness metrics.

This comprehensive evaluation helps ensure compliance with Article 9 and promotes the development of responsible and trustworthy AI systems.

5. Deployment

The next stage is to deploy your AI system in production. Let's look at deployment through the lens of the three quality attributes that are relevant to Article 9.

Risk identification. You'll first want to implement vulnerability scanning to identify security risks. The OWASP Machine Learning Security Top 10 (*https://oreil.ly/Ks7Jt*) is a good reference for understanding common security issues, vulnerabilities, and risks associated with machine learning systems. You might also use tools like OWASP ZAP or Nessus to scan for common vulnerabilities such as:

- Input manipulation attacks (ML01:2023)
- Data poisoning attacks (ML02:2023)
- Model inversion attacks (ML03:2023)
- Membership inference attacks (ML04:2023)
- Model theft (ML05:2023)
- AI supply chain attacks (ML06:2023)
- Transfer learning attacks (ML07:2023)
- Model skewing (ML08:2023)
- Output integrity attacks (ML09:2023)
- Model poisoning (ML10:2023)

Additionally, the following AI incident and risk trackers can help you stay informed about the current developments and keep your AI security strategy up-to-date:

- AI Risk Repository (*https://oreil.ly/4vrn_*)
- AI Incident Database (*https://oreil.ly/8dyrm*)
- OECD AI Incidents and Hazards Monitor (*https://oreil.ly/tVVZ1*)

Another important pre-deployment activity is manual or automated penetration testing. Penetration testing helps identify ML vulnerabilities before malicious actors can exploit them. It's essential for AI systems handling sensitive data or intellectual property. Tools like Metasploit and Burp Suite can be used to test various attack vectors. Compliance with the EU AI Act requires demonstrable security measures, and regular penetration testing, continuous monitoring, and incident response planning should be part of a comprehensive security strategy for AI systems.

Perform a security-focused code review of the deployment scripts and infrastructure-as-code, and assess operational risks in the production environment. You can evaluate the reliability and scalability of your cloud or on-premises infrastructure using tools like AWS Trusted Advisor or Azure Advisor. To mitigate supply chain risks, analyze all dependencies for known vulnerabilities in the National Vulnerability Database (*https://oreil.ly/euMDH*). Tools like OWASP Dependency-Check and GitHub Dependabot are good starting points.

During deployment, you should also plan for disaster recovery. Develop and test backup and restore procedures for data, models, and pipeline artifacts, and implement and validate failover mechanisms for critical components in the ML system.

Testability. Testability in the deployment phase hinges on AI system observability, including implementing continuous monitoring and alerting systems. The initial step is to establish key metrics that offer a holistic view of the AI system. Your metrics categories should include:

- Model performance metrics (e.g., accuracy, latency)
- System health metrics (e.g., CPU usage, memory usage)
- Business metrics (e.g., number of predictions, error rates)

Once the metrics are defined, set up alerting by defining appropriate thresholds. You can use tools like Prometheus with Alertmanager or CloudWatch Alarms to implement alerting based on predefined conditions.

You might also want to implement API testing, automated regression testing, and data and model validation tests to detect drift. You can use tools like Deepchecks, a holistic open source solution for AI and ML validation.

Value alignment. To implement continuous value alignment checks, regularly assess model outputs against defined ethical guidelines (examples of ethical metrics are demographic parity, equal opportunity, and representation balance). A useful way to identify these ethical values is to apply the Foundational Value Finder Framework, as outlined in Olivia Gambelin's book *Responsible AI* (*https://oreil.ly/hmXoe*). It unites the government, industry, and organizational ethical value sets.

6. Monitoring and maintenance

To implement the quality attributes associated with Article 9 during the monitoring and maintenance phase, several key tasks need to be addressed.

Risk identification involves continuously monitoring for data drift and model performance degradation using automated tools. Update the AI system's risk register regularly to reflect new insights gathered from operational usage. Risks should be categorized across technical, operational, ethical, and regulatory domains.

To ensure testability, periodic audits of model performance, system behavior, and fairness metrics are important. Introduce chaos engineering techniques, such as simulating data corruption, resource exhaustion, or network failures, to identify system vulnerabilities.

Maintaining value alignment requires regular reviews and updates of ethical guidelines and periodic stakeholder reviews to assess alignment between stakeholder expectations and system behavior.

Summary

Table 5-2 summarizes the AI engineering practices you should implement across the CRISP-ML(Q) phases to support the quality attributes associated with Article 9. Following the steps outlined here will help ensure ongoing compliance with the EU AI Act while maintaining system reliability and ethical alignment.

Table 5-2. Quality attributes relevant to Article 9 and corresponding AI engineering practices and tools

CRISP-ML(Q) phase	Quality attributes	AI engineering practices and tools
Business and data understanding	Risk identification	Stakeholder interviews, initial risk assessment, creation of risk register, FMEA
	Value alignment	Ethical impact assessments aligned with project goals
Data preparation	Risk identification	Data quality assessment, data privacy/security risks
	Testability	Data validation tests, versioning/lineage
	Value alignment	Ethical checks, fairness audits
Modeling	Risk identification	Model vulnerability assessments, failure modes
	Testability	Unit tests, integration tests
	Value alignment	Define metrics, ethical guidelines
Evaluation	Risk identification	Model interpretability analysis, adversarial testing
	Testability	Comprehensive test suites, A/B testing
	Value alignment	Evaluate against ethical guidelines
Deployment	Risk identification	Pre-deployment security audits, operational risks
	Testability	Continuous monitoring/alerting, regression testing
	Value alignment	Feedback mechanisms
Monitoring and maintenance	Risk identification	Continuous monitoring, risk register updates
	Testability	Model/system audits, chaos engineering
	Value alignment	Regular reviews and updates of ethical guidelines, stakeholder reviews

Checklist for compliance

The following is a practical checklist for aligning AI engineering practices with Article 9 of the EU AI Act across the CRISP-ML(Q) lifecycle. This framework supports regulatory compliance by integrating risk management, testability, and value alignment throughout each phase of the development process:

Pre-development (not a part of CRISP-ML(Q))

- Define risk assessment methodologies and tools to identify critical risks based on potential harms (e.g., safety, privacy, bias).
- Create a risk management plan aligned with EU AI Act requirements.
- Establish a centralized risk register and documentation strategy.

Business and data understanding

- Conduct an initial risk identification workshop with key stakeholders.
- Document potential AI risks in the risk register.
- Perform an ethical impact assessment.
- Align project goals with organizational values and EU AI Act compliance requirements.

Data preparation

- Assess data quality, completeness, and representativeness.
- Ensure datasets are free from discriminatory bias.
- Identify and document data-related risks (e.g., bias, privacy, drift).
- Implement data versioning and lineage tracking.
- Design and implement data validation tests, incorporating quality checks for completeness and correctness.

Modeling

- Conduct model vulnerability assessments.
- Validate the model architecture for explainability and robustness.
- Implement version control for model code and artifacts.
- Design and implement unit tests for model components.
- Document model architecture and design decisions.
- Implement integration tests for the full ML pipeline.
- Simulate edge cases and stress-test model behavior.

Evaluation

- Execute comprehensive test suites (unit, integration, system).
- Perform adversarial testing and document results (vulnerabilities, mitigation strategies).
- Evaluate performance with regard to business and ethical goals and the intended purpose of the system; include value alignment metrics such as fairness, explainability, robustness, safety, and accountability.
- Update the risk register based on evaluation results.
- Conduct A/B testing in controlled environments.
- Engage domain experts to validate evaluation metrics.

Deployment

- Conduct a pre-deployment security audit.
- Implement a continuous monitoring and alerting system.
- Set up automated regression testing.
- Establish feedback mechanisms for end users and stakeholders.
- Ensure that risk mitigation measures (e.g., rollback mechanisms) are operational.
- Integrate quality gate checks into the deployment pipeline.

Monitoring and maintenance

- Implement automated monitoring for data drift, concept drift, and model degradation.
- Define thresholds and set up alerting for critical metrics.
- Conduct regular internal audits of model and system performance.
- Perform periodic chaos engineering tests.
- Regularly update the risk register based on operational insights and regulatory guidance.
- Schedule periodic reviews of ethical guidelines and value alignment.

Further reading

As further reading, I recommend the NIST AI Risk Management Framework (*https://oreil.ly/ht2NM*) (AI RMF). This is important in the context of Article 9 because it offers a lifecycle-based approach to identifying, assessing, and mitigating AI risks, in line with the EU AI Act's requirements for continuous risk management in high-risk AI systems.

Article 10: Data and Data Governance

Article 10

Article 10 of the EU AI Act (*https://oreil.ly/v75QK*) mandates high-quality data and sound data governance practices for high-risk AI systems. It aims to ensure that these systems are developed, trained, validated, and tested using data that supports fairness, accuracy, and transparency.

Key points of Article 10 include:

Data quality
: Data used to train, validate, and test AI systems must be relevant, representative, and as free from errors and bias as possible to ensure fair and accurate outcomes.

Preprocessing requirements
: Mandatory preprocessing steps, such as data cleaning, normalization, and anonymization, must be applied to enhance the data's usability and minimize bias.

Data relevance and representativeness
: To ensure reliable outcomes, data used for training, validation, and testing must reflect the AI system's intended use cases and operational environment.

Bias monitoring
: Ongoing monitoring is required to detect and correct biases that could impact health, safety, or fundamental rights—particularly those leading to discrimination.

Documentation and transparency
: Comprehensive documentation is required, including clear descriptions of how the data was collected, selected, and processed.

Data governance practices
: Organizations must implement governance measures, including access control, data management policies, and versioning, to ensure continuous compliance with the Act.

Periodic review
: Data governance practices and datasets must be reviewed and updated regularly to maintain alignment with the AI system's evolving context and address newly identified risks.

As you may recall from Chapter 3, at its core, data governance ensures high data quality throughout the machine learning lifecycle, supports business objectives, and enables organization-wide data use by focusing on availability, usability, consistency, integrity, security, and compliance. That chapter also outlined data governance processes for each stage of the CRISP-ML(Q) framework, providing a practical approach to managing data responsibly across the development lifecycle that supports the creation of AI systems that are trustworthy, compliant, and sustainable.

Since Article 10 of the EU AI Act provides only a high-level explanation of the requirements regarding data and data governance, let's break down the quality attributes that support a comprehensive framework for implementing trustworthy AI through MLOps practices. In "Navigating the EU AI Act," Kelly et al. map Article 10 to 13 quality attributes for high-risk AI systems. These are:

Independence
: The extent to which datasets used for training, validation, and testing are isolated and unaffected by each other, preventing data leakage across sets.

Data completeness
: The extent to which the dataset contains all necessary data points and variables to support accurate predictions, covering the full range of use cases and features relevant to the AI system's purpose.

Currentness
: The degree to which the data is up-to-date and temporally relevant for its intended use case.

Data fairness
: The absence of bias, prejudice, or favoritism toward individuals or groups in the data, particularly in relation to protected characteristics.

Precision
: The level of exactness or granularity in the data measurements and representations.

Representativeness
: The extent to which the data and its distribution reflects the characteristics of the real-world population or scenario it is intended to model.

Consistency
: The uniformity of data (the degree to which it maintains its format, structure, and values) across the entire dataset and over time.

Accuracy
: The closeness of data values to their true or accepted real-world values.

Credibility
: The trustworthiness of the data sources and collection methods.

Temporality
: The degree to which the temporal characteristics of the data, including timeliness, aging, versioning, and lifecycle management, ensure its ongoing relevance and appropriateness. This is important for understanding how data changes over time and for making decisions based on current information.

Confidentiality
: The protection of sensitive information in accordance with privacy requirements and data protection regulations.

Compliance
: The degree to which data practices conform to applicable legal, ethical, and organizational standards and regulations.

Data traceability
: The ability to track data from its origin through its entire lifecycle, including all transformations, access points, and uses, supporting transparency, accountability, and auditability.

The quality attributes associated with Article 10 are distributed throughout the CRISP-ML(Q) lifecycle. Table 5-3 maps these attributes to each development phase and highlights practical AI engineering practices for implementing them.

Table 5-3. Quality attributes relevant to Article 10 and corresponding AI engineering practices and tools

CRISP-ML(Q) phase	Quality attributes	AI engineering practices and tools
Business and data understanding	Independence	Establish clear data governance policies that outline data acquisition procedures and criteria to ensure data independence.
	Data completeness	Perform thorough data exploration and profiling to identify missing data points, outliers, or insufficient representation and define strategies for addressing them.
	Currentness	Document data update frequencies and establish refresh procedures to maintain currentness.
	Data fairness	Analyze data for potential biases using fairness metrics and visualization tools; document and mitigate identified biases.
	Data traceability	Implement data versioning and logging practices from the outset to enable traceability of data provenance, transformations, and access across the lifecycle.

CRISP-ML(Q) phase	Quality attributes	AI engineering practices and tools
Data preparation	Precision	Define and enforce data quality rules for input data, including data types, ranges, and formats, and use data validation tools to ensure data precision.
	Consistency	Apply data cleaning techniques to address inconsistencies, such as duplicate entries and conflicting data formats.
	Accuracy	Implement data validation checks to identify and correct inaccuracies and errors in the data.
	Data traceability	Continue documenting data manipulation steps, including transformations, feature engineering and data cleaning procedures, to maintain traceability throughout the pipeline.
Modeling	Representativeness	Ensure the training data represents the target population or scenario accurately, using sampling techniques to address imbalances and improve representativeness.
	Data traceability	Log and version model training parameters, hyperparameters, datasets, and code to support full traceability of the development process.
Evaluation	Accuracy	Evaluate model performance using domain-relevant metrics on a strictly independent hold-out test dataset.
	Robustness	Conduct robustness testing by introducing variations in input data and assessing model performance under different conditions.
Deployment	Confidentiality	Implement security measures such as data encryption, authentication, and access control to protect sensitive data during model deployment and prediction serving.
Monitoring and maintenance	Currentness	Monitor incoming data for changes in distribution or characteristics that might signal data staleness or concept drift, and define thresholds and triggers for automated model retraining.
	Compliance	Regularly audit model performance and data usage to verify compliance with relevant regulations and ethical guidelines.

Key tools

When it comes to ensuring data quality, several key tools and technologies stand out. Among them are Great Expectations, Apache Griffin, Deequ, and TensorFlow Data Validation (TFDV), all of which play crucial roles in maintaining data integrity and reliability.

In terms of monitoring data and machine learning processes, tools like Prometheus, Grafana, MLflow, and Weights & Biases are invaluable. They help track performance and visualize trends effectively.

For compliance purposes, OpenLineage, Atlas, Collibra, and DataHub are go-to tools that assist organizations in managing and safeguarding their data assets, ensuring they adhere to industry regulations and standards.

Checklist for compliance

The following checklist can be used to ensure compliance with Article 10 throughout the CRISP-ML(Q) lifecycle. The key is to implement these practices systematically, maintain thorough documentation in all phases, and view compliance engineering as an ongoing process:

Business and data understanding

- Establish a data governance framework aligned with EU AI Act requirements.
- (Organizational) Define roles and responsibilities for data management.
- Define and document data quality metrics and standards.
- Maintain documentation of all data sources, including assessments of their credibility.
- Verify and record data licensing terms and usage rights for all datasets.
- Assess data protection requirements.
- Validate data source reliability.
- Profile existing datasets.
- Document known data quality issues.
- Assess data completeness requirements.
- Evaluate data representativeness.
- Check for potential biases in the data.

Data preparation

- Specify data validation requirements (e.g., schema validation, data type checks, range checks, functional dependency validation, consistency checks).
- Implement data quality checks (e.g., completeness, accuracy, consistency).
- Set up data validation pipelines.
- Implement data cleaning procedures.
- Implement data lineage tracking.
- Validate processed data quality.
- Document transformation rules.
- Validate transformed data.
- Implement data anonymization where required.
- Set up data versioning.
- Implement privacy-preserving measures.
- Set up secure data storage.
- Implement access controls.
- Document security measures.
- Set up audit logging.

Modeling

- Validate training data quality.
- Document the data splitting methodology.
- Implement a cross-validation strategy.
- Track data versions used for training.
- Track model versions.
- Track model lineage.
- Monitor data drift.
- Implement reproducibility controls.
- Track experiment results.
- Implement model validation procedures.
- Test model robustness.
- Validate model fairness.

Evaluation

- Evaluate model performance.
- Assess model fairness and check for biases.
- Validate model robustness.
- Conduct a risk assessment.
- Validate security measures.

Deployment

- Establish service level agreements for data quality attributes such as completeness, accuracy, timeliness, and consistency.
- Integrate quality gates into the deployment pipeline.
- Configure automated alerting mechanisms.
- Develop a structured incident response plan.
- Enable continuous monitoring of model performance in production.
- Design and test rollback procedures.

Monitoring and maintenance

- Continuously monitor data quality metrics.
- Track model performance indicators such as processing or inference time and error rates.
- Regularly assess fairness metrics across user groups.
- Monitor system health (e.g., uptime, resource utilization).

- Track business-critical metrics tied to revenue, customer experience, and compliance.
- Implement structured update procedures.
- Systematically log all changes and updates.
- Maintain an internal audit trail.

Next, we'll delve further into the requirements for technical documentation and the importance of keeping logs and records that document the system's performance.

Article 11: Technical Documentation and Article 12: Record-Keeping

Article 11

Article 11 of the EU AI Act (*https://oreil.ly/8TJP3*) mandates comprehensive technical documentation for high-risk AI systems, ensuring transparency, traceability, and accountability throughout their lifecycle. This requirement helps stakeholders and regulators verify a system's safety, compliance, and performance.

Key points of Article 11 include:

Comprehensive information
: Developers must prepare detailed documentation covering the design, development, and intended purpose of the AI system.

Traceability and reproducibility
: Documentation must enable the reproduction of results and provide traceability of the AI system's processes and decisions.

Content requirements
: The documentation should include details on the system's architecture, algorithms, data sources, and performance metrics.

Risk and compliance reporting
: The documentation must describe the risk management measures applied and how the system complies with the EU AI Act.

Availability to authorities
: Technical documentation must be made available to regulatory authorities upon request to facilitate compliance checks and audits.

Maintenance and updates
: Developers must keep the documentation up-to-date, reflecting all modifications, upgrades, or changes to the AI system.

According to Kelly et al., Article 11 maps to one key quality attribute: traceability. Documenting AI models is a central requirement of the EU AI Act, particularly as a means of assessing legal compliance. Both technical and quality management system documentation are critical components in the conformity assessment process.

For downstream providers incorporating a preexisting AI model into an AI system, a comprehensive understanding of the model and its functionalities is essential, both to facilitate the integration into their offerings and to ensure they fulfill their responsibilities under the EU AI Act and other applicable regulations (Recital 101 (*https://oreil.ly/kB5Pj*)). As such, the creator of the AI model is required to provide comprehensive technical documentation to downstream providers (Article 53(1b) (*https://oreil.ly/Xn8iw*)).

MLOps and documentation are closely related, as documentation plays a critical role in the lifecycle of machine learning (ML) projects and is essential for operationalizing models effectively. For example, documentation captures details about data preprocessing, feature engineering, model configurations, hyperparameters, and environment settings, enabling others (or the same team at a later time) to reproduce experiments and results reliably.

Furthermore, MLOps involves tracking all stages of the ML workflow—data preparation, model training, testing, deployment, and monitoring. Documenting each stage, including data sources, code versions, and model changes, supports traceability and accountability, which are vital for auditability, especially in regulated sectors. More importantly, robust documentation is essential for meeting regulatory standards, including the data protection and transparency requirements outlined in the EU AI Act.

What's more, according to DORA's 2023 Accelerate State of DevOps Report (*https://oreil.ly/sjTX3*), high-quality documentation has been linked to a 25% increase in team performance.

Technical documentation requirements

Article 11 outlines the requirements for the technical documentation of high-risk AI systems, although related obligations are found throughout Articles 8–15.[1] These requirements apply to both datasets and AI systems.

Technical documentation serves two primary purposes: providing instructions for users of the system and demonstrating regulatory compliance to authorities. As such, the intended audience spans technical teams, compliance teams (AI auditors and conformity assessment bodies), and end users. Table 5-4 outlines the relevant

1 To learn more about technical documentation, refer to the paper "Documenting High-Risk AI: A European Regulatory Perspective" (*https://oreil.ly/AoUII*) by Isabelle Hupont et al.

technical information elements under the EU AI Act. It provides an overview of key documentation types, their intended audiences, and the essential details each should contain.

Table 5-4. Overview of technical documentation requirements for datasets and AI systems

Document type	Target audience	Description	Key information elements
Data source documentation	Compliance teams	Documentation of data origins and collection methods	Sources, collection methods, and aggregation approaches
Dataset characteristics	All stakeholders	Documentation of dataset contents, coverage, and known limitations	Data types, scope, and limitations
Data processing documentation	Technical teams	Documentation of data handling procedures	Processing steps, quality controls, and preparation methods
Data quality metrics	Compliance teams	Documentation of quality assessment procedures	Quality metrics, validation results, and completeness checks
Population coverage analysis	All stakeholders	Documentation of dataset representativeness	Coverage metrics, demographic analysis, and usage context
Privacy protection documentation	Compliance teams	Documentation of privacy safeguards	Privacy measures, data protection controls
System purpose and scope	All stakeholders	Documentation of intended use and limitations	Use cases, constraints, and misuse prevention measures
Risk assessment documentation	All stakeholders	Documentation of risk analysis and controls	Risk assessment, mitigation measures
System operation documentation	All stakeholders	Documentation of system behavior and oversight	Operation procedures, human oversight measures
Technical architecture documentation	Technical teams	Documentation of system design and implementation	Architecture, components, development process
Performance documentation	All stakeholders	Documentation of system capabilities and limitations	Accuracy metrics, robustness measures, test results
Security documentation	All stakeholders	Documentation of security measures	Security controls, vulnerability management
Maintenance documentation	Technical teams	Documentation of system lifecycle management	Change procedures, version control, updates

Technical documentation for high-risk AI systems is a legal requirement and must be created prior to placing the systems on the market or putting them into service. It is essential to keep this documentation updated, as it serves to demonstrate compliance to regulatory authorities. Furthermore, it plays a crucial role in conformity assessment procedures, ensuring that all requirements are met. The documentation must be detailed enough to show compliance with all applicable regulations. Ultimately, it serves the needs of both users and regulatory authorities, providing transparency and assurance in the use of high-risk AI systems.

Managing documentation debt

Documentation debt refers to the accumulated costs and risks associated with incomplete, outdated, inconsistent, or missing documentation across the dataset, data processing, and AI system lifecycle. Organizations can minimize this debt by automating documentation generation as part of ML pipeline execution, taking care to capture the following elements:

- Data quality metrics and validation results
- Data lineage and transformation steps
- Feature definitions and characteristics
- Pipeline metadata, including execution parameters, data statistics and profiling, validation results, transformed datasets, evaluation metrics, and training logs
- Model versions, hyperparameters, and training outcomes

Another essential aspect of operationalizing documentation is applying version control to key documentation assets such as feature definitions and schemas, model documentation (such as model cards), ML pipeline configurations and parameters, training datasets, feature stores, data transformations, and preprocessing steps. Documentation versions should be tracked alongside code versions using Git-based version control systems, artifact repositories, model registries, and feature stores with versioning capabilities.

By automating these processes and utilizing appropriate tools and platforms, organizations can establish a robust documentation system that is integrated into their MLOps practices. This reduces manual effort, improves consistency, and helps ensure the AI system's ongoing compliance with the EU AI Act.

Existing frameworks for documenting data and AI systems

Documentation has long been a challenge in software engineering, and several mature approaches have emerged to address it. Table 5-5 outlines state-of-the-art documentation tools and methods for data and AI systems, highlighting widely adopted practices.

Table 5-5. Popular documentation approaches for data and AI systems

Approach	Origin	Format	Purpose	Coverage
Datasheets for datasets	Black in AI, Microsoft, and academia (2018)	Questionnaire-based documentation	Documents datasets, including collection procedures, intended uses, content, distribution, and maintenance	Strong on data provenance, scope, representation, and privacy considerations.
Dataset Nutrition Label	Harvard and MIT (2018, updated 2022)	Visual template with standardized fields	Provides standardized dataset information to drive higher data quality	Good for data quality, fairness, and completeness checks.
AI Factsheets	IBM (2019)	Customizable questionnaire templates for different stakeholders	Documents AI systems comprehensively through their lifecycle	Most comprehensive overall coverage of AI system documentation needs. Covers technical, performance, risk, and operational aspects.
Model cards	Google (2019)	Standardized information sheet	Documents model specifications and intended uses	Suitable for model performance, limitations, and use cases. Focus: Model-specific documentation and transparency.
OECD AI Classification Framework	OECD (2022)	Structured questionnaire	Standardized AI system classification and documentation	Comprehensive AI system classification framework. Institutional backing: International standard-setting organization.
Use case cards	European Commission, Joint Research Centre (2024)	Information sheet	Documents intended use cases of AI systems	Provides a high-level overview of use cases without technical details. Focus: Risk assessment under the EU AI Act.
AI Cards framework	European Commission, Joint Research Centre (2024)	Dual representation: visual human-readable and machine-readable specifications	Provides holistic documentation of AI systems and their risks	Covers technical specifications, context of use, risk management, and compliance. Recent development specifically for EU AI Act compliance.

When selecting a documentation framework, it is essential to choose one that aligns with your organization's specific needs and regulatory obligations. In practice, the most effective approach often involves combining multiple complementary documentation methods to ensure thorough coverage while maintaining usability. AI Factsheets and AI Cards currently offer the most comprehensive support, but organizations may benefit from supplementing them with more specialized tools, such as datasheets for datasets and model cards. Taking a "layered documentation" approach is a useful strategy, where the AI Cards framework is used for high-level system documentation, component-specific details are captured through datasheets and model cards, and greater technical depth is provided by using AI Factsheets.

Implementing machine-readable specifications that integrate with existing metadata management systems is crucial. This enables automated documentation generation, streamlining the process and improving consistency and efficiency. Finally, it's important to adapt the level of detail in documentation to suit different audiences (technical teams, compliance teams, and end users).

Now let's turn to the recordkeeping requirements outlined in Article 12, which closely relate to the technical documentation obligations in Article 11.

Article 12: Recordkeeping requirements for high-risk AI systems

Article 12

Article 12 of the EU AI Act (*https://oreil.ly/eFkXj*) sets out obligations for recordkeeping to ensure transparency, accountability, and traceability of high-risk AI systems. It emphasizes the need to maintain detailed logs and records to uphold accountability and ensure that high-risk AI systems operate transparently and can be evaluated throughout their lifecycle.

Key points of Article 12 include:

Comprehensive logging
: AI systems must maintain detailed logs documenting key operations, system performance, and anomalies.

Traceability
: Logs should provide sufficient detail to trace the AI system's activities, enabling incident investigation and auditability.

Data retention policy
: Records must be retained for a period appropriate to the AI system's intended purpose and associated risks.

Format and accessibility
: Records must be stored in a structured and accessible format to ensure they are usable for oversight and accountability purposes.

Availability for authorities
: Developers and operators must make records available to regulatory authorities upon request to assist in compliance checks.

Incident reporting support
: The records must support the investigation of failures, malfunctions, or adverse outcomes and aid with corrective actions.

In "Navigating the EU AI Act," Kelly et al. map Article 12 to eight quality attributes for high-risk AI systems:

Operability
: The ease with which an AI system can be operated, managed, and maintained effectively, including usability, reliability, and the ability to perform functions under stated conditions.

Non-repudiation
: The ability to ensure that actions or events within an AI system cannot be denied after they have occurred, preventing any party from falsely denying responsibility.

Traceability
: The ability to track and document every aspect of the AI system's data and decision-making processes, including data sources, transformations, model training, and predictions.

Self-descriptiveness
: The AI system's capacity to explain its structure, functionalities, and behaviors in understandable terms, including comprehensive documentation and the use of explainable AI techniques.

Accountability
: The obligation of individuals or organizations to accept responsibility for the AI system's actions and outcomes, involving clear role assignments and ensuring accountability for errors or negative impacts.

Self-monitoring
: The AI system's ability to autonomously observe and assess its performance and behavior, detecting anomalies, errors, or deviations from expected operations without external prompts.

User engagement
: The active participation of users with the AI system, involving designing systems that encourage user interaction, feedback, and collaboration.

Monitorability
: The extent to which the AI system's operations and performance can be observed and measured in real time or retrospectively, involving tools and processes to track system behavior, performance metrics, and compliance.

Table 5-6 maps these quality attributes to the CRISP-ML(Q) phases with specific AI engineering processes and tools.

Table 5-6. Quality attributes relevant to Article 12 and corresponding AI engineering practices and tools

CRISP-ML(Q) phase	Quality attributes	AI engineering practices and tools
Business and data understanding	Accountability	• Defined roles and responsibilities • Established governance frameworks
	User engagement	• Stakeholder involvement • Feedback mechanisms (surveys, focus groups)
	Self-descriptiveness	• Comprehensive documentation (data catalog)
	Traceability	• Metadata recording (data sources, collection methods) • Version control for documentation
Data preparation	Traceability	• Data versioning (DVC, LakeFS) • Data lineage tracking (Apache Atlas, OpenLineage)
	Accountability	• Assigned data stewardship (escalation paths) • Audit trails (Apache Ranger)
	Operability	• Automated data pipelines (Airflow, Luigi, Prefect) • Data validation (Great Expectations, TensorFlow Data Validation)
	Self-descriptiveness	• Data documentation (dictionaries, schemas) • Descriptive metadata
Modeling	Traceability	• Model versioning (MLflow, DVC, Git LFS) • Experiment tracking (Weights & Biases, Neptune.ai, Comet.ml) • Model documentation (diagrams, explanations)
	Self-descriptiveness	• Explainable AI techniques (SHAP, LIME, Integrated Gradients)
	Accountability	• Assigned modeling responsibilities (peer review) • Governance policies (performance, ethics)
	Operability	• Automated training pipelines (Kubeflow pipelines, TFX)
	Non-repudiation	• Immutable logs (append-only databases) • Secure model artifacts (digital signatures, checksums)
Evaluation	Traceability	• Evaluation logging (metrics, datasets, conditions) • Version control (evaluation code, documentation)
	Accountability	• Assigned evaluation roles (sign-off procedures) • Approval processes (performance, ethics)
	Non-repudiation	• Immutable evaluation records (timestamped) • Digital signatures (evaluation reports)
	Self-descriptiveness	• Evaluation documentation (metrics, visualizations, explainable AI)
	Operability	• Automated evaluation pipelines (CI/CD tools)
Deployment	Operability	• Continuous deployment (Jenkins, GitLab CI/CD, CircleCI) • Containerization and orchestration (Docker, Kubernetes)
	Non-repudiation	• Deployment logs (immutable, access-controlled) • Artifact signatures (cryptographic methods)
	Traceability	• Deployment documentation (architecture diagrams, artifact repositories)
	Accountability	• Deployment approvals (change management systems)
	Monitorability	• Monitoring setup (Prometheus, Grafana, Datadog) • Logging practices (structured logs)

CRISP-ML(Q) phase	Quality attributes	AI engineering practices and tools
Monitoring and maintenance	Self-monitoring	• Automated alerts (Alertmanager, PagerDuty) • Health checks (APIs, scripts, Kubernetes liveness/readiness probes)
	Monitorability	• Centralized monitoring systems (observability practices)
	Operability	• Log aggregation (Elastic Stack, Splunk) • Scalable infrastructure (cloud autoscaling)
	Accountability	• Assigned maintenance roles (ticketing systems) • Incident response plans
	Traceability	• Maintenance logs (change management logs) • Performance tracking
	User engagement	• Feedback collection (support portals, in-app forms) • User support (documentation, FAQs, help centers)

Interdependence of Articles 11 and 12

Articles 11 and 12 of the EU AI Act are closely connected and interdependent. As you've seen, Article 11 outlines comprehensive documentation requirements covering overall system design, technical specifications, development processes, and risk and quality management measures. Article 12 focuses specifically on the automatic recording of events and activities, capturing operational logs, behavioral data, and runtime information. In the context of compliance, technical documentation provides the framework for what needs to be recorded, while recordkeeping provides the operational evidence that the AI system performs in accordance with that documentation. Table 5-7 shows the correspondence between technical documentation and runtime recordkeeping elements.

Table 5-7. Correspondence between technical documentation and recordkeeping obligations

Article 11: Technical Documentation	Article 12: Record-Keeping
System specifications	Runtime behavior logs
Expected behaviors	Actual behaviors
Risk assessments	Incident logs
Design decisions	Operational metrics

Considering the technical requirements of Articles 11 and 12, one aspect that becomes apparent is that they share a common technical component: the metadata store.

Data and AI system metadata

Capturing and managing metadata is fundamental to meeting the documentation and recordkeeping obligations under Articles 11 and 12 of the EU AI Act. Metadata provides the foundation for systematic, auditable, and maintainable documentation by enabling traceability, demonstrating compliance, supporting collaboration, and ensuring documentation quality over time.

A robust metadata management system is key to maintaining the level of oversight, quality, and governance required for compliance, particularly as AI systems evolve and scale over time. Table 5-8 outlines the types of data and AI system metadata required for each of the documentation types listed in Table 5-4.

Table 5-8. Essential metadata for meeting compliance demands for Articles 9–15 of the EU AI Act

Document type	Data and AI system metadata		
Data source documentation	Source identification: • Source name/identifier • Source type (database, API, sensor data, etc.) • Source owner/maintainer • Source access method • Source version/timestamp • Data licensing information • Terms of use	Data collection methods: • Collection protocol identifier • Collection time frame (start/end dates) • Collection frequency • Collection tools/software used • Collection validation procedures • Sampling methodology • Sample size calculations	Aggregation approaches: • Aggregation rules • Merge procedures • Deduplication methods • Data harmonization steps • Source reconciliation procedures • Data lineage tracking
Dataset characteristics	Content description: • Data types (numerical, categorical, text, etc.) • Feature descriptions • Feature relationships • Data dictionary • Schema definition • Data formats • Encoding standards	Coverage information: • Temporal coverage • Geographical coverage • Demographic coverage • Domain coverage • Missing data patterns • Known biases • Edge cases	Known limitations: • Gaps • Quality issues • Coverage limitations • Usage restrictions • Technical constraints • Statistical limitations
Data processing documentation	Preprocessing steps: • Cleaning procedures • Normalization methods • Feature engineering steps • Data transformation rules • Outlier handling • Missing value treatment	Quality controls: • Validation rules • Data consistency checks • Integrity constraints • Quality metrics • Error handling procedures • Exception management	
Data quality metrics	Statistical measures: • Descriptive statistics • Distribution analysis • Correlation metrics • Data completeness rates • Error rates • Confidence intervals	Validation results: • Cross-validation metrics • Test results • Quality scores • Performance indicators • Benchmark comparisons	

Document type	Data and AI system metadata		
Population coverage analysis	Demographic metrics: • Population distributions • Representation ratios • Coverage gaps • Bias metrics • Fairness indicators	Usage context: • Target population description • Application domain • Use case scenarios • Environmental conditions • Operational constraints	
Privacy protection documentation	Privacy measures: • Anonymization methods • Pseudonymization techniques • Data masking rules • Access controls • Consent management • Deletion requests • Data retention policies	Data protection controls: • Security protocols • Encryption methods • Data segregation rules • Privacy impact assessments • Compliance checks	
System purpose and scope	Definition: • Primary objectives • Target users • Use case descriptions • Success criteria • Performance targets • Business context	Constraints: • Operational limitations • Technical constraints • Resource requirements • Environmental requirements • Regulatory restrictions	Misuse prevention: • Usage restrictions • Warning systems • Prevention mechanisms • Detection methods
Risk assessment documentation	Risk analysis: • Risk categories • Impact assessments • Probability metrics • Severity ratings • Risk matrices • Risk evolution tracking	Control measures: • Mitigation strategies • Control mechanisms • Monitoring procedures • Response plans • Recovery procedures • Review cycles	
System operation documentation	Operational procedures: • Startup procedures • Shutdown procedures • Maintenance routines • Error handling • Recovery procedures • Backup protocols	Human oversight: • Supervision roles • Decision authorities • Intervention protocols • Override mechanisms • Audit procedures • Training requirements	
Technical architecture documentation	Architecture specifications: • Component diagrams • Interface definitions • Data flows • Processing pipelines • Infrastructure requirements	Dependencies: • Technology stack • Libraries and frameworks • API specifications • Configuration settings • Deployment requirements • Resource specifications	

Document type	Data and AI system metadata	
Performance documentation	Accuracy metrics: • Performance measures • Error rates • Confidence scores	Robustness measures: • Stability metrics • Reliability scores • Resilience tests • Edge case handling • Failure modes • Recovery capabilities
Security documentation	Security controls: • Access controls • Authentication methods • Authorization rules • Data protection • Network security • Monitoring systems	Vulnerability management: • Security assessments • Threat models • Patch management • Incident response • Recovery procedures • Audit logs
Maintenance documentation	Change management: • Version control • Release procedures • Update protocols • Testing requirements • Rollback procedures • Documentation updates	Lifecycle management: • Maintenance schedules • Support procedures • Deprecation plans • Upgrade paths • End-of-life procedures • Archive requirements

Metadata systems are often overlooked or deprioritized, but they are key components of any data and ML platform for operationalizing documentation requirements and maintaining compliance with the EU AI Act. A well-designed metadata system provides the foundation for systematic documentation management, supports automation and quality control, and enables organizations to demonstrate compliance to regulatory authorities. To ensure effectiveness, organizations should treat metadata systems as integral to their data and AI governance infrastructure and periodically conduct internal test audits to verify that key information is easily accessible when needed.

Checklist for compliance

The following checklist defines a structured process you can follow to implement the technical documentation and recordkeeping requirements of Articles 11 and 12 of the EU AI Act. It uses a compressed version of the CRISP-ML(Q) lifecycle to streamline implementation across the business and data understanding, model development, and operational phases:

Business and data understanding

- Document intended purpose and use cases (business objectives and constraints, expected performance metrics).
- Establish recordkeeping infrastructure (data collection scope and methods, metadata tracking systems, logging requirements).
- Document data sources and specifications (data provenance, quality criteria, privacy and security controls, governance procedures).

Model training and operationalization

- Document model development environment (hardware specifications, software dependencies, tools and versioning).
- Document training methodology (model architecture, hyperparameters, algorithms, feature engineering steps).
- Implement pipeline logging (infrastructure usage, execution records, resource utilization).
- Implement training logs (metadata on training runs, performance metrics, data versioning, feature extraction).

Model deployment and serving

- Document deployment procedures (testing protocols, validation methods, release criteria).
- Document deployment architecture (infrastructure design, scaling, security measures).
- Implement deployment logging (event logs, configuration changes, versioning, access control).
- Document operational procedures (maintenance protocols, update routines, emergency response plans).
- Document serving infrastructure (API specifications, performance benchmarks, resource allocations, scaling policies).
- Implement prediction logging (inference logs, latency, errors, user feedback).
- Document monitoring strategy (metrics tracked, alerting thresholds, response procedures, maintenance schedules).
- Document monitoring system (tools used, automated alerts, performance metrics, health checks).

Teams should adjust this checklist based on their specific high-risk AI system and organizational context, while ensuring all regulatory requirements are addressed.

Further reading

For more in-depth information about the importance of metadata and documentation in software development, see:

- *Crafting Docs for Success: An End-to-End Approach to Developer Documentation* (*https://oreil.ly/8IY2w*) by Diana Lakatos (Apress)
- *Fundamentals of Metadata Management* (*https://oreil.ly/W5xiK*) by Ole Olesen-Bagneux (O'Reilly)
- "ML Lineage for Trustworthy Machine Learning Systems" (*https://oreil.ly/nlNfU*) by Mikko Raatikainen et al.

Article 13: Transparency and Provision of Information to Deployers and Article 14: Human Oversight

Article 13

Article 13 of the EU AI Act (*https://oreil.ly/E-Jt0*) mandates that deployers of high-risk AI systems receive adequate information to use these systems responsibly. It emphasizes transparency to support informed decision making and regulatory compliance and to ensure that deployers have clarity around their functionality, risks, and limitations. The goal is to equip operators with the information they need to use the systems safely and effectively.

Key points of Article 13 include:

Clear instructions
: Developers must provide detailed instructions on the proper setup, installation, and use of the AI system.

Operational requirements
: Documentation should explain specific conditions, limitations, and constraints under which the system is intended to operate.

Risk awareness
: Deployers must be informed about potential risks to health, safety, or fundamental rights and applicable mitigation strategies.

Human oversight guidelines
: Clear instructions must be provided on when and how human operators should intervene during the system's operation.

Performance metrics
: Information should be provided on expected performance across a range of scenarios and usage conditions.

Maintenance and updates
: Deployers must receive instructions on system maintenance and software updates and versioning, to ensure safe and reliable operation over time.

Contact and support information
: Developers must provide appropriate contact details for technical support and incident reporting.

Article 14

Article 14 of the EU AI Act (*https://oreil.ly/WBf-Q*) sets out requirements for human oversight to help ensure that high-risk AI systems operate safely and ethically. It underscores the importance of human involvement in monitoring system behavior and intervening when necessary to prevent adverse outcomes, thereby promoting accountability, safety, and the ability to respond effectively to unforeseen situations.

Key points of Article 14 include:

Oversight by design
: High-risk AI systems must include features that enable effective human oversight during their operation.

Prevention of harm
: Human oversight must be capable of preventing or minimizing risks to health, safety, and fundamental rights.

Intervention mechanisms
: Operators must be able to interrupt or override the system's actions if it behaves unexpectedly or unsafely.

Training for operators
: Individuals responsible for oversight must be given clear instructions on how and when to intervene.

Consideration of operational context
: Oversight strategies should reflect the specific use case and operating conditions of the system.

Managing increasing autonomy
: In systems that evolve toward greater autonomy, human intervention must remain possible at all times.

Continuous monitoring
: Deployers should regularly assess the system's performance to determine when human involvement is necessary for safe and reliable operation.

Articles 13 and 14 of the EU AI Act are closely connected, as they both deal with transparency and human oversight requirements for high-risk AI systems. However, they focus on different aspects, as depicted in Table 5-9.

Table 5-9. Similarities and differences between Articles 13 and 14

Feature	Article 13	Article 14
Primary focus	Transparency and user information	Human oversight and control
Scope	System capabilities and limitations	Technical design for oversight
Implementation	Documentation and communication	Technical measures and procedures
Key requirements	Transparency about AI system outputs and interpretations Information about accuracy and performance limits Documentation of AI system capabilities	Human oversight measures to monitor and control the AI system Design for human interpretability and understanding Documentation of oversight procedures and assessments
Relationship to risk management	Focus on transparency about potential risks	Focus on human oversight as a risk mitigation measure
Overall goal	Ensure users understand the system's capabilities and limitations	Enable effective human monitoring and control of high-risk AI systems

Article 13 quality attributes

Kelly et al. associate Article 13 with to the following quality attributes, along with self-descriptiveness:

User engagement
: The extent to which users are actively involved with and informed about the AI system, such as being able to opt in/out, challenge outputs, or provide feedback.

User transparency
: The degree to which the functionalities, capabilities, and limitations of the AI system are understandably communicated to users.

Interpretability
: The extent to which the reasoning and decision-making processes of the AI system can be understood and explained. An interpretable system allows users and stakeholders to comprehend how inputs are transformed into outputs, supporting trust and accountability.

Documentability
: The quality, completeness, and accessibility of documentation describing the AI system design, development, and operation. This includes information on data sources, model architectures, training processes, evaluation metrics, and system updates, supporting transparency and reproducibility.

Appropriateness recognizability
: The degree to which users can discern that they are interacting with an AI system rather than a human and assess whether it is appropriate for a particular context or task. This ensures that users can identify the system's limitations and intended use cases, preventing misuse or overreliance.

Table 5-10 maps these attributes to the CRISP-ML(Q) phases and outlines core AI engineering practices associated with each phase. This structure helps ensure systematic implementation of the requirements of Article 13 throughout the entire AI system lifecycle.

Table 5-10. Quality attributes relevant to Article 13 and corresponding AI engineering practices and tools

CRISP-ML(Q) phase	Quality attributes	AI engineering practices and tools
Business and data understanding	User engagement	• Involve users early through interviews, workshops, or cocreation exercises.
	Appropriateness recognizability	• Conduct feasibility studies and risk assessments. • Design mock interfaces to gather user feedback.
Data preparation	Documentability	• Maintain data lineage with tools like DataHub or Great Expectations.
	User transparency	• Annotate datasets clearly and provide metadata descriptions.
Modeling	Interpretability	• Use interpretable models (like decision trees).
	Documentability	• Implement versioning for models and scripts using Git and DVC. • Use techniques like feature attribution (SHAP, LIME). • Test explanations with users. • Automate documentation updates using pipelines. • Create a centralized repository for project documentation.
Evaluation	Appropriateness recognizability	• Ensure evaluation metrics are domain-appropriate.
	User engagement	• Test models with representative user groups.
Deployment	User transparency	• Deploy user-facing documentation alongside APIs or systems. • Use plain language in user-facing documentation.
	Documentability	• Utilize CI/CD pipelines (e.g., GitHub Actions, MLflow). • Publish ethical guidelines and disclaimers.
Monitoring and maintenance	User transparency	• Provide users access to monitoring dashboards.
	Interpretability	• Monitor explainability metrics.

Article 14 quality attributes

In addition to documentability, value alignment, accountability, and interpretability, Article 14 is associated with the following quality attributes for safety-critical AI systems:

Learnability
: The degree to which human operators can understand and learn an AI system's behavior, outputs, and decision-making processes. Learnability depends on the clarity and comprehensibility of system documentation, interfaces, and training materials; it reflects how quickly human operators can achieve competency in overseeing the system.

Fairness
: The extent to which the system produces outcomes that are unbiased and do not result in unjustified discrimination against any individual or group. Fairness ensures equitable treatment and decision making across different demographic groups.

Explainability
: The extent to which the internal logic and behavior of the system can be understood and interpreted by humans. Explainability enables stakeholders to comprehend how inputs are transformed into outputs.

Intervenability
: The capacity for human operators to influence or override the system's behavior and decisions, or halt the system if necessary.

Monitorability
: The degree to which the system's operations and performance can be continuously observed, measured, and analyzed. Monitorability facilitates early detection of issues such as drift, anomalies, and system failures.

User error protection
: The inclusion of design features that help prevent or mitigate errors caused by user interactions. This includes safeguards against incorrect inputs, misinterpretations, and unintended uses of the system.

Table 5-11 maps these quality attributes to the relevant AI engineering practices to fulfill the technical requirements of Article 14.

Table 5-11. Quality attributes relevant to Article 14 and corresponding AI engineering practices and tools

CRISP-ML(Q) phase	Quality attributes	AI engineering practices and tools
Business and data understanding	Fairness	• Assess potential biases in datasets using fairness auditing tools like Aequitas. • Define fairness metrics (e.g., demographic parity) as project requirements.
	Learnability	• Conduct user research to understand user learning capabilities and needs. • Define metrics like System Usability Scale (SUS) for usability and ease of learning.
Data preparation	Fairness	• Ensure representative and balanced datasets by applying techniques such as oversampling or undersampling. Use bias mitigation tools like Fairlearn or IBM's AI Fairness 360 to evaluate and reduce bias. • Create a data dictionary to promote transparency about feature definitions.
	Monitorability	• Use metadata tracking tools like DVC to document data transformations, ensuring traceability.
Modeling	Explainability	• Choose models that balance accuracy with interpretability, such as decision trees or linear models.
	Intervenability	• Introduce model checkpoints during training for human-in-the-loop interventions. • Integrate tooling like MLflow for easy rollback.
Evaluation	Explainability	• Utilize tools like SHAP or LIME to evaluate model predictions and make them understandable to nontechnical stakeholders.
	Fairness	• Evaluate the model on the fairness metrics defined earlier. • Implement subgroup performance tests.
	User error protection	• Simulate potential user interaction scenarios and evaluate how errors can be mitigated. • Create fallback strategies.
Deployment	Monitorability	• Simulate monitoring scenarios such as data drift or model decay. • Integrate model monitoring tools like Prometheus, Grafana, or AWS SageMaker Model Monitor to track model drift, bias drift, and other performance indicators.
	Intervenability	• Set up mechanisms for human intervention in case anomalies are detected, such as alert systems and override mechanisms.
Monitoring and maintenance	Learnability	• Provide regular training and clear documentation for users. • Establish a feedback loop to gather user input continuously.
	Monitorability	• Conduct regular audits to validate model behavior. • Implement automated retraining pipelines to address performance drift and ensure compliance.

Checklist for compliance

Since Articles 13 and 14 of the EU AI Act are closely related, as shown in Table 5-9, I've created a comprehensive joint checklist for integrating AI engineering best practices that align with the quality attributes associated with both of them. It defines a structured process you can follow to implement the requirements of Articles 13 and 14 throughout all phases of the development lifecycle:

Business and data understanding

- User requirement gathering: Engage end users in defining AI system requirements through interviews, surveys, or workshops.
- Expectation alignment: Ensure user expectations are documented and understood, along with all stakeholders' fairness expectations.
- Transparency requirements: Define user-specific transparency needs.
- User personas and goals: Create representative user personas to guide the design of user-facing transparency and oversight features.
- Explainability objectives: Establish clear interpretability goals aligned with user needs.
- Documentation standards: Set organization-wide standards for capturing system requirements, data sources, design decisions, and rationales.
- Requirement documentation: Use structured templates to document all information related to system requirements.
- Scope definition: Clearly define the AI system's intended use cases and limitations.
- Use case documentation: Develop detailed descriptions of appropriate and inappropriate use cases to prevent misuse.

Data preparation

- Data relevance validation: Involve users or domain experts in validating dataset relevance and quality. Analyze the dataset distribution, complete a data bias assessment, and log the results.
- Fairness-aware preprocessing: Apply preprocessing techniques to address bias or imbalances where necessary, and document decisions and justifications.
- Data catalog accessibility: Provide users with access to data catalogs, including metadata, schema descriptions, and data quality indicators.
- Feature explainability: Validate that data features are understandable and meaningful to users.
- Feature selection documentation: Record the rationale behind feature selection.
- Data source documentation: Maintain detailed records of data sources, collection methods, and preprocessing steps.
- Data versioning: Implement a version control system to track changes to the data over time.
- Contextual data labeling: Label and tag data to indicate the context in which it is appropriate.

Modeling

- Model selection input: Involve users or domain experts in model selection decisions to ensure they meet users' needs and expectations.
- Model architecture disclosure: Provide users with understandable information about the model architecture and its components.
- Use of interpretable models: Prefer inherently interpretable model types where possible.
- Explainability techniques: Implement techniques to explain complex or opaque models, if these are used. Validate explainability outputs with SHAP, LIME, or similar tools.
- Model documentation: Maintain complete documentation of model architecture, hyperparameters, and training processes.
- Model cards: Create model cards summarizing key information about each model (intended use, ethical considerations, limitations, evaluation results).
- Human override mechanisms: Implement mechanisms that allow human operators to override or intervene in model decisions when necessary, and document when and how they should be used.

Evaluation

- User testing sessions: Involve users in testing and evaluating model outputs.
- Evaluation results sharing: Provide stakeholders with accessible reports on evaluation outcomes.
- Explain evaluation metrics: Use understandable metrics and explain their implications to users.
- Evaluation procedures documentation: Thoroughly document evaluation methods and rationales, along with datasets used and results.
- Experiment tracking: Use tools such as MLflow or Weights & Biases to track experiments and results systematically.
- Contextual performance analysis: Evaluate model performance across different contexts (user groups, usage scenarios), and document findings.
- Model applicability testing: Validate that the models used are appropriate for the intended deployment contexts and use cases. Document limitations.
- Stress testing: Perform stress tests to assess model performance in various scenarios.

Deployment

- User control options: Implement mechanisms that allow users to control AI interactions (e.g., opt-in/opt-out features, adjustable system behavior settings).
- AI interaction disclosure: Clearly inform users when they are interacting with an AI system.
- Information accessibility: Provide easy access to information about how the AI system works.
- Decision explanations: Offer understandable explanations for AI decisions.
- Deployment documentation: Record details on deployment configurations, environments, and versions.
- AI system indicators: Use visual cues or labels to indicate AI-generated content or decisions.
- Usage limitations display: Clearly communicate the intended use cases and known limitations of the AI system.
- Alerting systems: Configure alerting mechanisms for data drift, model performance degradation, and other issues.

Monitoring and maintenance

- Feedback mechanisms: Provide channels for users to submit feedback and report issues.
- Update notifications: Inform stakeholders about system updates, significant changes, and issues that arise.
- Continuous explainability: Ensure that explanations remain accurate and relevant over time, and implement real-time explainability pipelines if necessary.
- Maintenance logs: Keep detailed records of maintenance activities, updates, and system changes.
- Documentation updates: Regularly revise technical and user-facing documentation to reflect the system's current state.
- Context drift monitoring: Monitor for changes in the operating environment that could affect the appropriateness or effectiveness of the system. Conduct regular fairness and performance audits.
- Misuse alerts: Set up alerting mechanisms for potential misuse or operation outside intended contexts.
- Feedback loops: Implement mechanisms for integrating user feedback into future system improvements, retraining, or governance decisions.

This checklist provides a structured way to ensure compliance with the joint requirements of Articles 13 and 14. Again, teams should revise the checklist based on their specific high-risk AI system and organizational context, while ensuring compliance with all regulatory requirements.

Article 15: Accuracy, Robustness, and Cybersecurity

Article 15

Article 15 of the EU AI Act (*https://oreil.ly/7bq1r*) establishes requirements to ensure that high-risk AI systems are accurate, reliable, and secure. It focuses on maintaining the technical integrity of AI systems to prevent malfunctions, reduce vulnerabilities, and guard against misuse. The article highlights the need for resilience, reliability, and safety across the AI system lifecycle, minimizing risks associated with errors, disruptions, or malicious interference.

Key points of Article 15 include:

Accuracy requirements
: High-risk AI systems must deliver consistent and precise results appropriate to their intended purpose, with a low rate of errors and incorrect outputs.

Robustness
: Systems must be resilient to various conditions, including potential operational disruptions or changes in the input data.

Handling adverse scenarios
: Systems should be designed to maintain functionality or fail gracefully under unexpected or adverse conditions.

Cybersecurity measures
: Developers must implement robust cybersecurity safeguards to protect the system from unauthorized access, tampering, or attacks.

Resilience to manipulation
: AI systems should be designed to be resistant to intentional manipulation or exploitation by bad actors.

Ongoing monitoring and testing
: Accuracy, robustness, and security must be continuously tested, monitored, and improved throughout the system's lifecycle.

Incident response
: Developers and operators must have protocols in place to detect and address security incidents promptly, minimizing damage and ensuring rapid recovery.

According to Kelly et al., to guarantee the implementation of accurate, reliable, and secure AI systems, the requirements stated in Article 15 can be mapped to the following quality attributes, as well as appropriateness recognizability and self-descriptiveness:

Functional correctness
: The degree to which the system produces outputs that accurately reflect its intended functionality and specified behavior for given inputs.

Faultlessness
: The extent to which the system operates without defects, malfunctions, or unintended behavior throughout its lifecycle, ensuring reliability and consistency.

Robustness
: The system's ability to maintain stable performance and functionality under a wide range of conditions, including adversarial inputs, edge cases, or unexpected environmental changes.

Functional adaptability
: The capacity of the system to adapt to changing requirements, environmental conditions, or use contexts without significant performance degradation.

Fault tolerance
: The system's ability to continue functioning correctly (or in a degraded mode) even when faults or failures occur.

Integrity
: The extent to which the system's data and operations are protected against unauthorized access or alterations, ensuring trust in its behavior and outputs.

Resistance
: The ability of the system to defend against attacks, tampering, or unauthorized manipulations, maintaining secure and reliable operation.

Table 5-12 summarizes the AI engineering practices you should implement throughout the development lifecycle to support these attributes.

Table 5-12. Quality attributes relevant to Article 15 and corresponding AI engineering practices and tools

CRISP-ML(Q) phase	Quality attributes	AI engineering practices and tools
Business and data understanding	Functional correctness	Define measurable goals using JIRA.
	Self-descriptiveness	Document assumptions using Confluence or GitHub wikis.
Data preparation	Faultlessness	Implement data validation pipelines with Great Expectations.
	Integrity	Secure data with encryption (AWS KMS, GCP KMS) and access controls.
	Robustness	Include data augmentation techniques for edge cases.

CRISP-ML(Q) phase	Quality attributes	AI engineering practices and tools
Modeling	Robustness	Use adversarial training frameworks like CleverHans or IBM ART.
	Functional adaptability	Utilize AutoML tools (H2O.ai, DataRobot) for adaptability.
	Fault tolerance	Design models with redundancy (ensemble methods) for fault tolerance.
Evaluation	Functional correctness	Use metrics like precision, recall, F1 score, and confusion matrix.
	Robustness	Evaluate models with stress testing and adversarial scenarios.
	Appropriateness recognizability	Assess model transparency with explainability tools (SHAP, LIME).
Deployment	Faultlessness	Use CI/CD pipelines (Jenkins, GitHub Actions, ArgoCD) for bug-free deployments.
	Integrity	Sign model artifacts with secure hash algorithms (SHA-256).
	Resistance	Apply NIST Cybersecurity Framework principles: identify vulnerabilities, secure environments, detect threats.
Monitoring and maintenance	Functional correctness	Implement real-time performance monitoring with Grafana dashboards.
	Self-descriptiveness	Log decisions and anomalies with Elastic Stack.
	Fault tolerance	Design failover mechanisms with Kubernetes health probes.
	Resistance	Apply active threat detection with AWS GuardDuty or Azure Security Center.

Checklist for compliance

Building an AI system that complies with Article 15 of the EU AI Act requires a comprehensive approach that addresses the related dimensions of accuracy, robustness, and cybersecurity. The following checklist (which can be adapted according to context) outlines practical steps that can be taken to support compliance throughout the system's lifecycle. It integrates AI engineering best practices aligned with the quality attributes described in the previous section into each development phase:

Business and data understanding

- Identify potential data quality issues through profiling and exploratory analysis.
- Document known data limitations and risks that could impact system reliability and correctness.
- Ensure training data represents diverse operational scenarios, including potential edge cases.
- Define robustness requirements based on system objectives and identified risks (e.g., resistance to common attacks such as feature perturbation or injection of adversarial examples, performance degradation thresholds under stress conditions).

Data preparation

- Validate datasets for accuracy, duplicates, outliers, and completeness using tools such as Great Expectations.
- Maintain end-to-end data lineage and document all preprocessing steps to support traceability.
- Apply data augmentation techniques to simulate edge cases and stress-test model generalization.
- Use adversarial testing to ensure robustness.
- Encrypt data in transit and at rest.
- Enforce strict access controls to ensure secure handling of sensitive data.

Modeling

- Define and track performance metrics to comprehensively assess functional correctness, robustness, and security (e.g., precision, recall, F1 score, mean absolute error, adversarial robustness score, attack success rate, system uptime, and throughput).
- Implement unit and integration tests for model components.
- Use exception handling mechanisms in code to manage unexpected inputs or processing errors.
- Conduct code reviews and apply static code analysis tools (e.g., SonarQube) to detect defects early.
- Use adversarial training techniques to improve robustness.
- Use interpretable models or apply explainability tools (e.g., SHAP, LIME) to clarify model behavior.
- Use metadata management tools (e.g., MLflow, Neptune.ai) to track model lineage.
- Sign model artifacts with secure hash algorithms (e.g., SHA-256) to ensure their integrity and authenticity.
- Protect model training environments from unauthorized access.
- Conduct security assessments and penetration tests during development to identify and address potential vulnerabilities.
- Evaluate system behavior under adversarial attack scenarios and mitigate high-level threats (e.g., gradient masking).

Evaluation

- Validate model outputs against ground truth data.
- Assess the model's accuracy using holdout datasets and cross-validation techniques.
- Conduct regression testing to ensure updates do not introduce new errors.
- Evaluate model performance against adversarial inputs and out-of-distribution data.
- Perform stress testing to determine performance limits and evaluate system behavior in extreme or unexpected conditions.

Deployment

- Implement CI/CD pipelines to automate testing and validation prior to deployment.
- Monitor real-time performance to ensure stability and consistency.
- Apply redundancy mechanisms to mitigate failures in production.
- Deploy redundant models or ensemble models for fault tolerance.
- Secure deployment pipelines using role-based access controls and encrypted communications.
- Monitor for cybersecurity threats using tools like AWS GuardDuty.
- Develop and periodically test incident response plans for security breaches and failures.

Monitoring and maintenance

- Monitor edge case behavior and retrain models as new data becomes available.
- Periodically reassess the system's robustness to ensure it can handle evolving operational or environmental conditions.
- Conduct regular security audits to verify the integrity of deployed systems.
- Encrypt backups and secure access to sensitive data and systems.
- Continuously monitor for emerging threats and implement mitigations to maintain system security.
- Use intrusion detection systems to detect unauthorized access or anomalous activity.

By integrating these practices into the AI lifecycle, documenting them thoroughly, and continuously evaluating performance against accuracy, robustness, and security requirements, AI engineering teams can support compliance with Article 15. Close collaboration between AI engineers, information security teams, and risk and compliance stakeholders will be key.

Further information

The following frameworks and resources offer practical guidance for implementing the technical requirements of Article 15 and building trustworthy, reliable, and secure AI systems:

- NIST Cybersecurity Framework (*https://oreil.ly/2mQel*)
- NIST Privacy Framework (*https://oreil.ly/kTfwZ*)
- *Machine Learning for High-Risk Applications* (*https://oreil.ly/dRyWk*) by Patrick Hall, James Curtis, and Parul Pandey (O'Reilly)

Conclusion

This chapter has explored the intersection of the EU AI Act and AI engineering, presenting a framework for achieving and demonstrating compliance through robust engineering practices. As you have seen, data and AI governance, monitoring, alerting, and documentation are not merely best practices but foundational elements for compliance with the EU AI Act.

We examined Articles 9 through 15 of the Act here, translating their high-level requirements for high-risk AI systems into actionable technical specifications aligned with the CRISP-ML(Q) lifecycle. By mapping these requirements to relevant quality attributes for safety-critical AI systems, this chapter provides a practical roadmap for organizations to develop, deploy, and manage high-risk AI systems responsibly and transparently. (See Table 5-13 for the complete mapping.) A key takeaway is the central role of documentation in assessing and demonstrating compliance. A robust metadata management system is also essential, both for meeting the documentation requirements of Article 11 and for ensuring traceability, as mandated by Article 12.

AI governance is an emerging discipline, and its implementation varies across industries. Consequently, achieving compliance with the EU AI Act presents real challenges, and there is a need for an engineering-level approach to meet the Act's requirements. This chapter, along with the previous ones, represents an initial effort to establish principles for proactive compliance through comprehensive AI engineering practices—practices that serve as enablers of trustworthy AI, which is the core motivation behind the EU AI Act.

The concept of AI engineering for the EU AI Act introduced here blends law, ethics, and MLOps, with an emphasis on continuous compliance through monitoring and documentation. In the next chapter, we will examine the requirements for limited-risk AI systems and explore strategies for proactive compliance through AI engineering in that context.

Table 5-13. Mapping the EU AI Act requirements to quality attributes for high-risk AI systems

Quality attribute	Article 9	Article 10	Article 11	Article 12	Article 13	Article 14	Article 15
Risk identification	✓						
Testability	✓						
Value alignment	✓					✓	
Independence		✓					
Data completeness		✓					
Currentness		✓					
Data fairness		✓					
Precision		✓					
Representativeness		✓					
Consistency		✓					
Accuracy		✓					
Credibility		✓					
Temporality		✓					
Confidentiality		✓					
Compliance		✓					
Data traceability		✓		✓			
Traceability			✓	✓			
Operability				✓			
Non-repudiation				✓			
Self-descriptiveness				✓	✓		✓
Accountability				✓		✓	
Self-monitoring				✓			
Monitorability				✓		✓	
User error protection				✓		✓	
User engagement					✓		
User transparency					✓		
Interpretability					✓	✓	
Documentability					✓	✓	
Appropriateness recognizability					✓		✓
Learnability						✓	
Fairness						✓	
Explainability						✓	
Intervenability						✓	

Quality attribute	Article 9	Article 10	Article 11	Article 12	Article 13	Article 14	Article 15
Functional correctness							✓
Faultlessness							✓
Robustness							✓
Functional adaptability							✓
Fault tolerance							✓
Integrity							✓
Resistance							✓

CHAPTER 6

AI Engineering for Limited-Risk AI Systems

The previous chapter translated Articles 9 to 15 of the EU AI Act into actionable specifications for high-risk AI systems within the CRISP-ML(Q) lifecycle, providing practical checklists to support responsible development and management. It also introduced the concept of AI engineering in the context of EU AI Act compliance.

This chapter shifts focus to the Act's requirements for limited-risk AI systems, with particular attention to transparency obligations. It explores how organizations can address these requirements proactively through MLOps. See Figure 6-1 for a visual of the steps to take to move toward compliance with the EU AI Act.

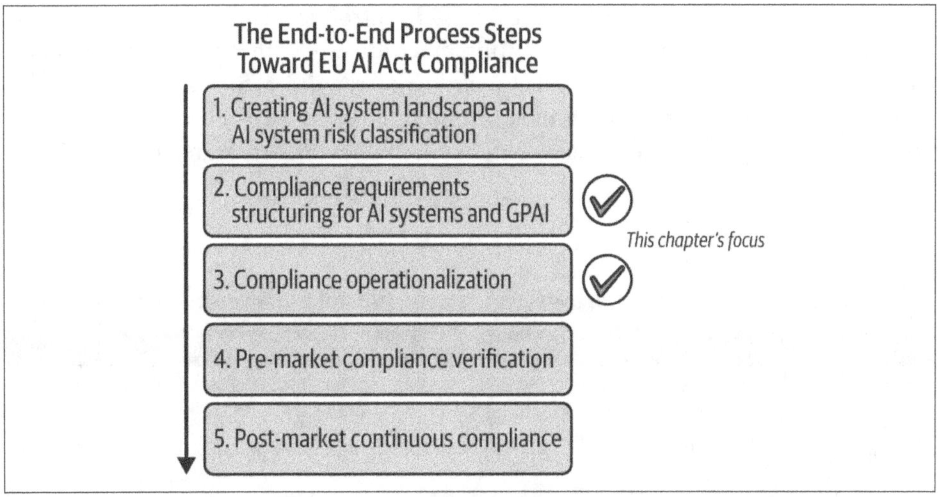

Figure 6-1. This chapter focuses on the requirements for limited-risk AI systems and the operationalization of compliance for such systems. See Chapter 1 for an explanation of the end-to-end process steps toward EU AI Act compliance.

The two guiding questions for this chapter are:

- To comply with the EU AI Act, what requirements must limited-risk AI systems fulfill?
- What processes, structures, and AI engineering practices need to be established to comply with the Act with regard to transparency obligations?

As you may have noticed, I mention both compliance and transparency obligations here. Let's examine the difference between these two concepts.

Compliance Assessment Versus Transparency Obligation

A compliance or conformity assessment is a mandatory process for high-risk AI systems to ensure they meet the EU AI Act's requirements, often involving third-party evaluation. Transparency obligations are less strict and are a broader requirement for all AI systems interacting directly with humans. Let's quickly take a closer look at each before diving deeper into the transparency obligations laid out in the Act.

A conformity assessment is a formal process by which a provider demonstrates that an AI system meets the requirements outlined in Chapter III, Section 2 of the EU AI Act. This process ensures compliance with legal obligations and may involve a third-party evaluation by a notified body (an independent organization designated by Member States to assess high-risk AI systems). The primary objective is to verify that the system conforms to EU regulatory standards before it is placed on the market.

Article 50 of the EU AI Act (*https://oreil.ly/cc73j*) introduces transparency obligations that apply to all AI systems intended to interact directly with humans, regardless of their risk classification. These obligations do not require a formal assessment but instead aim to prevent deception or harm by imposing specific duties on providers and deployers to inform individuals that they are interacting with an AI system.

Table 6-1 compares conformity assessments and transparency obligations under the EU AI Act.

Table 6-1. Key differences between conformity assessments and transparency obligations

Feature	Conformity assessment	Transparency obligation
Applicability scope	High-risk AI systems only	AI systems interacting with humans, broadly applicable
Main goal	Ensure compliance with technical and legal requirements	Promote user awareness and prevent deception
Nature	Formal process, which requires third-party assessment	Informative and clarity-focused
Process	Technical evaluations and compliance checks	Labeling, information disclosure
Responsibility	Providers	Providers and deployers

Feature	Conformity assessment	Transparency obligation
Outcome	Certificate and EU declaration of conformity	Awareness and understanding for users
Relation to other laws	Part of EU harmonization law, when applicable	In addition to other national or EU transparency laws

In sum, a conformity assessment is a rigorous, technical process aimed at ensuring that high-risk AI systems are safe and fully compliant with the EU AI Act, while transparency obligations are designed to ensure that users are aware they are interacting with an AI system, regardless of its risk classification. In this chapter, we'll explore what those obligations entail and how they can be addressed in practice.

Understanding Transparency Obligations

As I explained in Chapter 4, the term "limited risk" is not explicitly defined in the EU AI Act. Instead, the Act outlines three main categories: prohibited AI practices under the unacceptable risk category (Article 5), high-risk AI systems (Article 6), and AI systems with specific transparency obligations (Article 50).

"Limited-risk" AI systems are generally understood to be those that are not explicitly prohibited or high risk but are still subject to transparency requirements when they interact directly with humans. Article 50 sets out the transparency obligations for both providers and deployers of AI systems. These obligations apply to *all AI systems intended to interact directly with natural persons*, regardless of their risk level. Table 6-2 summarizes the key provisions.

Table 6-2. Overview of transparency obligations for providers and deployers of AI systems according to Article 50 of the EU AI Act

Transparency obligation	Description
Informing users of AI interaction	Providers must inform users when they are interacting with an AI system, unless it's reasonably obvious or the system is used for law enforcement purposes (e.g., detecting, preventing, investigating, or prosecuting crimes). This applies to chatbots and content-generating tools.
Marking synthetic content	Providers of AI systems that generate synthetic content (audio, images, video, text) must clearly mark these outputs as artificially generated or manipulated. The labels should be machine-readable and easily detectable, signaling the content's non-authentic nature. This requirement does not apply to assistive editing tools or systems that do not significantly alter the original input.
Disclosing deepfakes	Providers of AI systems that generate deepfakes (described by Article 3(60) as "AI-generated or manipulated image, audio or video content that resembles existing persons, objects, places, entities or events and would falsely appear to a person to be authentic or truthful") must clearly label these outputs as artificial. The labels should be machine-readable and easily detectable. This obligation does not apply to systems that provide standard editing functions, do not significantly alter the original data, or are used for law enforcement purposes.

Transparency obligation	Description
Additional transparency measures for emotion recognition and biometric categorization	Deployers of emotion recognition and biometric systems must clearly inform users about how these technologies work and how their data is used, with particular attention to accessibility for individuals with disabilities. Note that meeting the Act's transparency requirements does not ensure compliance with other legal standards, such as the GDPR.

Article 50 requires that AI systems intended to interact directly with natural persons be properly designed to support that interaction, as well as mandating that individuals be clearly informed that they are engaging with an AI system. This information should be provided at the start of the interaction. For instance, an AI system with a chat interface triggers this transparency obligation, and users should be informed of its artificial nature the first time they engage with it.

Here are some additional examples of systems that require disclosure:

- AI systems like Jasper AI or Voice.ai that create or modify content (audio, images, videos, or text) must clearly label their outputs as artificially created or altered.
- AI systems that generate deepfakes must clearly state that the content is artificially created or manipulated. This is in addition to the general requirement to mark all synthetic content.
- Emotion recognition and biometric categorization systems like Affectiva (by Smart Eye), which analyze facial expressions or biometric data to infer emotions or classify individuals, require deployers to inform users about the system's operation.
- AI systems that generate or manipulate text, such as social media content bots, AI-powered news writing systems like Narrative Science, and large language models (e.g., OpenAI's GPT models) that produce news articles, financial updates, weather reports, and other public-interest content must disclose that the content was artificially generated or manipulated.

According to Article 50, all disclosures of this type must be clear, easily noticeable, and accessible to all users. General site-wide disclaimers are insufficient. The disclosure must be made before the actual exposure to the content in question.

Now that you have an idea of what the key transparency obligations look like, let's turn our attention to how AI engineering practices can support effective implementation.

Aligning AI Engineering with SMACTR and CRISP-ML(Q) for Transparency

As discussed earlier, a conformity assessment is a formal process that requires a third-party audit. However, this audit is typically conducted after deployment, when the system might already have negatively impacted users. Inioluwa Deborah Raji et al. address this in their widely cited paper "Closing the AI Accountability Gap: Defining an End-to-End Framework for Internal Algorithmic Auditing" (*https://oreil.ly/9RVsg*), in which they propose an internal audit framework designed to guide the practical implementation of ethical AI development: SMACTR (Scoping, Mapping, Artifact Collection, Testing, and Reflection). SMACTR provides a structured approach for organizations to ensure that their AI systems align with their stated ethical principles and values. The framework is intended to be used throughout the entire AI system development lifecycle, not just at a single point in time, and it aids organizations in preparing effectively for third-party conformity audits.

The Five Stages of the SMACTR Framework

Let's start by examining the five stages of the SMACTR framework:

Scoping
: Clarifies the objectives of the audit by reviewing the motivations and intended impact of the system and confirming the principles meant to guide system development. This stage also involves mapping out use cases and identifying analogous deployments to anticipate potential harm.

Mapping
: Connects the documents produced during the Scoping phase to the stakeholders that will be involved in testing and reviewing. FMEA should begin in this stage (for more on FMEA, see "Failure Mode and Effects Analysis" on page 109).

Artifact Collection
: Gathers key documents and evidence needed to support ethical and technical evaluation, including an ethical review of the system's use case and a social impact assessment. Prerequisite documents from system and engineering teams typically include a declaration of ethical objectives and a product requirements document (PRD).

Testing
: Involves a thorough audit of the model's performance, considering both technical and ethical aspects.

Reflection
: Focuses on reviewing the entire development process and identifying opportunities for improvement in the future.

As visualized in Figure 6-2, each stage has its own set of documentation requirements, which help ensure the framework supports accountability and transparency.

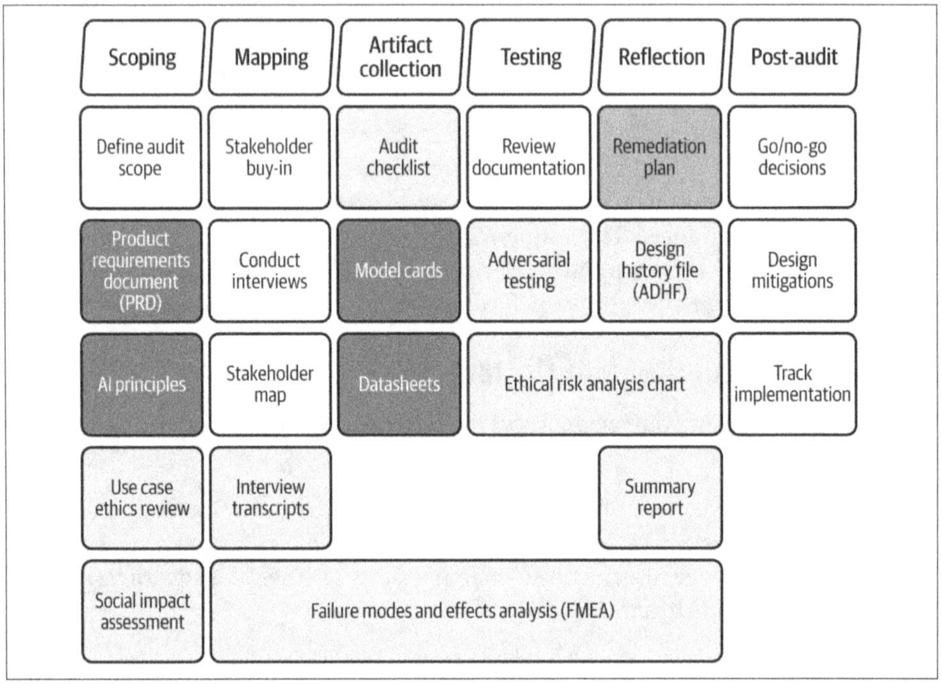

Figure 6-2. Overview of the SMACTR framework (source: https://oreil.ly/9RVsg)

Table 6-3 summarizes the purpose, key activities, and expected outcomes of each stage, as outlined in the paper introducing the framework.

Table 6-3. The stages of the SMACTR framework

SMACTR stage	Purpose	Activities	Outcomes
Scoping	Clarify the audit's objective by reviewing the AI system's motivations and intended impact. Define the project's scope and the ethical principles that should guide its development.	• Review the product or request document specifying the AI system's requirements and expectations. • Identify the intended use cases and potential areas of harm or social impact. • Map out analogous deployments either within the organization or from competitors to anticipate potential issues. • Confirm the ethical principles and values that are meant to guide product development. • Define a risk analysis centered on the failure to achieve the ethical principles.	A clear understanding of the audit's objectives, the intended impact of the AI system, and the ethical guidelines that should be followed. Key documentation to create includes AI system (project) scope documents, initial risk assessments, and ethical review reports.
Mapping	Identify all relevant stakeholders to ensure that the audit considers the perspectives and interests of all parties involved, including users, developers, and other affected groups.	• Identify all relevant stakeholders who may be affected by the AI system. • Determine the potential impact of the system on each stakeholder group.	A comprehensive stakeholder map and a clear understanding of the potential impacts of the AI system on different groups.
Artifact Collection	Gather all relevant documentation and data related to the development and deployment of the AI system. This information is essential for the auditors to thoroughly evaluate the system and identify potential risks and ethical concerns.	• Collect project-related documents, technical specifications, and relevant data. • Gather information about data sources, data preparation steps, model training details, and evaluation results. • Gather documentation related to the system's development.	A complete set of documents, data, and other artifacts related to the AI system, which facilitates analysis. This documentation may include data quality assessments, model cards, training logs, and performance reports.
Testing	Evaluate the AI system's performance and identify any potential issues or risks that may arise during its operation. This goes beyond standard technical testing to include ethical implications and biases.	• Conduct technical tests to assess the model's accuracy, robustness, and reliability. • Evaluate the model's fairness and identify any potential biases that may lead to discriminatory outcomes. • Assess the model's performance under various conditions, including edge cases and potential adversarial scenarios. • Use both technical metrics and ethical considerations for evaluation.	A thorough understanding of the system's performance, limitations, and potential risks, focusing on both technical and ethical aspects. This includes performance reports and bias detection analysis.

SMACTR stage	Purpose	Activities	Outcomes
Reflection	Analyze the results from the previous phase and evaluate them in light of the original scoping goals. This step focuses on summarizing findings, assessing how well ethical risks were addressed, and proposing improvements for the future.	• Evaluate the outcomes of the Testing stage with regard to the project's original scoping goals. • Identify any ethical principles that may be jeopardized when the AI system is deployed. • Based on the test results, formulate recommendations for further mitigating identified risks and ensuring responsible use of the system. • Develop a risk mitigation plan in collaboration with engineering teams.	An algorithmic use-related risk analysis, including a risk mitigation plan that addresses the identified failures and potential risks. This will include a reflection on the ethical implications of deploying the AI system.

How the SMACTR Framework Aligns with the EU AI Act

The SMACTR framework is intended for pre-deployment auditing and can be used to support compliance with the EU AI Act. Its emphasis on embedding ethical considerations throughout the AI development lifecycle directly aligns with the Act's objectives and requirements. Let's look at some of the key areas of alignment:

Proactive and preventative auditing
: The SMACTR framework promotes a proactive approach to ethical AI development by integrating audit processes into the design and development phases. This is in contrast with traditional external audits, which often occur after deployment, when risks may have already caused harm. This preventive orientation aligns well with the EU AI Act's requirements for risk assessment and mitigation: by using SMACTR, AI engineers can anticipate and address potential risks before they become problems. While the framework wasn't developed specifically for the EU AI Act, its focus on "urgent governance," which emphasizes auditing not only for system reliability but also for societal harm, makes it a good fit for the Act's goal of protecting fundamental rights.

Emphasis on transparency and documentation
: SMACTR produces structured documentation at each stage, forming a comprehensive audit trail. This aligns with the EU AI Act's requirements for comprehensive technical documentation and traceability, particularly for high-risk AI systems. The documentation that is generated, including artifacts such as model cards and datasheets, supports information sharing along the AI value chain and can serve as evidence of due diligence in addressing ethical concerns and meeting regulatory requirements.

Alignment with ethical principles and values
: The EU AI Act is grounded in the concept of trustworthy AI and builds on the ethical guidelines developed by the High-Level Expert Group on AI. The SMACTR framework is designed to help organizations align their AI systems with their stated ethical principles and values and enables them to evaluate how well the systems uphold those principles in practice.

Risk assessment integration
: The Scoping stage of the framework involves a structured risk analysis that goes beyond technical reliability, mapping use cases and identifying potential sources of harm and social impact. Tools such as FMEA and anticipatory "What if…?" questions support this process. This broader risk-based approach, which incorporates ethical and societal considerations, aligns well with the EU AI Act's emphasis on comprehensive risk management.

Accountability and responsibility
: SMACTR explicitly promotes accountability by defining roles and responsibilities throughout the AI development lifecycle. This aligns with the EU AI Act's emphasis on traceability, transparency, and explainability and defined obligations for providers, deployers, and other stakeholders. The Mapping stage of the framework, in particular, can help establish an internal record of individual accountability.

As you can see, the SMACTR framework is not only a tool for ethical AI development but also a practical mechanism for supporting compliance with the EU AI Act. Its focus on proactive auditing, detailed documentation, alignment with ethical principles, integrated risk assessment, and accountability makes it especially suitable for guiding AI engineering teams in meeting the Act's regulatory requirements. The framework can be implemented in full or in a streamlined form, depending on the desired level of rigor. It can also be adapted to different risk levels and specific system requirements, making it applicable across a wide range of use cases.

Crucially, SMACTR can be integrated with AI engineering practices to ensure that ethical and transparency considerations are addressed throughout the AI system lifecycle. By integrating SMACTR with the CRISP-ML(Q) methodology, AI engineers can embed transparency and compliance measures in all stages of development.

The following sections outline how to integrate SMACTR into the CRISP-ML(Q) lifecycle and provide a step-by-step engineering guide to help organizations meet transparency obligations under the EU AI Act. For each phase of the lifecycle, I'll start by examining the relevant transparency requirements, then describe the corresponding CRISP-ML(Q) activities, show how SMACTR can be applied, and identify the key artifacts that support compliance and traceability.

Business and Data Understanding Phase

In the business and data understanding phase, several transparency requirements need to be addressed to ensure that users are aware when they are interacting with an AI system and that synthetic content is clearly identified. Key requirements in this phase include:

Document the intended purpose of the AI system
: Clearly document the intended purpose of the AI system, specifying what it is designed to do and the problem it is meant to solve.

Define interaction points with humans
: Identify all points where the AI system will interact directly with humans. This includes user interfaces, chatbots, or any other mechanism where a natural person will engage with the system.

Identify synthetic content generation capabilities
: Determine whether the AI system can generate or manipulate audio, image, video, or text content. If so, document this capability, as any synthetic output must be clearly marked.

Plan notification mechanisms
: Develop a plan for notifying users that they are interacting with an AI system. This may involve implementing visible notifications, clear labeling, and other accessible methods.

CRISP-ML(Q) activities

In the business and data understanding phase, the following CRISP-ML(Q) activities are crucial:

Define scope and success criteria
: Clearly define the project's goals and the criteria for success. This includes identifying measurable outcomes and establishing KPIs for the AI system.

Assess data availability and quality
: Evaluate the data available for training and validation, considering its quantity, relevance, accuracy, and completeness.

Evaluate feasibility
: Assess the technical and operational feasibility of the project to determine whether its goals are achievable with the available resources and technologies.

Design data collection strategy
: If there's not enough existing data, design a strategy for collecting additional data. Specify how new data will be sourced, stored, and managed.

SMACTR integration

The SMACTR framework enhances the CRISP-ML(Q) process by integrating ethical considerations and auditability from the beginning. The Scoping, Mapping, and Artifact Collection stages are relevant to the business and data understanding phase. Here are the key tasks:

Scoping (ethical review of system use case)
: Conduct an ethical review of the AI system's intended use. This involves considering who might be affected by the system and what the potential social impacts might be.

Mapping (stakeholder identification)
: Identify all internal and external stakeholders who will be involved in or affected by the AI system. This could include developers, product managers, end users, and individuals whose rights may be impacted.

Artifact Collection (initial documentation gathering)
: Begin gathering initial documentation for the AI system. This includes project proposals, requirements documents, and statements of ethical objectives.

Key artifacts

By the end of the business and data understanding phase, the following key artifacts should be produced to meet the requirements of the EU AI Act:

Project scope document
: A document that clearly defines the project's objectives, scope, and success criteria. This should include details about what the AI system aims to achieve and the boundaries of the project.

Ethical review report
: A report that outlines the ethical implications of the AI system, including potential risks and harms, and documents whether the system aligns with a set of ethical values or principles.

Stakeholder map
: A visual representation of all stakeholders, showing their roles and relationships to the AI system. This map should clarify participant dynamics and provide context for interpreting the final audit report.

Data quality assessment
: A report assessing the availability, quality, and suitability of the data for the project. This document should identify any data gaps or potential biases that need to be addressed in the next phase.

Initial transparency requirements document
: A document that outlines the preliminary transparency requirements based on Article 50. This includes interaction points with humans, any synthetic content generation, and planned notification mechanisms.

Table 6-4 summarizes the content of these artifacts.

Table 6-4. Summary of key artifacts produced during the business and data understanding phase

Artifact	Content
Project scope document	• Project objectives • Success criteria • Resource requirements • Timeline • Constraints • Dependencies
Ethical review report	• Impact assessment • Risk analysis • Mitigation strategies • Compliance evaluation • Ethics board recommendations
Stakeholder map	• Involved parties • Roles and responsibilities • Communication paths • Decision authority levels
Data quality assessment (assessment criteria)	• Completeness • Accuracy • Consistency • Timeliness • Privacy compliance
Initial transparency requirements document	• System purpose declaration • Human interaction points • Synthetic content capabilities • Notification mechanisms • Documentation requirements • Compliance checklist

Data Preparation Phase

In the data preparation phase, the focus is on guaranteeing that the data used to train the AI system is well documented and auditable. This is crucial for transparency, accountability, and enabling deployers and users to understand how the AI system makes decisions. Here's how the transparency requirements of Article 50 translate into practical steps in this phase:

Implement data lineage tracking
: Establish a system for tracking the origin and data flows. This includes recording where the data comes from, any transformations it undergoes, and how it is used. This is important to ensure that the data used by the system can be traced back to its original source, which can help to identify and correct potential issues. Technically, this requires components such as source system tracking, transformation history, and version control integration.

Document data transformations
: All transformations applied to the data, such as cleaning, normalization, or aggregation, must be clearly documented. The documentation should describe what transformations were applied, why they were applied, and their impact on the data.

Establish audit trail
: Create a robust audit trail by logging all data preparation activities, including who made the changes, when they were made, and what specific changes were implemented. An audit trail ensures that there is a record of all data preparation steps, which is essential for maintaining accountability and demonstrating compliance with transparency requirements.

Create metadata management system
: Develop a system for managing metadata about the data, such as its format, type, source, and any associated quality metrics. A well-structured metadata management system is key for understanding the data and its characteristics and enables better data governance. It also supports the traceability and reusability of ML assets, such as data, features, and models.

CRISP-ML(Q) activities

The key activities for a structured approach to data preparation within machine learning projects during this phase include:

Data cleaning and validation
: Identify and correct any errors or inconsistencies in the data. This includes handling missing values, correcting typos, and ensuring data conforms to the defined standards.

Feature engineering
: Create new features from the existing data that are relevant to the modeling task. This might involve transforming existing variables, creating interaction terms, or extracting other meaningful information to enhance model performance.

Data transformation
: Convert the data from its raw format into a suitable format for machine learning algorithms. This may involve normalizing numerical data or encoding categorical data, for example.

Data documentation
: Record the characteristics of the data including its sources, data types, and limitations, and document any issues or biases present in the data.

SMACTR integration

The Artifact Collection, Testing, and Reflection stages of the SMACTR framework can be integrated into all the remaining CRISP-ML(Q) phases. Here are the key activities for the data preparation phase:

Artifact Collection (data documentation)
: Create detailed documentation about the data and all processing steps. This should go beyond basic recordkeeping.

Testing (initial data quality verification)
: Perform rigorous validation of data quality and transformation effectiveness to ensure that the data preparation process meets both technical requirements and compliance standards and that it is aligned with transparency and ethical goals.

Reflection (data preparation impact analysis)
: Consider the broader implications of the data preparation process. Analyze how each transformation might affect different groups or communities, and reflect on potential ethical concerns such as bias or unfair outcomes.

Key artifacts

By the end of the data preparation phase, several key artifacts should be produced to meet the requirements of the EU AI Act. These include:

Data quality reports
: Detailed reports on the quality of the data, highlighting any issues or limitations. These reports should specify what metrics were used, what problems were found, and how they were resolved.

Feature documentation
: Clear descriptions of all features used in the model, including how they were engineered and what they represent. This documentation should also explain the rationale behind the feature engineering choices.

Data lineage documentation

Records that trace the origin of the data and any transformations applied. This documentation should show the entire path the data takes, from its source to its final use in the system.

Transformation logs

Detailed logs of all data transformations, including the date, time, user, and specifics of each change. These logs serve as a verifiable record of the data transformation process.

Metadata schema

A defined structure and format for metadata, ensuring consistency in how data is documented. The metadata schema provides a clear framework for classifying and tracking data.

Table 6-5 provides an overview of the content of each of these artifacts.

Table 6-5. Summary of key artifacts produced during the data preparation phase

Artifact	Content
Data quality reports	Validation checks: • Schema validation • Business rule compliance • Constraint verification • Format consistency Data quality assessments, e.g.: • Completeness: (metric: null percentage; threshold: <0.05; validation result: pass/fail) • Accuracy: (metric: error rate; threshold: <0.01; validation result: pass/fail)
Feature documentation	• Feature name • Description (business meaning) • Source (original data source) • Transformations (list of applied transformations) • Dependencies (parent features) • Validation rules (business constraints)
Data lineage documentation	• Operation ID • Timestamp • Data transformation type • Input data: source (input location), version • Output data: destination (output location), version
Transformation logs	• Transform ID • Method: transformation function, input parameters, validation results • Metadata: timestamp, responsible user, code version
Metadata schema	• Technical metadata: data types, schema version, storage format • Business metadata: owners, update frequency, sensitivity level • Operational metadata: processing history, quality metrics, dependency map

Modeling Phase

The core focus of the CRISP-ML(Q) modeling phase is to select and train models, optimize hyperparameters, and evaluate model performance. The following actions support compliance with Article 50's transparency requirements in this phase, ensuring that an AI system's decision-making process is interpretable, traceable, and reproducible:

Implement version control for models
: Use a version control system (such as Git) to track all changes made to the model's code, parameters, and configurations. This not only enables reproducibility but also provides the ability to revert to previous versions when necessary.

Document model behavior and intent
: Develop comprehensive documentation that clearly explains how the model works, its intended applications, and its limitations. This should include details about the model's architecture, the training process, the datasets used, and evaluation methodology. In the previous chapter, I gave a detailed overview of the types of documentation that can be created for AI systems. For example, model cards can be used to provide a concise summary of the model's key characteristics (intended use, performance metrics, limitations, ethical considerations, and an overview of the evaluation data, scope, and associated risks).

Establish explainability mechanisms
: Incorporate explainability tools or techniques to enhance understanding of the model's decision-making process. For example, you might use feature importance analysis or surrogate models to provide insights into how the model arrives at its predictions.

CRISP-ML(Q) activities

The key activities during the modeling phase include:

Model selection
: Select the most appropriate model architecture based on the problem definition and requirements.

Training and validation
: Train the selected model using the prepared data, and use a hold-out validation set to fine-tune hyperparameters and evaluate its performance. Document the entire training process.

Performance evaluation
: Assess the model's performance using appropriate metrics, focusing on both technical accuracy and fairness across different subgroups.

Model optimization
: Fine-tune the model to improve performance, considering factors such as accuracy, fairness, and robustness.

Make sure to thoroughly document all of these processes, along with the rationale behind all of your decisions.

SMACTR integration

The following activities show how the SMACTR stages of Artifact Collection, Testing, and Reflection can be integrated into the modeling phase:

Artifact Collection
: Document all relevant information about the model, including its architecture, training details, and performance metrics.

Testing
: Thoroughly evaluate the model's performance, considering both technical and ethical aspects. Include tests for fairness, accuracy, and robustness across different subgroups.

Reflection
: Continuously assess the broader ethical implications of the model, including potential impacts on fundamental rights and societal outcomes. Document the model selection rationale and the ethical considerations behind modeling choices.

Key artifacts

Table 6-6 lists the artifacts that should be generated and maintained during the modeling phase.

Table 6-6. Summary of key artifacts produced during the modeling phase

Artifact	Content
Model cards	Concise documents summarizing the model's intended use, performance metrics, limitations, and ethical considerations. (See the Model Card Toolkit (*https://oreil.ly/5fcMI*).)
Training logs	Comprehensive records of the training process, including hyperparameters, data used, and performance metrics at each stage.
Performance reports	Detailed analyses of the model's performance, including accuracy, precision, recall, and other relevant metrics. Also include results from fairness testing and bias detection and mitigation strategies.
Explainability documentation	Structured summaries of the methods used for model interpretation and the insights gained from them.
Version control records	Logs from the version control system showing all changes made to the model's code and configurations. This ensures full traceability and enables reproducibility.

Technical implementation guide

The following infrastructure components enable teams to implement the practices outlined in the previous sections and support the transparency requirements of Article 50:

Version control
: Use a version control system such as Git to track changes to data, models, and code, to ensure transparency and facilitate rollbacks. You may want to adopt a dual tracking approach, using DVC for data versioning and MLflow for model versioning.

Metadata tracking system
: Implement a robust metadata tracking system to record model versions, training data, evaluation results, and explainability information. The components of this system will include:

  - A scalable database (e.g., PostgreSQL) for structured metadata
  - A document store (e.g., MongoDB) for unstructured data and logs
  - A searchable index (e.g., Elasticsearch) for quick retrieval

MLOps platform
: Use an MLOps platform that supports versioning, experiment tracking, and pipeline automation. Options include Managed MLflow and Unity Catalog (Databricks), Weights & Biases, and Metaflow, to name a few.

Evaluation Phase

The CRISP-ML(Q) evaluation phase focuses on validating the AI model's performance on unseen data and refining the model as needed prior to deployment. To meet the transparency obligations outlined in Article 50 of the EU AI Act, the following practical steps should be implemented:

Record and track model predictions and confidence levels
: Establish a system that logs all model predictions along with their associated confidence scores. This system should support easy retrieval and analysis to help users understand how the AI system generates its outputs. In addition to the predictions themselves, log any intermediate steps or features that contribute to these outcomes.

Verify notification mechanisms
: Evaluate whether the system clearly informs users that they are interacting with an AI. The notification should describe the system's purpose, data sources, and known limitations. Test the effectiveness and visibility of the disclosure in the user interface, and make sure it is accessible to all users.

Test content marking processes

If the AI system generates synthetic content (audio, images, videos, or text), it must have the capability to mark the content as artificial in a machine-readable format. Verify that these markers are detectable and compliant with deepfake disclosure requirements, if applicable, to enhance transparency and promote accountability.

Validate documentation completeness

Ensure all documentation is complete and up-to-date, including information on the intended use of the AI system, data sources, model cards, training logs, and performance reports. The documentation should be crafted in a way that is easily understandable for both deployers and end users, facilitating smooth communication and comprehension of the system's functionality and purpose.

CRISP-ML(Q) activities

The main activities of the evaluation phase are:

Model validation

Assess the model's accuracy and generalization ability by using use case–specific metrics on unseen data. Employing techniques such as cross-validation can improve the robustness of the model, enabling a more reliable evaluation of its capabilities.

Performance assessment

When evaluating a model's performance, it's essential to consider not just accuracy but also fairness, robustness, and explainability. It's also important to track the following:

- Predictive performance across different continuous-training executions
- Metadata and artifacts generated throughout the pipeline to support debugging, reproducibility, and lineage analysis (the ability to track a trained model back to its training dataset, including all intermediate artifacts and metadata)
- Hyperparameters used during training
- All evaluations performed by the pipeline
- Processed data snapshots after transformation steps, if feasible
- Data summaries such as descriptive statistics, schemas, and feature distributions

Documenting these metrics in the evaluation report and model card enhances transparency. Aligning them with the model's intended use is crucial for producing relevant and meaningful assessments.

Business goal alignment
: Verify that the model's performance aligns with the original business goals and success criteria. Confirm that the model's outputs are relevant and valuable for the intended use case.

Compliance verification
: Verify that the system's functionalities and documentation comply with the EU AI Act and any other applicable laws or industry standards.

SMACTR integration

Here are the main SMACTR integration activities for the evaluation phase:

Artifact Collection (test results)

- Gather all test results and performance data to be used in the impact assessment.
- Ensure all AI system artifacts are well documented and clearly presented.
- Collect comprehensive data on the model's behavior and performance under a variety of conditions.

Testing (comprehensive system testing)

- Conduct thorough testing of the entire AI system, including the model, data pipelines, and user interfaces. The tests should cover a range of scenarios, including edge cases and potential adversarial inputs.
- Ensure all tests are documented and results are properly recorded.

Reflection (system impact analysis)

- Document potential risks and limitations, including sources of bias and fairness concerns.
- Assess whether the AI system aligns with the organization's defined ethical principles.

Key artifacts

Table 6-7 provides a summary of the artifacts that should be produced during this phase.

Table 6-7. Summary of key artifacts produced during the evaluation phase

Artifact	Content
Evaluation reports	Document all evaluation activities, including model validation, performance metrics, and business goal alignment. Include a summary of the model's strengths, weaknesses, and limitations.
Compliance verification documents	Provide evidence of compliance with the transparency requirements of Article 50 and other relevant regulations. Clearly demonstrate how the system meets legal and ethical obligations.

Artifact	Content
Test results	Compile the findings of model and system tests, including inputs, outputs, and any errors found. Include performance data and error analysis.
Impact assessments	Analyze the system's effects on stakeholders, considering potential ethical and societal implications. Document any identified biases and risks.
Audit reports	Summarize findings from the evaluation phase, including compliance checks and ethical assessments. Provide recommendations for improvements, and include a social impact analysis.

Available tools and technologies

Integrating transparency into MLOps workflows requires robust tools for explainability, monitoring, and validation. The following tools and technologies can be used to implement best practices and support compliance with the EU AI Act:

Explainability tools
: These help make the model's decision-making process more interpretable and understandable. Examples include:

- SHAP, for understanding feature importance
- LIME, for explaining individual predictions
- Explainable Boosting Machines (EBMs), for creating inherently interpretable models

Monitoring and logging tools
: These are essential for tracking system performance in real time and monitoring for fairness, and potential biases. Examples include:

- Prometheus, for time-series data and alerts
- Grafana, for data visualization and dashboards
- Elastic Stack, for log management and analysis
- Model Card Toolkit, for standardizing and documenting key information about AI models via structured model cards

Testing frameworks
: These facilitate thorough testing of the entire AI system. Examples include:

- PyTest, for writing and running tests of Python-based AI applications
- TensorFlow Testing, for testing TensorFlow models and pipelines

Deployment Phase

The deployment phase marks the transition of the AI system into a live production environment. The following actions are essential for meeting transparency requirements under Article 50 during this lifecycle phase:

Deploy notification systems
: Users must be informed that they are interacting with an AI system before they engage with the system (unless it is obvious). These disclosures must be clearly visible within the system interface and include an explanation of the system's purpose, data sources, and any known limitations. User disclosures must be clear, concise, and accessible to everyone. Test the notification system thoroughly to ensure it works properly in the production environment.

Implement content marking
: Use content marking mechanisms that clearly identify synthetic content (audio, images, video, or text) as artificially generated or manipulated. For systems that produce deepfakes, explicit disclosure is required to inform users that the content is synthetic.

Enable monitoring
: Activate monitoring tools to observe the system's real-time performance. Monitor for data drift, model performance degradation, and the emergence of biases. The monitoring system should also track user interactions, content generation events, and model deployments.

Establish audit logging
: Implement a comprehensive audit logging framework to record all relevant system activities (user interactions, content generation or manipulation events, errors, etc.). The logs should include model versioning details, transparency notifications, and compliance verification results. The audit logging system should be robust and secure while adhering to data protection regulations.

CRISP-ML(Q) activities

This phase typically involves the following key activities:

System integration
: Integrate the AI model with the rest of the production environment. This requires end-to-end testing to ensure that all components are correctly connected and functioning as intended.

Production deployment
: Deploy the AI model into the production environment using established CI/CD pipelines. Validate that the deployed system is functioning as expected by running tests in the live environment.

Monitoring setup

Configure monitoring tools to track key metrics and performance indicators (defined in the earlier CRISP-ML(Q) phases) such as accuracy, fairness, robustness, and explainability. Set up alerting mechanisms to notify stakeholders of any issues or anomalies that arise.

Documentation finalization

Ensure that all relevant documentation, including user manuals, system architecture diagrams, dataset documentation, and model cards, is complete and accurately reflects the current state of the deployed system. Finalizing documentation is an often overlooked step that is essential for transparency and providing end users and stakeholders with a clear understanding of the deployed system.

SMACTR integration

The deployment phase incorporates SMACTR's Artifact Collection, Testing, and Reflection stages through the following activities:

Artifact Collection (final documentation)

- Gather final versions of all documentation, including system architecture diagrams, data flow schematics, dataset and model cards, and compliance records.
- Confirm that the documentation reflects the complete process, from development to deployment.

Testing (production verification)

- Perform a final verification of the system's performance in the live environment.
- Ensure that the system continues to operate as expected and that all transparency mechanisms are functioning correctly.
- Continuously monitor the model for performance degradation, fairness issues, and potential bias drift.

Reflection (deployment readiness assessment)

- Ensure all necessary safeguards are in place to protect users and support responsible AI deployment.
- Conduct a final review of the entire system to confirm it meets all technical, ethical, and legal requirements.

Key artifacts

By the end of the deployment phase, several key artifacts should be available to meet the transparency obligations of the EU AI Act. As usual, I've summarized them in Table 6-8.

Table 6-8. Summary of key artifacts produced during the deployment phase

Artifact	Content
Deployment configurations	Document the configurations and settings used for deploying the AI system into production. Include infrastructure setup, software versions, and any dependencies.
Monitoring dashboards	Set up monitoring dashboards to provide real-time visibility into the system's performance. Dashboards should display key metrics and include alerting mechanisms for potential issues and anomalies.
System documentation	Compile all documentation related to the deployed system, including architecture diagrams, deployment details, API specifications, and user guides. Make sure this documentation is accessible to all stakeholders.
Compliance records	Maintain records demonstrating compliance with Article 50 transparency obligations and any other applicable regulations. Ensure these records are accessible for audit purposes.
Incident response plans	Establish clear procedures for identifying, containing, and resolving incidents in the production environment. Include communication protocols for notifying relevant stakeholders.

Available tools and technologies

Here are some tools and technologies that can support the implementation of transparency during the deployment phase:

Metadata tracking systems
: These enable traceability by tracking user interactions, content generation events, model deployments, and compliance verification results. Examples include:

  - Databases: PostgreSQL (for structured metadata), MongoDB (for unstructured data)
  - Searchable index: Elasticsearch (for quick retrieval)

MLOps platforms
: These support model deployment, versioning, and lifecycle management. Popular examples include:

  - Kubeflow, an open source platform for deploying and managing machine learning workflows on Kubernetes
  - MLflow, for managing the complete ML lifecycle
  - Vertex AI, Google Cloud's managed ML platform for building, deploying, and scaling ML models

CI/CD tools
: These automate the deployment pipeline, ensuring consistency and traceability. They include:

  - GitLab CI/CD, an integrated solution for version control and automated deployments
  - GitHub Actions, for automating ML workflows within the GitHub ecosystem

Monitoring and logging tools
: These provide real-time observability into system behavior, supporting transparency and bias detection. Examples include:

  - Prometheus, for time-series data and alerts
  - Grafana, for data visualization and dashboards
  - Elastic Stack, for log management and analysis

Explainability tools
: These help make the AI system's decisions interpretable in a live environment. They include:

  - SHAP, for understanding feature importance
  - LIME, for explaining individual predictions

Monitoring and Maintenance Phase

The monitoring and maintenance phase is crucial for ensuring continued compliance with the EU AI Act and the reliability and ethical performance of the AI system in the long term. Relevant transparency requirements include:

Monitor notification delivery
: Regularly verify that user-facing transparency notifications are clear, accessible, and delivered at the appropriate moments. Track delivery frequency and success rates to identify gaps and areas for improvement, and use these insights to improve the user experience and build trust in the AI system.

Track content marking effectiveness
: Continuously validate that synthetic content is consistently and accurately marked in a machine-readable, detectable format and that this marking persists even after any modifications to the content. Monitor for instances when content is not marked correctly, and take corrective actions to address these issues.

Log compliance status
: Record any system configuration changes or behaviors that could impact compliance. Ensure that compliance logs are stored securely and are readily available for audits.

Maintain an audit trail
: Keep a detailed record of all system activities, including user actions, content creation events, model updates, and configuration changes. The audit logs should include timestamps, user IDs, and clear descriptions of what actions were taken. Review these logs regularly to detect any unusual activity or potential problems, to maintain the system's reliability and performance and guide necessary improvements.

CRISP-ML(Q) activities

Core activities in this phase of the lifecycle include:

Data drift and model decay detection

- Implement mechanisms for detecting data drift, where the characteristics of the input data change over time.
- Monitor for changes in the distribution of input features and flag any significant shifts that could impact the model's performance.

Performance monitoring

- Continuously track key performance metrics such as accuracy, precision, recall, and F1 score, fairness indicators, feature attributions, and error rates. Also include serving efficiency metrics such as latency (responsiveness and health of the model service), throughput (volume of predictions handled within a given time), and resource utilization (CPU, GPU, and memory usage, for cost and performance optimization).
- Monitor these metrics over time to identify performance degradation or drift.
- Establish thresholds for acceptable performance and set up alerts to notify stakeholders of any significant deviations.

Model updates

- Establish a structured process for updating models in response to performance degradation, data drift, or changing business requirements.
- Use version control to track model updates and roll back to previous versions if necessary.
- Ensure that all model updates are thoroughly tested and validated before deployment to production.

System maintenance

- Perform regular maintenance to address bugs, security vulnerabilities, and performance issues.
- Schedule downtime as necessary and communicate maintenance activities to users in advance.

Keep detailed records of all monitoring and maintenance activities and ensure that system documentation remains up-to-date.

SMACTR integration

Here are the main SMACTR integration activities for the monitoring and maintenance phase:

Artifact Collection (ongoing documentation)

- Continuously collect and update all relevant documentation, including monitoring reports, maintenance logs, and update records.

Testing (continuous monitoring)

- Implement continuous monitoring of the AI system, with a focus on ethical considerations including fairness, bias, and accountability.
- Regularly evaluate the system's impact on different user groups to ensure it does not perpetuate or amplify existing biases.
- Set up mechanisms for reporting and addressing any ethical concerns that arise.

Reflection (regular assessments)

- Conduct regular assessments of the system's performance and compliance with transparency obligations.
- Review the ethical and social implications of the system while it is in production.
- Use insights from these assessments to identify areas for improvement and guide updates to the design, deployment, or governance strategies.

Key artifacts

Table 6-9 summarizes the artifacts that should be produced and maintained during this phase.

Table 6-9. Summary of key artifacts produced during the monitoring and maintenance phase

Artifact	Content
Monitoring reports	• Generate regular reports summarizing system performance and providing details on any identified issues or anomalies, such as data drift. • Include visualizations and metrics to illustrate the system's overall health and performance.
Maintenance logs	• Maintain detailed logs of all maintenance activities, including changes to system configurations, data, or code. • Record the purpose of each activity, along with the steps taken and the outcome. • Ensure the logs are securely stored and available for audits.
Update records	• Maintain version control for all model and system updates. • Ensure that you can roll back to previous AI model versions if needed or have a rule-based fallback mechanism in place.
Compliance reports	• Produce periodic reports documenting adherence to Article 50 and other applicable regulations. • Include metrics related to notification delivery, content marking effectiveness, and audit trail maintenance. • Highlight any areas of noncompliance and actions taken to address these.
Audit trails	• Maintain a complete audit trail of all system activities, including user interactions, content generation events, model deployments, and changes to system configurations. • Ensure audit logs are securely stored and accessible to relevant stakeholders for audit and compliance verification purposes.

Available tools and technologies

In addition to the tools mentioned in the previous sections, supporting SMACTR integration during the monitoring and maintenance phase requires the following:

Tools for data drift detection
: These monitor input data and model predictions over time to detect shifts that could impact performance or fairness. Examples include:

  - TensorFlow Data Validation, for automatically detecting data anomalies and drift in TensorFlow pipelines
  - Evidently AI, an open source tool for monitoring data quality and model performance
  - NannyML, a library for detecting data drift and model degradation

Compliance and auditing tools
: These help organizations define, enforce, and monitor compliance policies while maintaining secure audit trails. Examples include:

  - Open Policy Agent (OPA), for defining and enforcing governance and compliance controls
  - Cloud Security Command Center, for compliance monitoring and security checks in cloud-based environments like Google Cloud

Congratulations! You've just walked through the complete process of integrating the SMACTR framework into the CRISP-ML(Q) AI system development lifecycle. This integration extends the technical workflow with an internal algorithmic audit process, enabling teams to proactively identify and mitigate potential harms prior to deployment. It ensures transparency and supports compliance throughout every phase, from business and data understanding to ongoing monitoring and maintenance.

For reference, Table 6-10 maps the SMACTR stages to the CRISP-ML(Q) phases.

Table 6-10. SMACTR and CRISP-ML(Q) integration

CRISP-ML(Q) phase	SMACTR stage				
	Scoping	Mapping	Artifact Collection	Testing	Reflection
Business and data understanding	✓	✓	✓		
Data preparation			✓	✓	✓
Modeling			✓	✓	✓
Evaluation			✓	✓	✓
Deployment			✓	✓	✓
Monitoring and maintenance			✓	✓	✓

Technology Trend: AI Governance Platforms

An AI governance platform is a comprehensive, distributed system designed to manage complex workflows, handle large volumes of data, and integrate with diverse AI systems. It comprises a set of rules, processes, frameworks, and tools that organizations can use to support the ethical and responsible development and deployment of AI systems.

The primary function of an AI governance platform is to align AI initiatives with organizational principles, legal requirements (such as the EU AI Act), and ethical standards. You can think of it as a central control system that helps organizations track and manage all their AI-related activities—much like how a financial management system tracks monetary transactions and ensures regulatory compliance.

These platforms typically provide a centralized inventory of all AI systems in use across the organization and assist in classifying them according to the EU AI Act's risk levels. This is crucial because different risk classifications require different compliance measures.

Governance platforms offer built-in risk assessment tools that help identify potential compliance gaps and suggest remediation measures. For instance, if an AI system is used for hiring and classified as high risk, the platform can help track whether it's being regularly tested for bias and fairness as required by the legislation.

AI governance platforms also provide tools for documenting and monitoring AI systems throughout their lifecycle. This includes tracking how AI models are developed, trained, and deployed, what data they use, and how they perform in production. They often include features for automatically generating technical documentation and maintaining audit trails as well, which is helpful as the EU AI Act requires extensive documentation, particularly for high-risk AI systems.

Governance workflows are another critical feature. These help manage the approvals required before deploying AI systems, ensure regular reviews are conducted, and maintain records of key decisions and changes. To give a practical example, imagine a large bank using AI for credit scoring. Its AI governance platform might support the following functions:

- Document how the credit scoring model was developed.
- Track the data used during training.
- Monitor performance for accuracy and fairness.
- Generate required compliance reports.
- Alert relevant stakeholders if the system starts showing signs of bias.
- Maintain records of all model updates and approval processes.

In the context of the EU AI Act, these platforms are becoming increasingly valuable. The Act introduces strict requirements for documentation, risk management, human oversight, and accountability. While it doesn't explicitly require organizations to use an AI governance platform, having one in place can significantly ease the compliance burden, especially for organizations managing multiple AI systems.

Leading Platforms

Several notable AI governance platforms are available at the time of writing, including the following:

Credo AI
: Specializes in model risk management and compliance assessments, with a strong focus on generative AI

Monitaur
: Provides an ML Assurance platform for building scalable AI governance programs

Fairly AI
: Offers tools for real-time monitoring, auditing, and automated compliance management

Modulos
: Features an agentic AI governance platform that automates compliance with trustworthy AI standards

Holistic AI
: Delivers enterprise-level oversight of AI projects and inventory management

Further Reading

To learn more about AI governance platforms, check out the following resources:

- Domo's Top 8 AI Governance Platforms for 2025 (*https://oreil.ly/tuYhZ*)
- "What Is an AI Alignment Platform?" (*https://oreil.ly/FtsGt*) by Andrew Burt, Mike Schiller, and Ben Lorica
- Edwin Wenink's Ethical Tools Landscape (*https://oreil.ly/rn8_p*)

Conclusion

Transparency obligations under the EU AI Act focus on user awareness and preventing deception. Unlike the conformity assessments required for high-risk AI systems, which are formal processes that verify legal compliance, transparency obligations apply to all AI systems that interact directly with humans, regardless of their risk classification. Their primary goal is to ensure that individuals are clearly informed when they are interacting with an AI system and understand its purpose and limitations.

This chapter has provided a practical, detailed guide for AI engineers seeking to achieve proactive compliance with the transparency requirements set out in Article 50 of the Act. As you've seen, integrating the SMACTR framework with the CRISP-ML(Q) methodology provides a robust and auditable process for responsibly developing and deploying AI systems and supports transparency throughout the AI lifecycle.

The next chapter will discuss the implications of the EU AI Act on developing and deploying general-purpose AI models and systems. We'll examine the specific rules and obligations for GPAI and explore the conditions under which these systems might be classified as high risk, with corresponding stringent requirements.

CHAPTER 7

Toward Trustworthy General-Purpose AI and Generative AI

The EU AI Act, which came into effect in August 2024, is the world's first comprehensive legal framework for AI. Up to this point, this book has focused primarily on how the Act's risk-based approach applies to predictive AI systems. However, the Act also includes provisions for *general-purpose AI* (GPAI)—a relatively late addition spurred by the rapid rise of large language models (LLMs) such as GPT and BERT, along with the broader emergence of generative AI technologies during the period when the legislation was being drafted. This addition was intended to address a key regulatory challenge: how to govern AI models that are not tied to a specific task and can be adapted to a wide range of downstream uses.

The EU AI Act aims to balance innovation and risk mitigation by promoting research and development while safeguarding fundamental rights. As such, it does not apply to GPAI models developed and used solely for prototyping or for research and development purposes prior to being placed on the market or put into service. In general, the rules for GPAI models and systems are less stringent than those for high-risk AI systems—unless they are deemed to present a systemic risk (defined as "a risk that is specific to the high-impact capabilities of general-purpose AI models, having a significant impact on the Union market due to their reach, or due to actual or reasonably foreseeable negative effects on public health, safety, public security, fundamental rights, or the society as a whole, that can be propagated at scale across the value chain").

This chapter lays out the requirements for EU AI Act compliance for GPAI and generative AI. It also introduces the concept of GenAIOps—the application of MLOps principles to the development and deployment of generative AI applications. As in the previous chapters, the focus will be on how AI engineering principles and practices can be applied to meet the transparency obligations of the EU AI Act in this rapidly evolving domain.

The EU AI Act and Generative AI

The notion of "general-purpose" AI (also known as "foundation models") was introduced into the EU AI Act relatively late in the negotiations between the European Parliament and Council. The rapid emergence and widespread adoption of generative AI systems like ChatGPT, DALL·E, and Midjourney during the legislative process revealed that the Act's initial focus on AI systems with specific, identifiable risks stemming from clearly defined use cases was too narrow. General-purpose AI was added as a distinct category primarily to address concerns around quality control and copyright protection related to training data, while also allowing for the assessment of systemic risks, as elaborated in Chapter V of the Act. The regulations governing these models are relatively limited in scope, focusing mainly on requirements for documentation and transparency (Article 53) and obligations for cooperation with relevant authorities (Article 91).

Generative AI, or GenAI, offers numerous potential benefits, including enhanced decision making, increased productivity, and the ability to generate novel content. GenAI technologies can be used in a wide range of domains, such as education, research, and customer service, to automate tasks and improve operational efficiency.

However, these technologies also pose significant risks. These include the potential for bias and discrimination, the generation of inaccurate or misleading information, and various form of misuse (e.g., creating deceptive content, or deepfakes). Misuse tends to fall into two broad categories:[1]

Exploitation of GenAI capabilities
: Tactics that leverage the features of GenAI models to create harmful outputs or support malicious activities. For example, AI robocalls can imitate real people and take actions on their behalf, and synthetic content can be generated to create fake social media accounts to promote a specific agenda or to fabricate identification documents.

Compromise of GenAI systems
: Tactics that involve attacking or manipulating the GenAI systems, targeting model or data integrity vulnerabilities. Examples include prompt injection (manipulating model prompts to enable unintended or unauthorized outputs); compromising the privacy of training data to extract personal information;

1 For more information, see the paper "Generative AI Misuse: A Taxonomy of Tactics and Insights from Real-World Data" (*https://oreil.ly/DDpPc*) by Nahema Marchal et al.

bypassing restrictions on the model's safeguards (known as jailbreaking); and model extraction (reverse engineering to obtain details on the model's architecture, parameters, or training data).

The EU AI Act aims to mitigate these risks by imposing certain obligations on the providers of generative and general-purpose AI systems to ensure that they are developed and deployed responsibly.

GPAI Systems and Transparency Obligations

GPAI systems that interact directly with humans, including those that generate synthetic content, are subject to the following transparency obligations under Article 50 of the EU AI Act:

Informing users of AI interaction
: Providers must inform users when they are interacting with an AI system, unless it's reasonably obvious or the system is used for law enforcement purposes (e.g., detecting, preventing, investigating, or prosecuting crimes). This applies to chatbots and content-generating tools.

Marking synthetic content
: Providers of AI systems that generate synthetic content (audio, images, video, text) must clearly mark these outputs as artificially generated or manipulated. The labels should be machine-readable and easily detectable, signaling the content's non-authentic nature. This requirement does not apply to assistive editing tools or systems that do not significantly alter the original input.

Disclosing deepfakes
: Providers of AI systems that generate deepfakes (described by Article 3(60) as "AI-generated or manipulated image, audio or video content that resembles existing persons, objects, places, entities or events and would falsely appear to a person to be authentic or truthful") must clearly label these outputs as artificial. The labels should be machine-readable and easily detectable.

Regulating General-Purpose AI

The EU AI Act introduces specific regulations for GPAI models and systems, focusing on transparency, documentation, and risk management. In this section, I'll first define what constitutes a GPAI model or system under the Act and explain the criteria for determining whether a GPAI model presents systemic risk. I will then outline the obligations for providers of GPAI models and deployers of GPAI systems, including the increased obligations for providers of GPAI models deemed to pose systemic risks.

Definition and scope

The EU AI Act defines a *GPAI model* as an AI model with significant generality that can perform a wide range of distinct tasks. These models are typically trained on large amounts of data, often using self-supervised learning techniques, and are designed to be integrated into various downstream systems or applications.

The Act defines a *GPAI system* as an AI system based on a GPAI model that can serve a variety of purposes, either as a standalone application or as a component integrated into other AI systems. As a reminder, the Act defines an AI system as "a machine-based system that is designed to operate with varying levels of autonomy and that may exhibit adaptiveness after deployment, and that, for explicit or implicit objectives, infers, from the input it receives, how to generate outputs such as predictions, content, recommendations, or decisions that can influence physical or virtual environments."

It's important to distinguish between the model and the system it powers. The Act regulates both providers of GPAI models and deployers who use or integrate these models into AI systems. The obligations for deployers of GPAI systems are generally the same as for other AI systems, with specific oversight powers granted to the AI Office in the European Commission.

Systemic risk criteria

The EU AI Act establishes a two-tiered regulatory approach for GPAI models:

General obligations
: All providers of GPAI models must meet baseline transparency and compatibility requirements.

Systemic risk
: If a GPAI model is classified as having systemic risk, it triggers additional regulatory oversight and extra obligations. The criteria for this classification are outlined in Table 7-1.

Table 7-1. Criteria for systemic-risk GPAI models

Criterion	Description of systemic risk
High-impact capabilities	The model has significant potential to cause harm due to its broad range of functionalities. Risks include major accidents, disruption of critical infrastructure, threats to public health or safety, impacts on democratic processes, national or economic security risks, generation of illegal or discriminatory content, lowering barriers to development of chemical, biological, radiological, and nuclear (CBRN) weapons technology, or the ability of models to make copies of themselves or train other models autonomously.
FLOPs threshold	The model requires more than 10^{25} floating-point operations per second (FLOPs) during training. This indicates a potential for high-impact capabilities.

Criterion	Description of systemic risk
Commission decision based on equivalent capabilities or impact	Even if the FLOPs threshold is not met, the European Commission can classify a model as posing systemic risk if it demonstrates a potential for high-impact capabilities based on the assessment criteria in Annex XIII.
Additional factors considered by the Commission	Additional factors that are taken into account include the number of parameters, quality and size of the training dataset (e.g., number of tokens), computational resources used for training (FLOPs, cost, time, energy consumption), input and output modalities, and degree of autonomy or scalability.
Contesting the presumption of systemic risk	A provider can contest the presumption of systemic risk by presenting sufficiently substantiated arguments demonstrating that, even if the FLOPs criterion is met, the model does not actually present systemic risks due to its specific characteristics. General arguments are not sufficient.

Obligations for providers of GPAI models

All providers of GPAI models, regardless of their systemic risk classification, are subject to a set of general obligations under the EU AI Act. These obligations are intended to promote transparency, accountability, and responsible development of powerful AI models. There are simplified requirements for providers offering GPAI models under free and open licenses, provided that these models do not present systemic risk. The core obligations (as outlined in Article 53 (*https://oreil.ly/Xn8iw*)) include:

Technical documentation
: Providers must create and maintain comprehensive technical documentation including details about the model's design specifications, training and testing processes, and evaluation results. This documentation must enable regulatory authorities to assess the model's compliance with the EU AI Act and must be provided to the AI Office and national competent authorities upon request.

Documentation for downstream providers
: Given that GPAI models are often integrated into other AI systems, the EU AI Act requires providers to furnish downstream providers with documentation that enables them to understand the model's capabilities, limitations, and known risks. For example, if the model is known to exhibit bias in certain contexts, this must be disclosed so that downstream providers can take appropriate mitigation steps in their AI systems.

Copyright compliance
: GPAI models are trained on vast amounts of data, often including copyrighted material. Consequently, providers must implement a policy to comply with EU copyright law (in particular, the EU Copyright Directive (*https://oreil.ly/6l3Hq*)), including measures to identify and respect any copyright restrictions on the data used to train the model and documentation of how such restrictions have been addressed.

Training data summary

To promote transparency and accountability, providers must publish a detailed summary of the data used to train their GPAI models. This should provide information about the types and sources of data used, as well as any known limitations or biases in the data.

EU representative

Providers based outside the European Union must appoint an authorized representative within the EU. This representative acts as a point of contact for authorities and is responsible for ensuring that the provider complies with its obligations under the EU AI Act.

Additional obligations for providers of GPAI models with systemic risk

GPAI models with systemic risk are subject to more stringent requirements due to their potential for causing significant harm. In addition to the general obligations outlined in the previous section, providers of these models must comply with the following obligations, specified in Article 55 (*https://oreil.ly/2fYcc*):

Model evaluation

Conduct regular rigorous evaluations of the models using standardized protocols and tools. This includes adversarial testing to identify vulnerabilities and potential risks. The goal is to ensure that the model is robust, reliable, and does not pose unacceptable risks.

Risk mitigation

Proactively assess and mitigate potential systemic risks associated with use of the models. Identify potential harms related to fundamental rights, health and safety, or security, and implement documented measures to minimize those risks.

Incident reporting

Establish a system for tracking, documenting, and reporting serious incidents related to use of the models. Incidents must be reported to the AI Office and relevant national authorities, and appropriate corrective actions must be taken and documented.

Cybersecurity

Implement robust safeguards to protect the models and the infrastructure on which they operate. This is crucial to prevent unauthorized access, data breaches, and malicious use.

Obligations for deployers of GPAI models

The EU AI Act applies to all deployers who operate an AI system under their own authority in a professional capacity. When deployers integrate GPAI models into their AI systems, they may incur additional responsibilities under the Act, particularly if the resulting systems are classified as high risk. These obligations include:

Using the system as intended
: The system must be used in accordance with the provider's instructions and for its intended purpose.

Human oversight
: Appropriate human oversight mechanisms must be established—for example, human review of the system's outputs, the ability to intervene in the system's operation, and clear assignment of responsibility for the system's decisions.

Data quality
: The input data provided to the system must be relevant, accurate, and representative. This is crucial to prevent biased or inaccurate outputs and to ensure that the system operates as intended.

Monitoring
: System performance must be monitored and any issues reported to the provider. This includes monitoring for unexpected outputs, performance degradation, or other indications that the system is not functioning correctly.

Recordkeeping
: System logs must be maintained for the purposes of incident investigation and demonstration of regulatory compliance.

Transparency
: AI systems that generate or manipulate content that is published to inform the public on matters of public interest must clearly disclose that the content is synthetic.

Predictive ML Versus GPAI

Before we turn our attention to operationalizing EU AI Act compliance for GPAI, let's briefly reflect on the differences between predictive and generative AI to better understand where generative AI diverges and why the discipline of GenAIOps has emerged.

Machine learning is a broad field, but at its core, most models can be categorized into two distinct paradigms: predictive ML and GPAI (see Figures 7-1 and 7-2 for concrete examples of each). While both rely on statistical learning, they differ in their goals, methodologies, and applications.

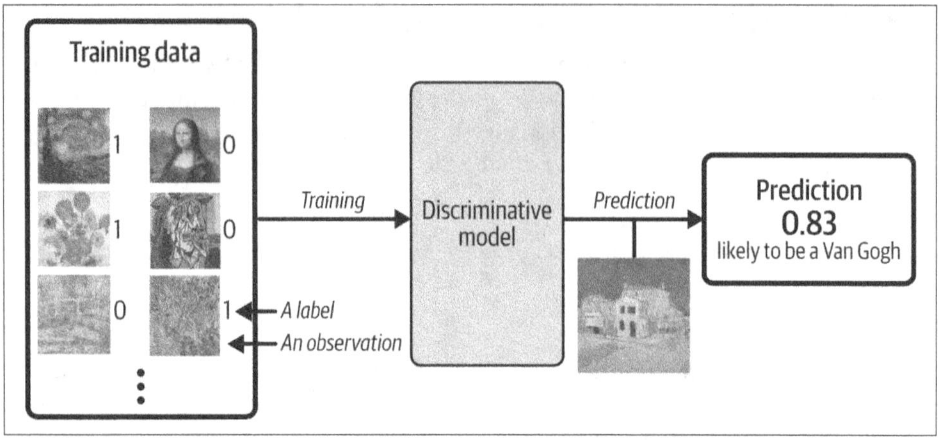

Figure 7-1. A visualization of predictive ML—a discriminative model trained to predict whether a given image is painted by Vincent van Gogh. Image from the book Generative Deep Learning, *2nd edition, by David Foster (O'Reilly). Used with permission.*

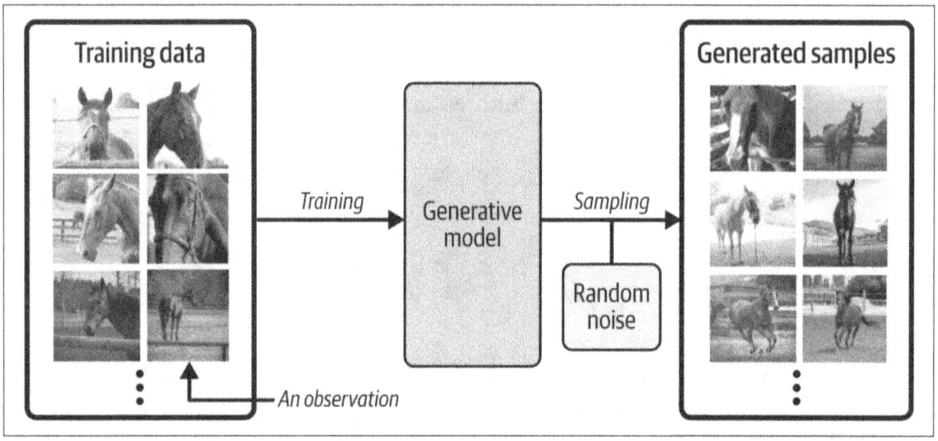

Figure 7-2. A visualization of generative AI—a generative model trained to generate realistic photos of horses. Image from the book Generative Deep Learning, *2nd edition, by David Foster (O'Reilly). Used with permission.*

At its core, predictive ML is about answering the question "What's likely?" It focuses on estimation, forecasting, and pattern recognition. Predictive models analyze historical data to make informed forecasts or decisions. They learn patterns from structured datasets and aim to provide numerical outputs, classifications, or recommendations on input features.

GPAI, on the other hand, is an umbrella category that includes many generative models—particularly foundation models such as LLMs. Generative AI can therefore be thought of as a subset of GPAI. Most state-of-the-art generative models (such as

GPT-4, DALL·E, and Stable Diffusion) are classified as GPAI under the EU AI Act. This includes models that are general-purpose (used across many tasks or systems) and models that are made available to others for downstream use or fine-tuning.

At its core, generative AI is about answering the question "What's possible?" It moves beyond predictions to creating new content. Instead of mapping inputs to predefined outputs, generative models learn the statistical distribution of their training data and generate new, plausible data points that fall within that learned distribution.

Table 7-2 provides a structured comparison of predictive ML and GPAI.

Table 7-2. Predictive ML and GPAI—a side-by-side comparison

Feature	Predictive ML	GPAI
Primary goal	Solve a well-defined, narrow task (e.g., fraud detection, loan scoring)	Provide broad capabilities that can be adapted to many tasks and use cases
Data input	Domain-specific structured or unstructured data (e.g., tabular data, images)	Massive and diverse cross-domain datasets (e.g., internet text, code, audio, images)
Output	Prediction, classification, regression, or recommendation for a specific task	Versatile outputs: text, code, reasoning, vision tasks, language understanding, etc.
Downstream use	Purpose-built systems with known users and applications	Can be adapted and fine-tuned by third parties for diverse and evolving applications
Examples	Predictive maintenance models, fraud detection systems	GPT-4, Gemini, LLaMA, Mistral, DALL·E
Algorithms	Decision trees, XGBoost, CNNs, RNNs	Large-scale Transformer-based architectures, foundation models (e.g., LLMs, vision language models)
Evaluation	Task-specific metrics: accuracy, F1 score, AUC-ROC, MAE/RMSE	Evaluated across a wide range of tasks using general benchmarks (e.g., MMLU, HELM), robustness, bias, toxicity

GenAIOps—Operationalizing EU AI Act Compliance for GPAI

GenAIOps is the systematic extension of DevOps and MLOps principles to meet the unique challenges of developing, deploying, and maintaining GPAI models and systems, including LLMs, image and video generators, and other foundation models. While traditional MLOps focuses on managing predictive models, GenAIOps must support the adaptation and governance of powerful generative models that may be used for a wide range of downstream tasks. This includes practices such as prompt engineering, retrieval-augmented generation (RAG), foundation model fine-tuning, and real-time monitoring for issues like hallucinations, bias, and safety risks. These needs introduce additional complexity in areas ranging from data governance to infrastructure, safety monitoring, and responsible use—especially in the context of compliance with regulatory frameworks like the EU AI Act.

Figure 7-3 visualizes the operational stages for GPAI models and how they map to the CRISP-ML(Q) development phases.

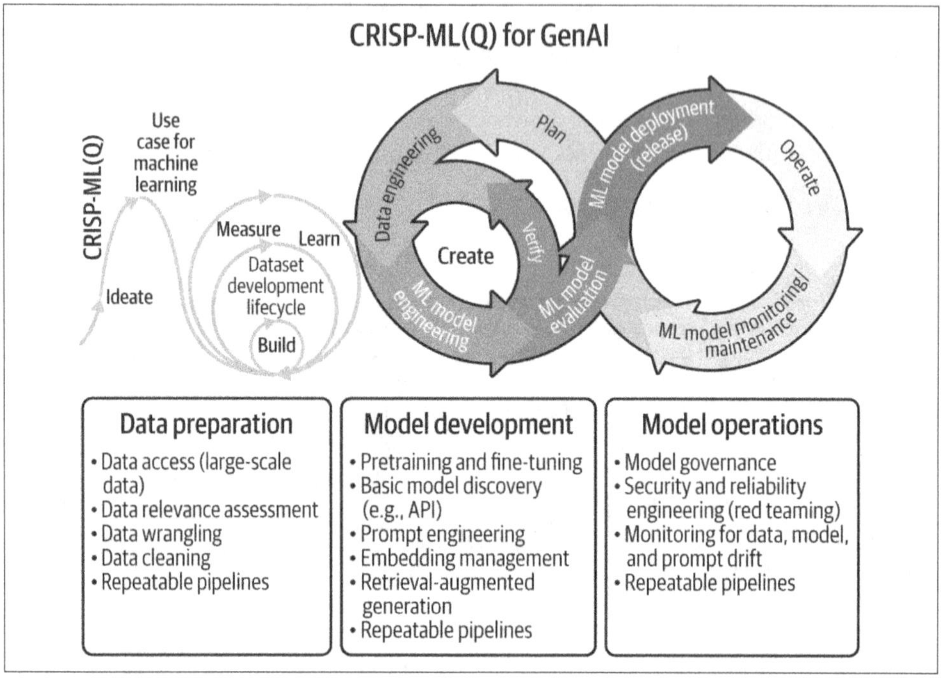

Figure 7-3. CRISP-ML(Q) framework for GPAI models and systems

Key Components

GenAIOps integrates automated pipelines, model versioning, and observability with inference optimization, safety guardrails, and compliance workflows to create a comprehensive framework for responsible GPAI deployment. This approach ensures that GPAI models operate with transparency and auditability in production environments while addressing concerns about misinformation, synthetic content attribution, and compliance with applicable regulatory requirements.

Key components of GenAIOps include the following (summarized in Figure 7-4):

Prompt engineering infrastructure
: Tools for managing prompt creation, testing, versioning, and orchestration, in particular for complex reasoning chains and RAG systems.

Inference optimization
: Techniques such as quantization, caching, and model distillation to reduce latency, cost, and resource usage in deployment environments.

Continuous evaluation
: Real-time monitoring systems to detect hallucinations and performance drift, and mechanisms to collect human feedback for ongoing model refinement.

Safety and content controls
: Automated content filtering, watermarking, red-teaming protocols, and risk assessment workflows to ensure responsible and secure AI outputs.

Governance and compliance
: Transparent documentation (e.g., model cards), content provenance systems, and comprehensive audit trails to meet evolving regulatory requirements and ethical standards.

Foundation model adaptation
: Fine-tuning workflows, reinforcement learning from human feedback (RLHF), and parameter-efficient methods (e.g., LoRA) to customize models for specific downstream use cases.

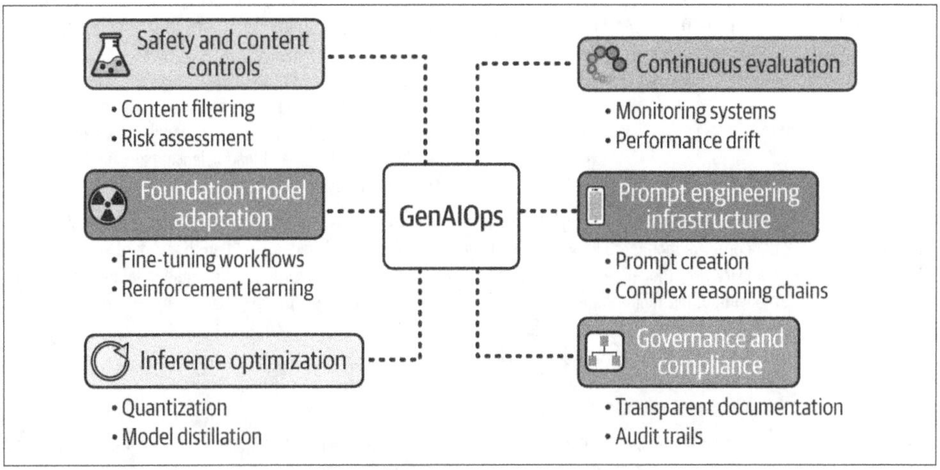

Figure 7-4. Key components of GenAIOps

How GenAIOps Extends MLOps

The core goals of MLOps, which is mainly focused on the lifecycle of predictive ML models, are reproducibility, scalability, and continuous delivery. GenAIOps retains these goals but adapts them to the specific needs of GPAI. For example, generative AI applications must operate on unstructured data at scale, incorporate prompt engineering and human-in-the-loop feedback mechanisms, and ensure that outputs are not only high quality but also safe, transparent, and appropriately labeled. Table 7-3 outlines key differences between MLOps and GenAIOps across several areas, such as data management, model training and adaptation, model deployment and inference, monitoring, and ethics and regulations.

Table 7-3. Key differences between MLOps and GenAIOps

Aspect	MLOps (predictive ML)	GenAIOps (GPAI)
Data management	Focuses on curated, labeled datasets, feature engineering, and versioning of training data pipelines. Data is often structured and tabular or limited to task-specific corpora.	Handles massive, unstructured datasets (text, images, audio). Embraces synthetic data generation for augmentation and requires robust data filtering to remove toxic or biased content from training corpora (to avoid amplifying harms). Uses embedding management (vector representations of data) in place of traditional feature stores to enable RAG, typically via vector databases.
Model training and adaptation	Models are trained from scratch or with transfer learning, with hyperparameter tuning and model selection based on task-specific data. Models are typically smaller and trained to converge on labeled data.	Starts from large, pretrained foundation models. Uses parameter-efficient fine-tuning (e.g., LoRA, adapter layers), prompt engineering, and few-shot learning instead of full retraining. Techniques like direct preference optimization (DPO) and RLHF are applied to align model behavior with human preferences. Experiment tracking must include prompt versions and chain configurations, not just model parameters.
Model deployment and inference	Models are deployed as microservices or batch jobs behind REST APIs, using standard scaling, CI/CD, and version control. Inference usually involves a single-model prediction call (e.g., a classification API).	Deployment requires specialized infrastructure (GPUs or TPUs, high memory usage). Focuses on real-time inference for generative outputs, often with streaming responses due to longer outputs (e.g., for chatbots). Frequently involves orchestrating multiple models and tools and managing prompt pipelines and session context. Optimization techniques such as model quantization, caching of outputs, and load balancing are applied to manage heavy inference loads.
Monitoring and continuous improvement	Model performance (accuracy, latency) and data drift are monitored in production. User feedback may trigger periodic retraining or model updates. Rollback mechanisms minimize downtime in case of failures. When using third-party models, custom evaluation sets may be needed to detect behavioral changes between versions.	Output quality and safety risks (hallucinations, toxicity, bias) are monitored, in addition to standard performance metrics. Requires continuous evaluation loops and human feedback to guide improvements.
Regulatory and ethical considerations	Focuses on fairness, bias mitigation, explainability, and compliance in decision-making contexts (e.g., loan approvals). Models are accompanied by comprehensive documentation (e.g., model cards, bias audits).	Faces new ethical and regulatory challenges: GPAI models can produce misinformation, harmful content, and deepfakes and can potentially be used for impersonation. Must support emerging requirements, such as labeling AI-generated content and ensuring transparency and traceability.

GenAIOps Tools, Workflows, and Frameworks to Support Transparency

GenAIOps builds on MLOps by adding capabilities like prompt management, chain-of-thought orchestration, synthetic data generation, and stringent output controls to address the unique demands of GPAI. It's also essential for ensuring transparency in GPAI models and systems, as mandated by regulations like the EU AI Act. The transparency obligations outlined in Article 50 of the Act, which we discussed in detail in

Chapter 6, apply to both providers and deployers of generative AI systems (as well as predictive ML systems). Meeting these obligations and effectively managing GenAI-related risks requires cross-disciplinary collaboration among data engineers, model developers, user experience designers, and ethics and compliance teams. The following GenAIOps tools and workflows can support this effort:

Prompt and chain management
: Frameworks like LangChain and NVIDIA NeMo can be used to orchestrate complex prompt workflows and ensure that required system prompts (including AI self-identification) are consistently included in user interactions. These tools also support prompt versioning, testing, and traceability.

Content watermarking and metadata
: Libraries and APIs compliant with the C2PA (Content Provenance and Authenticity) standard are increasingly being integrated into image and video generation pipelines. For example, OpenAI's DALL·E API automatically adds C2PA metadata (*https://oreil.ly/djcGb*) to its outputs. There are also third-party services, such as Stability's Stable Diffusion plug-ins or Steg.AI (*https://oreil.ly/PGrpq*), that insert invisible watermarks into images for later verification. GenAIOps pipelines can call these services post-generation. For text-based content, research into statistical watermarking is also advancing.

Monitoring and detection services
: To complement watermarks, GenAIOps can integrate deepfake detection models and content moderation AI into the monitoring stack. For instance, an enterprise might deploy a vision model that scans newly uploaded videos for signs of manipulation. If AI-generated media lacks the required disclosure, the detection system can flag it for review. Cloud providers are beginning to offer APIs for this purpose (e.g., Azure's Video Authenticator and AWS's Rekognition).

Guardrails and policy enforcement
: Guardrail frameworks such as NVIDIA NeMo Guardrails or the open source Guardrails AI library can be used to enforce policy at runtime by intercepting model outputs before they reach the user. They can automatically append disclaimers or block content that should be labeled as synthetic but isn't. For example, if a user prompts a GPAI model to generate a fake image of a person, a guardrail can attach a "Fake Image" label to the output. Similarly, an audible cue can be injected into audio content. These enforcement steps are configured directly within the inference pipeline.

Logging and versioning
: Prompts, responses, and content artifacts can be comprehensively logged using platforms like MLflow, Weights & Biases, or Arize AI that support GenAIOps features. These logs provide a robust audit trail that can verify, for example, whether a watermarking function ran and what output it produced.

In the remainder of this chapter, we'll explore how the SMACTR framework introduced in the previous chapter can be integrated into the different phases of the CRISP-ML(Q) lifecycle, providing a practical foundation for operationalizing compliance in the development and deployment of GPAI models and systems.

Aligning AI Engineering with SMACTR and CRISP-ML(Q) for Transparency

Chapter 6 provided a detailed guide for AI engineers on achieving proactive compliance with the transparency requirements outlined in Article 50 of the EU AI Act. This section applies the same approach to GPAI models and systems, incorporating GenAIOps principles. By integrating the SMACTR framework with the CRISP-ML(Q) methodology, teams can establish a robust, auditable process for responsible development and deployment of general-purpose AI.

Business and Data Understanding Phase

GenAIOps is generally broken down into three main operational phases (see Figure 7-3). The initial phase encompasses tasks related to use case definition and data requirements planning that precede full-scale data engineering. It also includes early data engineering activities such as clarifying the application's purpose and identifying data sources. For example, before building an LLM-powered system, teams must define the business problem (e.g., "customer support chatbot" versus "code generation assistant") and assess what data and model capabilities are needed to solve it efficiently. This aligns closely with the business and data understanding phase of the CRISP-ML(Q) methodology.

The first step is translating business goals into ML/LLM objectives—that is, determining what you want the model to do, and what data or base models that will require. For instance, if the goal is to develop a Q&A chatbot, GenAIOps teams must decide whether to use an existing Q&A model or fine-tune a base LLM, and identify the relevant domain data. This reflects CRISP-ML(Q)'s emphasis that business objectives and data constraints should be considered jointly to avoid building "the right answers to the wrong questions."

Early alignment on objectives, success criteria, and constraints shapes all subsequent work. CRISP-ML(Q) calls for success metrics to be defined at the business, ML, and system levels. GenAIOps expands this by requiring that user experience goals and ethical considerations also be addressed from the start—including expectations for model behavior, tone, and safety.

Implementation

Integrating CRISP-ML(Q) practices into GenAIOps at this stage means rigorously documenting requirements, constraints, and success criteria. In practice, the engineering team should convene domain experts, data scientists, and LLM engineers to define the scope of the GenAI application before development begins. The success criteria will go beyond classic metrics like accuracy or ROI to include measures of output quality (e.g., fluency, relevance) and safety (e.g., absence of harmful or biased content). An early feasibility assessment is crucial; if a required dataset is unavailable or the task is ill-suited to LLMs, that should be determined up front.

In GenAIOps, this phase often involves selecting an initial base model appropriate to the task. For example, the choice between a proprietary LLM like GPT-4 or a smaller open source model will depend on business needs and constraints such as cost, latency, and data privacy. Similar to algorithm selection in predictive ML projects, base model selection in GenAI is a key decision that should be guided by the problem scope and data requirements. For example, if the application involves sensitive or domain-specific content, a smaller fine-tuned model trained on proprietary data might be preferred over a general-purpose LLM. Documenting the decision and its rationale will help maintain clarity and transparency as the project progresses.

SMACTR integration

The Scoping and Mapping stages from the SMACTR framework are most relevant in this initial phase.

In the Scoping stage, the team conducts a preliminary risk assessment and an ethical review of the intended use cases. For a GenAI project, this involves asking how the application might affect users or stakeholders (e.g., "Could the chatbot give harmful advice or leak private data?"). Defining the ethical AI principles the project will follow is also part of this stage. Key outputs, such as a social impact assessment, help ensure the application's design considers and takes steps to mitigate potential harms and aligns with the organization's values and AI ethics guidelines.

In the Mapping stage, the focus shifts to identifying stakeholders and collaborators. In a GenAIOps context, this means mapping who needs to be involved—for example, data owners for access to data sources, compliance or legal experts if user data or intellectual property is involved, and end-user representatives. This stakeholder map promotes accountability and traceability by clarifying who is responsible for which inputs and decisions.

Incorporating Scoping and Mapping into the business and data understanding phase helps teams working on GenAI projects mitigate strategic risks before any data is collected or model work begins, reducing the chances of building a misaligned or unsafe product.

Table 7-4 provides an outline of key artifacts that should be produced during this phase.

Table 7-4. Summary of artifacts produced during the business and data understanding phase

SMACTR stage	Key artifacts
Scoping	• Preliminary risk assessment • Ethical review of intended use cases • Definition of ethical AI principles for the project • Statement of alignment with corporate values and AI ethics guidelines
Mapping	• Identification of stakeholders and collaborators (e.g., data owners, compliance/legal experts, end users) • Stakeholder map

Data Preparation Phase

CRISP-ML(Q)'s data preparation phase, in a GenAI context, includes steps such as gathering large-scale text data, cleaning and filtering it, and preparing it for model input (for example, performing tokenization and formatting). If the GenAI solution involves fine-tuning an LLM or training a domain-specific model, this phase will incorporate assembling the fine-tuning dataset and any prompt templates. It may also involve setting up a knowledge base for retrieval-augmented generation, which is a unique data component in GenAIOps not typically present in traditional ML pipelines. The goal of the data preparation phase remains the same—to ensure that the data fed into the model is high quality, relevant, and appropriately prepared—whether it's tabular data for classic ML or unstructured text and prompt data for LLMs.

Data quality directly affects model success. CRISP-ML(Q) emphasizes robust data handling by selecting the right data, cleaning it to remove noise, normalizing it, engineering features, and standardizing formats. GenAIOps extends MLOps to address the unique challenges of working with GenAI models. One major difference is that traditional feature engineering is unnecessary for LLMs. Instead, GenAIOps focuses on prompt engineering and data curation—for example, crafting prompt examples or structuring input/output pairs to teach the model a task. Another key difference is scale and diversity: GenAI applications often require large-scale data collection with an emphasis on diversity and representativeness to avoid bias or blind spots. If labeling is needed for fine-tuning or RLHF data, GenAIOps might use semi-automated techniques such as pre-labeling with another model or active learning.

Implementation

Data preparation involves implementing systematic data quality checks and creating thorough documentation. In practice, the engineering team should treat the text corpora or prompt datasets with the same discipline as curated ML datasets. Key activities include:

Data selection and sourcing
: Identify and collect data from multiple sources (e.g., internal documents, public datasets, web-scraped text) relevant to the use case. GenAIOps emphasizes automating this process and continuously ingesting new data if the application requires up-to-date information.

Data cleaning
: Filter out problematic content, such as profanity, personally identifiable information, or offensive text, to prevent the model from learning undesirable patterns. Both MLOps and GenAIOps stress the importance of dataset heterogeneity to reduce bias and overfitting. Tools like Data-Juicer (*https://oreil.ly/5wr6H*) can help with auditing dataset diversity.

Data structuring
: In traditional ML, this involves tasks like normalizing values or formatting comma-separated values. In GenAI, it includes tokenizing raw text, splitting documents, and adding prompt prefixes or suffixes. It can also involve prompt engineering at the dataset level—that is, constructing input/output pairs that demonstrate the task for fine-tuning or evaluation.

Embeddings
: GenAI data prep should account for dynamic data, meaning that if the application will retrieve documents at runtime (RAG), the team will need to set up an indexed vector database and pipelines to update it with new content. This is an extra operational consideration in GenAIOps to keep a knowledge base fresh.

Documentation
: For GenAIOps, recording details like data sources, preprocessing steps, and known limitations of the dataset is crucial. This supports transparency (e.g., via datasheets for datasets) and helps ensure auditability if issues arise later.

SMACTR integration

The Artifact Collection stage of SMACTR is particularly relevant during data preparation. As the team curates the dataset, they should also compile audit artifacts, including a comprehensive checklist to verify that all required documentation is in place and datasheets that capture data lineage, assumptions, etc. This implements quality assurance by design. Before modeling starts, auditors or internal QA reviewers should confirm that the dataset meets defined standards and that any potential biases or data limitations have been logged. For GenAI projects, this step helps surface issues like skewed representation in training data (say, underrepresentation of certain user demographics in a chatbot's training data) so they can be addressed (e.g., by augmenting the dataset with more representative samples).

The insights from the Scoping stage also feed into data preparation. For instance, if privacy risks were identified, the data pipeline should incorporate appropriate mitigation steps such as data minimization or anonymization.

Finally, the team should begin planning for how data-related risks will be handled in testing. SMACTR's Testing stage often draws on documented issues and failures, so any concerns that are identified during the data preparation phase should be noted (e.g., "Our dataset might not cover slang—possible failure mode for the chatbot").

Table 7-5 summarizes the key artifacts that should be produced during the data preparation phase. By treating data as an auditable artifact, supported by checklists, datasheets, and bias analysis, GenAIOps can incorporate SMACTR's accountability early in the pipeline.

Table 7-5. Summary of key artifacts produced during the data preparation phase

SMACTR stage	Output
Artifact Collection	• Datasheets (data documentation) detailing data lineage, assumptions, etc. • Log of identified biases or limitations in the dataset
Scoping	• Documentation of privacy risks that might require additional data privacy controls during preparation or training
Testing (planning during data prep)	• Notes on potential data-related risks • Preliminary plans for how these risks will be handled in testing

Modeling Phase

In GenAIOps, during the modeling phase the base model is chosen or built and adapted to the task. The base model selection and domain adaptation steps include prompt engineering, fine-tuning, or RAG. For a traditional ML project, modeling entails selecting algorithms, tuning hyperparameters, and training the model from scratch on prepared data. In a GenAI project, you're usually starting with a preexisting model, such as a large pretrained transformer, so "modeling" is more about *adapting* that model: choosing which LLM to use as a starting point, deciding whether to fine-tune it or use it via prompting, and implementing those adaptations. For example, if building a custom chatbot, the team might take a base model like GPT, fine-tune it on their domain data, and craft a prompt strategy.

CRISP-ML(Q) underscores modeling practices such as ensuring reproducibility of experiments, trying multiple modeling techniques, and aligning the model choice with business objectives. In GenAI application development, the choice of model and the corresponding prompt or fine-tuning strategy must align with the use case constraints (latency, accuracy, etc.), and experiments should be tracked. A key difference in generative modeling is the iterative experimentation with prompts. In structured ML, once you choose an algorithm and features, training is relatively straightforward. But with LLMs, achieving the desired output often requires interactive prompt tuning and tweaking parameters such as temperature settings. This means the modeling phase in GenAIOps can be highly iterative and exploratory, often interleaving with evaluation. You might prompt the model, observe its output, adjust the prompt or use in-context few-shot examples, and repeat. Still, the underlying focus remains on optimizing the model's behavior to meet predefined success criteria.

Another difference from traditional ML is the scale and tooling involved: training a classical ML model might involve a scikit-learn pipeline or custom code, whereas in GenAIOps, you might leverage specialized frameworks such as Transformers and parameter-efficient fine-tuning libraries and utilize distributed training or serving if fine-tuning a large model. In addition, the complexity of LLMs means that experiment tracking and versioning are even more crucial. Every prompt template or fine-tuned checkpoint is a variant that should be carefully managed (to avoid the "pipeline jungle" problem).

GenAIOps treats the model as an artifact to configure (select and tune) rather than invent from scratch, emphasizing configuration management and performance optimization. For example, model compression and GPU optimization are part of "modeling" in GenAIOps.

Implementation

Bringing CRISP-ML(Q)'s discipline into GenAI application development means adopting systematic experimentation and robust model management practices that support compliance with regulations such as the EU AI Act. Practically, this involves several key activities:

Model selection and establishing a baseline
: Just as a data scientist might test multiple algorithms, a GenAIOps team should evaluate different base LLMs—such as GPT-5, Mistral, or LLaMA-2—on a representative sample of tasks. The goal is to select the model that best balances performance with business and technical constraints, guided by the success criteria defined during the initial phase. The CRISP-ML(Q) approach emphasizes defining baseline model performance. In GenAI, that could mean using an off-the-shelf model to generate some outputs and evaluating those before customization.

Prompt and fine-tuning experimentation
: If fine-tuning is planned, each training run should be treated as an experiment, with proper versioning of training data, code, and resulting model checkpoints. Similarly, prompt designs—like few-shot or chain-of-thought designs—should be

versioned and documented. This will ensure that results can be traced to the exact models and configurations that produced them. Tools like Weights & Biases or MLflow can be integrated into the GenAIOps pipeline to track prompt parameters and model versions.

Quality assurance techniques
: CRISP-ML(Q) recommends integrating specific quality assurance practices during modeling, such as reproducibility checks and model stability assessments. For GenAI, this might include unit tests on prompts to verify that a fixed set of test inputs consistently produces the expected output formats, or static analysis to verify that fine-tuning has not degraded key model capabilities.

Addressing risks in model design
: If earlier phases flagged certain risks, bias mitigation techniques should be applied—for example, embedding alignment, incorporating moderation models into the generation pipeline, or choosing a smaller, more controllable model over a larger, less interpretable one. In addition, GenAIOps often involves adding guardrails at the model interface—such as rules-based filters or rejection sampling—to ensure that outputs meet quality and compliance requirements. This aligns with CRISP-ML(Q)'s focus on mitigating risks during development.

Throughout these steps, maintaining a "transparency trail" is encouraged by SMACTR. This means documenting design decisions such as why a specific model or prompt strategy was chosen, how configurations were set, and any known trade-offs. For example, you might want to create early drafts of model cards capturing the intended use, architecture, and limitations of the model.

By the end of the modeling phase, the engineering team should have not only a tuned model and pipeline ready for evaluation but also a comprehensive set of documentation and artifacts, guaranteeing that the modeling process is reproducible and well understood.

SMACTR integration

During the modeling phase, the key SMACTR stages to focus on are Artifact Collection and Testing (planning). The artifacts should include a design history file or similar documentation detailing the modeling decisions. This documentation might contain architecture diagrams (especially if the application includes multiple components, like an LLM and a vector database), records of hyperparameters or prompt scripts, and any ethical considerations incorporated into the model design (for instance, "we decided not to fine-tune on user chat logs containing sensitive data to preserve privacy").

SMACTR recommends using an audit checklist to verify that essential model documentation, such as model cards and associated data documentation, is complete and accessible. By the end of the modeling phase, these artifacts should be largely finalized.

Although the Testing stage formally begins during the next phase (evaluation), preparation for testing should start during modeling. The team should prioritize which risks to test based on earlier risk mapping. For example, if a failure mode of concern is the model generating toxic language, the modeling phase might incorporate a toxicity classification head or plan for adversarial prompt testing. Essentially, SMACTR encourages baking in testability by ensuring the model includes hooks or supporting tools to facilitate the intensive testing to come.

To enforce accountability and ownership of quality, individual engineers or researchers should be assigned responsibility for various model components or experiments, tracing who fine-tuned which version, who designed which prompt set, etc.

By integrating SMACTR into the modeling phase, the GenAI team treats the model not as a black box but as a transparently developed component ready for rigorous audit and testing. Table 7-6 summarizes the core artifacts produced during this phase.

Table 7-6. Summary of key artifacts produced during the modeling phase

SMACTR stage	Output
Artifact Collection	• Design history file or documentation of modeling decisions (architecture diagrams, hyperparameters, prompt scripts, ethical considerations) • Model documentation (model cards) • Near-complete data documentation
Testing (planning during modeling)	• Prioritized risks to test based on earlier risk mapping • Integration of testability features (e.g., toxicity classification head, adversarial prompt testing plans) • Plans for intensive testing
Mapping	• Identification of individuals responsible for model components or experiments (accountability)

Evaluation Phase

This phase aligns directly with the model evaluation stage in the GenAIOps lifecycle. After the model or prompt is developed, a thorough assessment of its performance against the previously defined success criteria should be conducted. In GenAIOps, evaluation is an ongoing, multifaceted process. It includes quantitative evaluation where applicable (e.g., accuracy on a benchmark or BLEU score for a translation task) as well as qualitative evaluation such as human judgment of output quality, user feedback loops, etc. It may also extend to assessing system behavior through techniques like red teaming or probing the model with adversarial or unusual inputs. In practice, the evaluation phase for GenAI often overlaps with deployment, involving shadow deployments or A/B testing with real users. Here, we'll focus on the core pre-deployment evaluation steps.

CRISP-ML(Q) frames evaluation as verifying the model's fitness for purpose by assessing its ability to meet the defined success criteria. Similarly, GenAIOps must determine whether the GenAI application meets business needs, quality standards, and thresholds for technical metrics. Both approaches involve testing on holdout datasets or scenarios.

Traditional ML evaluation typically uses well-defined metrics like accuracy, precision, root mean square error (RMSE), and static test datasets. GenAI evaluation is more complex, because generative outputs can't be easily captured by a single scalar metric. Evaluation in GenAI remains an unsolved problem. For example, given the same inputs, the behavior of the model might change over time, and maintaining consistent outputs may require prompt adjustments. GenAI evaluation often involves human rating of outputs for correctness or preference, adversarial testing to expose failure modes or undesirable behavior, and specialized generative quality metrics such as BLEU or ROUGE scores or perplexity.

GenAI evaluation must also consider ethical and safety dimensions: a model might have great accuracy but fail due to biased or toxic outputs. Therefore, fairness and safety audits must be incorporated. In CRISP-ML(Q), evaluation is iterative; if the model fails to meet the defined criteria, you return to modeling or even data prep. But in GenAIOps, evaluation is often continuous due to nondeterministic outputs and evolving usage. Techniques like "golden sets"—carefully curated test prompts with expected answers for regression testing—are becoming standard.

CRISP-ML(Q) demands rigorous validation against objectives. GenAI expands the scope of evaluation to include open-ended output quality and ethical risk testing alongside traditional performance metrics.

Implementation

In the evaluation phase, the engineering team should implement a robust evaluation strategy incorporating:

Benchmark testing
: Evaluate the LLM on a dataset of questions or tasks with known answers. For instance, for a code generation model, maintain a suite of programming problems where correct outputs are known and measure success rate. This is analogous to a test set in traditional ML. The benchmarks should be versioned so that improvements and regressions are tracked over time.

Quality metrics
: Define quantitative metrics appropriate to the use case. These might include BLEU or ROUGE scores for text similarity if a reference output is available, diversity metrics, or response latency. Incorporating user satisfaction scores or ratings into the evaluation loop is often useful, if the application can gather feedback.

Human and adversarial evaluation

Given the open-ended nature of generative models, humans should assess a sample of outputs for factors like correctness, coherence, and safety. Adversarial testing, which involves deliberately testing the model with challenging or sensitive prompts to observe its behavior, is also strongly encouraged during the Testing stage. For example, a tester might ask a chatbot inappropriate or policy-violating questions to see whether it responds with disallowed content. The results can be summarized in an ethical risk analysis chart, as suggested by SMACTR, rating failure modes by severity and likelihood.

Automated monitoring in evaluation

Use automated tools to evaluate outputs at scale. An emerging GenAIOps practice is using "watcher models" or classifiers to flag problematic content. For instance, toxicity detectors such as Llama Guard or Azure's Prompt Shields can scan a large sample of outputs to estimate the percentage that might be harmful or inappropriate. These tools add a layer of quality assurance beyond simple metrics.

Comparison and validation

If multiple model versions or prompt variants were developed, evaluate them side by side. A/B testing can be done offline (with evaluators blind to which model produced which output) to choose the best version. This resembles ensemble/hyperparameter selection in CRISP-ML(Q), but in GenAI it may involve comparing two prompt templates.

Documentation

Documentation remains critical throughout evaluation. Teams should record what tests were run, the outcomes, and the decisions made based on those results. If the model fails certain tests, document whether the issues will be addressed or accepted with mitigations. For instance, if an LLM occasionally produces outputs that are slightly incorrect but harmless, the team might decide that's acceptable for the business context; however, if it sometimes produces a privacy violation, that would trigger a model revision.

The evaluation phase in GenAIOps is also where "go or no-go" decisions are made for deployment. The engineering team should define clear launch criteria, such as "fewer than 1% of outputs flagged as offensive" or "at least 85% of test questions answered correctly." If the model fails to meet these thresholds, the process loops back to the modeling or even the data preparation phase to address the shortcomings through fine-tuning, prompt redesign, or data augmentation.

SMACTR integration

The Testing stage of SMACTR aligns directly with the evaluation phase. The framework recommends techniques such as adversarial testing to assess performance, and the production of artifacts such as an ethical risk analysis chart. In a GenAI context, this means paying special attention to verifying the model's compliance with ethical and risk-related requirements identified during the Scoping stage. Teams should use risk assessment tools like Failure Mode and Effects Analysis (FMEA) to list potential failure modes, such as "model gives legal advice" or "model outputs biased language," and implement tests to cover each identified risk.

The Testing stage also focuses on ethical compliance. To evaluate high-priority ethical risks or known issues arising from the training data or model design, teams may create and execute a checklist of ethical tests, including questions like "Does the model hallucinate facts?" or "Does it stereotype?"

This phase also lays the groundwork for the Reflection stage. Gather all evaluation results and insights to feed into a mitigation plan. For example, if testing reveals that the model struggles with a particular category of inputs, make a note of that for post-deployment monitoring or retraining.

Artifact Collection continues throughout this phase. Evaluation reports, risk charts, and test results should be saved as part of the transparency trail. The evaluation phase for GenAI applications effectively becomes an audit of the model's readiness. As well as verifying accuracy and performance, you should also test for safety, fairness, and robustness, with documented evidence to show stakeholders such as regulators that due diligence was done before deployment. Table 7-7 summarizes the key SMACTR artifacts for this stage.

Table 7-7. Summary of key artifacts produced during the evaluation phase

SMACTR stage	Output
Testing	• Performance assessment using methods like adversarial testing • Ethical risk analysis chart • FMEA or similar risk assessment • Tests for identified failure modes • Checklist of ethical tests (e.g., hallucination, stereotyping)
Reflection	• Gathered results and insights from evaluation to inform a mitigation plan
Artifact Collection	• Evaluation reports, risk charts, and test results

Deployment Phase

The CRISP-ML(Q) deployment phase focuses on delivering the model into production and making sure it meets business requirements in real-world operation. Other key activities include user acceptance testing and producing documentation. In GenAIOps, this phase covers multiple operational steps, such as integration and orchestration (CI/CD), security and reliability engineering, and the actual model deployment. Once a model is considered ready, it must be integrated into the application infrastructure, served to end users, and maintained with proper MLOps and GenAIOps practices.

As in traditional MLOps, deployment in GenAIOps involves pushing the model or pipeline to production by setting up API endpoints or embedding the model into an application. It also includes tasks like continuous delivery of prompt or model updates, implementing safety controls such as rate limiting, monitoring for misuse, and ensuring the system can scale and remain reliable under load.

Given the dynamic nature of GenAI applications, teams may frequently update prompts or swap in improved models, making a CI/CD pipeline essential. The security and reliability aspects of this stage reflect CRISP-ML(Q)'s quality assurance mindset. The main goal is to ensure that the deployed model doesn't expose vulnerabilities (such as prompt injection) and remains robust.

Implementation

In practice, deploying a GenAI application with CRISP-ML(Q) principles means paying attention to engineering best practices and safety as the model goes live. Key considerations in the deployment phase include:

CI/CD for prompts and models
: Establish automated pipelines to move updated prompts or model versions through testing and into production. For example, similar to unit tests in software deployment, if a prompt template is updated to improve performance, a CI pipeline should run the evaluation suite and promote the change only if it passes. Likewise, infrastructure-as-code should be used to deploy model servers or services. This ensures reproducibility by creating a consistent environment and provides traceability regarding which version of the model or prompt is in use.

System integration and performance optimization
: Unlike simple ML deployments, GenAI applications often have multiple components (frontend, backend, model APIs, databases, vector stores, etc.). Integration involves connecting these and making sure data flows correctly—for instance, a user query routes to the LLM, which might call a knowledge base before returning a response. Depending on nonfunctional requirements such as cost, speed, and scalability, you may need to optimize for latency and throughput. Because large models can be expensive or slow to run, you might want to apply techniques like model quantization, caching frequent responses, or using smaller distilled models for specific requests.

Monitoring setup

Although monitoring is the next formal phase in CRISP-ML(Q), the groundwork is laid during deployment. Implement logging for model inputs and outputs, set up dashboards and alerts for key metrics (error rates, response times, etc.), and track usage patterns. GenAIOps best practices recommend integrating observability from the moment a model is deployed. Tools like Prometheus and Grafana are commonly used for infrastructure monitoring, along with custom monitors for model behavior.

Safety mechanisms

For GenAI applications, guardrails such as content filters, user authentication and authorization, rate limiting, and fallback mechanisms should be put in place at deployment time. For instance, if the LLM is part of a user-facing app, you might integrate a moderation API or a simple rules engine to check model outputs. If an output violates policy (e.g., contains hate speech), the system can block or sanitize the response. You should also plan for failover: if the LLM service is unavailable, the system should default to a safe fallback such as a simpler response or a static message. These safety and reliability measures help ensure the live system is resilient and complies with the requirements of the EU AI Act.

Staged rollouts

Teams may choose to do a shadow deployment, where the model generates outputs in response to real user queries without the user seeing them, to collect performance data in production-like conditions. This is similar to a pilot or beta test in CRISP-ML(Q), providing assurance that the model works as expected before full launch.

Documentation and training

Ensure that the operations team (which may be the same as the development team) has clear documentation on how to roll back deployments, how to intervene if something goes wrong, and what the known issues are. In CRISP-ML(Q), deployment concludes with documentation being delivered to maintainers; in GenAIOps, this may take the form of runbooks or playbooks. For example, a playbook might say: "If monitoring shows a spike in slow responses, consider disabling complex features or scaling up compute resources."

SMACTR integration

The SMACTR framework encourages a "deploy responsibly" mentality, treating deployment not as the end goal, but as a moment to verify that everything done so far aligns with ethical, quality, and safety standards and to set up mechanisms for ongoing vigilance once the model is in production.

In this phase, the Reflection stage of SMACTR should be activated. Before going live, the team should reflect on whether the development process met the initial ethical and risk-related objectives. Concretely, this means reviewing evaluation results and determining whether any remaining risks are unacceptable. For example, the Reflection stage might lead to a risk mitigation plan: "We observed that the model sometimes gives outdated information. Mitigation: Display a disclaimer or schedule regular retraining."

SMACTR's Reflection stage also calls for producing an algorithmic audit summary report, which is a summary of key findings, risk decisions, and ethical considerations throughout the project. For a GenAI deployment, this could be distilled into something like a model card plus a responsible AI deployment checklist that is filed for governance purposes.

Table 7-8 provides an overview of the artifacts that should be produced during the deployment phase, particularly as part of the SMACTR framework's Reflection stage.

Table 7-8. Summary of key artifacts produced during the deployment phase

SMACTR stage	Output
Reflection	• Review of evaluation results • Decision on acceptability of residual risks • Risk mitigation plan (e.g., disclaimers, retraining schedules) • Algorithmic audit summary report (or model card and responsible AI deployment checklist) • Plan for periodic post-launch audits (internal reviews) • Maintenance of traceability (model version, deployment date, evaluation)

Model Monitoring and Maintenance Phase

In GenAIOps, once an LLM-powered application is deployed, teams must continuously monitor its performance, capture data on real-world use, and maintain or improve the model over time. This phase, often called *model operations*, is analogous to the CRISP-ML(Q) monitoring and maintenance phase.

Maintenance in a GenAI context can take several forms, such as fine-tuning a model on new data, switching to a new model version, updating prompts, refreshing the knowledge base in a RAG pipeline, or retraining if the domain has changed significantly. The monitoring and maintenance phase is specifically intended to address the risk of model degradation in evolving environments, where data drift, changing user needs, or concept drift may occur post-deployment.

In traditional ML, monitoring typically focuses on data drift, model drift, and core performance metrics—for instance, detecting if the distribution of the input data has changed enough to reduce accuracy and trigger retraining. Some of those concepts apply to GenAI as well: user queries may evolve over time, making the original model or prompt less relevant. However, GenAI introduces additional challenges, such as monitoring the content of outputs to detect inappropriate or factually incorrect answers and tracking user interaction patterns to detect potential misuse.

Feedback loops are especially critical in GenAI: models can be improved using techniques like RLHF or fine-tuning based on logged errors and failures. CRISP-ML(Q) emphasizes continuous quality control but focuses more on technical degradation and planned retraining, whereas GenAI maintenance involves active, sometimes real-time, management of model behavior.

Finally, integrating monitoring throughout the pipeline is essential. Without proper monitoring and maintenance, a model's performance and utility will likely decay over time, and safety can quickly degrade. The dynamic, nondeterministic nature of GenAI applications makes this phase even more critical and complex.

Implementation

For a GenAI application, the monitoring and maintenance phase involves several ongoing practices, many of which parallel classic MLOps but are adapted for GenAI-specific challenges and metrics:

Live performance monitoring
: Track the model's outputs in production, monitoring for quality and reliability. This may involve statistical indicators such as the percentage of queries answered successfully or user ratings (if available), as well as technical metrics like latency and error rates. In a GenAI chatbot, for instance, frequent rephrasing of questions by users might signal poor initial responses. Setting up alert thresholds is important. For example, if the rate of content flagging by a moderation filter doubles overnight, the team should be alerted to investigate potential model drift or misuse.

Data and usage drift
: Unlike traditional ML, where input features can be directly compared, GenAI may require monitoring embeddings of user queries or clustering them to detect topic shifts. In a RAG-based system, for example, monitoring might reveal user interest in a new product that isn't yet in the knowledge base.

Logging and audit
: Maintain detailed logs of interactions, with appropriate privacy safeguards, to support retrospective analysis and auditing. These logs can feed into a feedback dataset. In addition, teams might periodically label a random sample of interactions to assess satisfaction or accuracy, helping to build an ongoing evaluation dataset to use for quality tracking.

Retraining or model updates
: Decide on a schedule or criteria for when to retrain or update the model. In cases where the base model is provided via an API (like OpenAI's GPT), retraining might not be feasible. However, teams can still fine-tune adapters and switch to newer model versions as they become available (e.g., upgrading from GPT-3.5 to

GPT-4). Each update should pass through a condensed version of the evaluation and deployment lifecycle.

Prompt and system maintenance
: Maintenance is also important for the surrounding system. Teams may refine prompt templates based on observed performance or introduce new safety rules in response to emerging failure cases. Because GenAI applications can be highly sensitive to prompt changes, treat these with the same caution as code changes—test before rollout and monitor performance closely.

User feedback and iteration
: Provide channels for user feedback (thumbs up/down for responses, reporting issues, etc.), and establish a process for analyzing and acting on this feedback regularly.

Risk management
: If new misuse patterns emerge—for example, if users find a new way to get the model to produce disallowed content—the team should respond quickly, updating filters, modifying prompts, or adjusting model behavior to block these vulnerabilities.

SMACTR integration

Monitoring and maintenance corresponds to an ongoing cycle of Reflection and renewed Scoping in SMACTR terms. While the Reflection stage is originally framed as a pre-deployment audit, its core activity—evaluating outcomes against initial goals and risks—should continue periodically post-deployment.

For a GenAI application, this could mean scheduling regular internal audits or postmortems. For example, after a month of production use, the team might review questions such as:

- Are there new ethical concerns arising from how the model is being used?
- Did our mitigation plan hold up, or do we need new measures?

This continuous reflection can lead to updates to the risk mitigation plan and may even trigger a fresh round of Scoping if the application's purpose or usage context evolves. For instance, if the system is used in a higher-stakes environment than originally intended, the team should revisit and rescope ethical and operational risks.

SMACTR also calls for documentation of incidents, meaning teams should maintain a history of design changes and keep a log of any significant failures and how they were addressed. This is analogous to treating the algorithmic use-related risk analysis and audit summary report as living documents, updated with real-world findings over time.

Additionally, the Mapping stage may need to be revisited if new stakeholders emerge. For example, customer support might get involved to handle user reports about the system, or legal teams might need to review compliance with regulations such as the EU AI Act. Maintenance processes should ensure that these stakeholders are identified and looped into governance and oversight activities.

Finally, monitoring effectively functions as continuous testing in production. The SMACTR framework emphasizes that monitoring and audits help identify emerging threats and act quickly. The engineering team should treat monitoring data not just as operational information but as audit evidence. Every anomaly should be investigated for root causes, every significant output error analyzed for potential broader impacts, and oversight responsibilities clearly assigned. This is especially important for risk mitigation in GenAI, where issues like model bias or inappropriate outputs can lead to reputational or legal consequences.

All notable outputs for the monitoring and maintenance phase for each SMACTR stage are outlined in Table 7-9.

Table 7-9. Summary of key artifacts produced during the monitoring and maintenance phase

SMACTR stage	Output
Reflection (ongoing)	• Periodic internal audits or postmortems • Evaluation of results relative to original goals and risks • Updates to the risk mitigation plan (living document) • Documentation of incidents (design history, failure logs) • Maintenance of algorithmic use-related risk analysis and audit summary report (living documents)
Scoping (renewed)	• Rescoping and reassessment of risks if the application's scope expands or changes
Mapping (revisited)	• Inclusion of new stakeholders (e.g., customer support, legal teams) and clarification of their oversight roles
Testing (continuous)	• Monitoring as continuous testing in production • Identification of emerging threats • Investigation of anomalies and significant output errors • Clear assignment of oversight responsibility

Conclusion

This chapter explored the core aspects of the EU AI Act as they apply to general-purpose AI models and systems, along with the practical role of GenAIOps in supporting compliance and fostering trustworthy AI. As outlined here, the Act establishes a structured regulatory framework for GPAI, requiring documentation, disclosure, and risk mitigation measures to be embedded into providers' workflows. GenAIOps extends traditional MLOps practices to meet the unique challenges of GPAI, enabling engineering teams to build systems that are compliant with regulatory requirements, resilient, scalable, and aligned with societal expectations. By integrating the SMACTR framework, organizations can further enhance CRISP-ML(Q) by embedding accountability mechanisms that address GPAI-specific risks such as hallucination and ethical misalignment.

Achieving compliance, however, is not a one-time task. It demands a proactive, ongoing approach in which transparency, accountability, and ethical reflection are integrated throughout the AI development lifecycle. From data preparation and model fine-tuning to deployment and continuous monitoring, teams must adopt structured, auditable processes to ensure their systems remain reliable and interpretable and meet ethical standards. This is particularly crucial for managing risks such as bias, misinformation, and unintended model behaviors. GenAIOps provides an operational framework that allows organizations to implement these safeguards systematically, bridging the gap between regulatory compliance and real-world AI development and deployment.

Final Words and Future of AI Policymaking

As we conclude our journey through AI governance, engineering practices, and the EU AI Act, it's important to reflect on what has been covered and look to the future. We began by exploring the foundational landscape of the EU AI Act's risk-based approach and how it introduces crucial obligations, even for systems not classified as high risk. A key insight is that the Act requires transparency for all AI systems intended to interact directly with natural persons, regardless of their risk level (primarily through Article 50).

We then turned to the practical world of AI development and deployment, recognizing that compliance is not a post-deployment afterthought but a process that must be integrated throughout the AI system lifecycle. The adoption of structured methodologies such as CRISP-ML(Q), alongside ethical frameworks like SMACTR, emerges as a proactive catalyst for responsible and compliant development. By aligning the phases of CRISP-ML(Q), from business and data understanding to monitoring and maintenance, with SMACTR principles, organizations can systematically address ethical considerations, manage risks, and fulfill transparency requirements at every stage.

A recurring theme throughout this book has been the critical importance of documentation and robust metadata management. These are foundational for traceability, internal audits, demonstrating compliance, and fostering transparency. Key artifacts generated throughout the development process, such as the project scope document, ethical review report, stakeholder map, data quality assessment, and initial transparency requirements document, serve as evidence of due diligence and ethical consideration. Further documentation, such as data quality reports, feature documentation, evaluation reports, compliance verification records, deployment configurations, and monitoring logs, helps establish a comprehensive compliance trail.

The rapid emergence and widespread adoption of GPAI and generative AI models during the legislative process introduced new challenges, prompting the EU AI Act to incorporate specific provisions to address them. In this evolving landscape, the principles of MLOps—extended into GenAIOps—remain vital for managing these complex systems. They support transparency, logging, and version control to create auditable trails, enabling teams to operationalize compliance while maintaining flexibility and performance.

As you have seen, navigating the landscape of AI regulation requires more than just understanding the rules—it demands a fundamental shift in how AI systems are engineered and governed. Proactive compliance, embedded within engineering workflows and supported by comprehensive documentation, is the path forward.

The landscape of AI technologies is evolving at a remarkable pace. An example of this is the emergence of retrieval-augmented generation and agent-based architectures. To keep pace, we must continually learn about new technologies and stay informed about regulatory updates, best practices, and emerging methodologies for AI governance.

In the Preface, I quoted Fei-Fei Li, the founding codirector of the Stanford Institute for Human-Centered AI (HAI) and CEO and cofounder of World Labs, who remarked (*https://oreil.ly/_PUIb*): "Now more than ever, AI needs a governance framework." She laid out three fundamental principles for the future of AI policymaking:

1. AI engineering should *prioritize empirical validation over speculation*, ensuring models are rigorously tested with real-world data and transparent benchmarks. This means engineers should rely on scientifically grounded methods, avoiding hype and focusing on practical applications rather than speculative scenarios. Standardized frameworks like ISO/IEC AI guidelines, NIST's AI Risk Management Framework, or SMACTR can be integrated into development workflows to promote reliability, fairness, and robustness.
2. Engineers must *adopt risk-aware, pragmatic development practices, balancing innovation with responsible deployment* by integrating continuous monitoring and adherence to ethical standards. This includes incorporating risk assessment early in development, leveraging iterative prototyping to surface and address unintended consequences, and continuous post-deployment monitoring to detect bias or misuse. AI systems should be designed with built-in safeguards and governance mechanisms, especially in high-stakes areas like defense or healthcare.
3. Lastly, *collaboration and open access* should be central, promoting open source contributions, knowledge sharing, and cross-sector partnerships to strengthen the AI ecosystem while maintaining accountability. Engineers can support this by sharing research findings, building reusable frameworks, and creating or contributing to tools that lower barriers to entry for startups and academic institutions.

Ultimately, building trustworthy AI is both a technical challenge and a responsibility shared by the whole organization. As engineers, researchers, and practitioners, we shape not only what AI can do, but how it affects the world. By embedding ethics, transparency, and accountability into every stage of development, we can ensure that the systems we create are not only powerful, but worthy of the trust placed in them.

APPENDIX A

Designing AI-Powered Applications

This appendix explores a general approach to designing *AI-powered applications*—software applications that incorporate machine learning models to power one or more of their core features.

In recent years, there has been growing interest in the concept of "AI products" and the application of "product thinking" (*https://oreil.ly/NKBgD*) to ML- and AI-enabled systems. This approach focuses on AI capabilities not just as technical components, but as integral features that solve real user problems. Figure A-1 shows an example of an AI product: the O'Reilly Learning Platform's generative AI assistant, *Answers*. This assistant is designed to help users interact with book content and conduct research across the publisher's book corpus using natural language queries.

I define an AI product as a software solution that:

Delivers value
: AI products provide meaningful value to users, stakeholders, or systems, whether by automating tasks, enabling new capabilities, improving efficiency, reducing costs, enhancing user experience and interactivity, boosting productivity, or generating new content.

Incorporates AI technologies
: AI products utilize technologies such as machine learning, deep learning, natural language processing (NLP), and computer vision to enable or enhance functionality.

Interacts and adapts
: AI systems can interpret and respond to inputs (such as data, user interactions, or other systems) in a way that is perceived as intelligent, and often they can learn from those interactions and adapt and improve over time.

Integrates operationally
: AI systems can be integrated into broader systems or processes, whether software systems (like mobile or web apps) or real-world processes (e.g., in manufacturing or customer service).

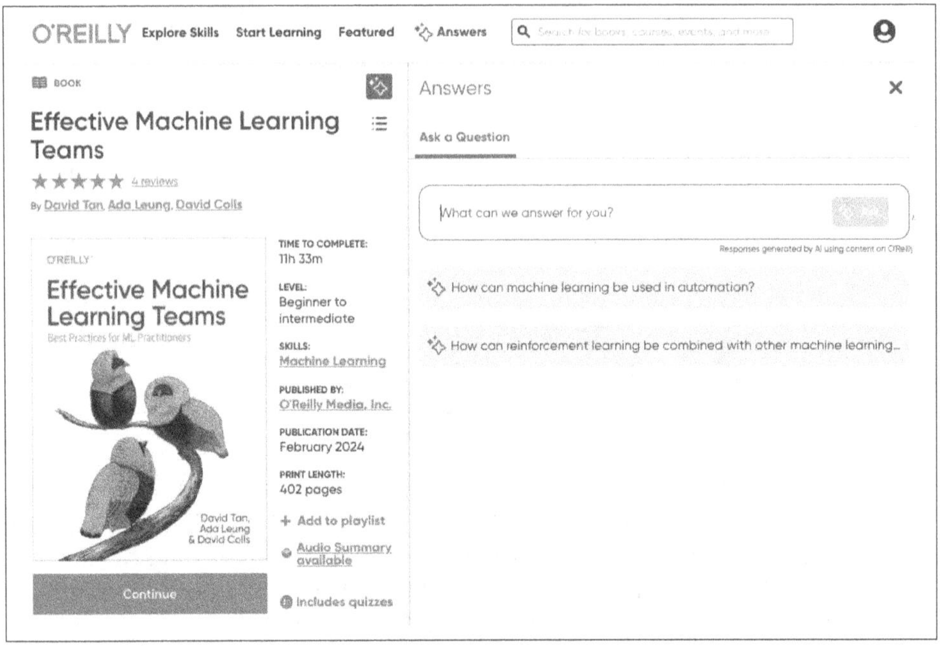

Figure A-1. An example of an AI product

In general, AI enhances software products, but it is seldom the product itself. Next, we'll turn our attention to the design process for AI products. Note that in this context, I use the terms *AI products* and *AI systems* interchangeably.

Backward Thinking for Designing AI Systems

It's important to start an AI endeavor with the business goal in mind, because only about 10% of AI PoCs (*https://oreil.ly/Ha6oK*) succeed in production. Often, alignment to the business problem—solving real users' pain points (*https://oreil.ly/MRKCZ*)—is the reason for this success.

Backward thinking provides a strategic framework for scoping, planning, and executing ML projects. Starting with the end in mind (*https://oreil.ly/Si4EX*) helps maximize the chances of delivering a useful solution while avoiding common pitfalls like poorly defined objectives, irrelevant features, and misaligned architectures.

It does, however, require a clear and accurate vision of the end goal, making it less suitable for exploratory research where the exact objectives are uncertain or in cases where problem decomposition is particularly complex.

Key benefits of a backward-thinking approach include:

Clear scope up front
: Starting with the desired outcome and working backward helps to define project requirements, feasibility, and success metrics. This prevents scope creep and keeps development focused.

Business-aligned AI products
: By tying AI development to concrete goals, backward thinking ensures that the end product delivers real value and solves the original business problem.

Minimum viable data
: Working backward from the desired output helps clarify which input features and datasets are needed.

Narrowed solution space
: With a well-defined end goal, developers can research and select among model architectures that have been proven to work well for similar problems in the past.

Iterative-incremental development
: Backward thinking encourages starting with simple prototypes, rapidly testing ideas, and incrementally increasing complexity. This agile approach surfaces issues early and allows for faster iterations.

The Machine Learning Canvas

To apply the backward-thinking approach in practice, teams can use a strategic planning tool such as the Machine Learning Canvas (*https://oreil.ly/32fj3*) (see Figure A-2). This framework helps anticipate hidden costs, identify bottlenecks, specify requirements, and create a clear roadmap for an ML project.

By aligning stakeholders on the end goal and value proposition from the outset, the Machine Learning Canvas helps ensure that the ML solution is designed to address user needs, rather than being solely technology-driven.

Throughout the planning process, the canvas keeps the focus on end-user value, placing the user and their needs and the overall software architecture requirements at the center of all decision making and technology choices. One of its key benefits is its structured approach to defining the ML task and prediction requirements. In addition, the canvas prompts early identification of data requirements and constraints, helping teams assess feasibility and start planning for data collection and labeling. Crucially, filling it out helps teams to consider how models will be used, monitored, and updated over time. This holistic view encourages a more thorough, forward-looking approach to ML project planning and execution.

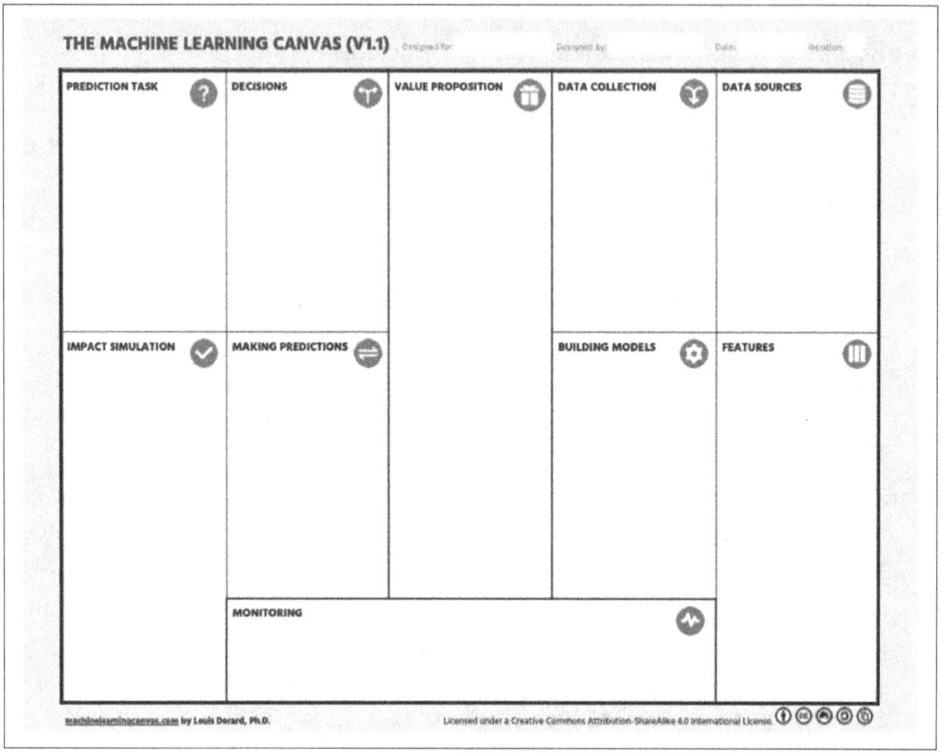

Figure A-2. The Machine Learning Canvas, developed by Louis Dorard (source: https://oreil.ly/32fj3)

The canvas also serves as a tool for collaboration between different roles, such as data scientists, software engineers, and AI product managers. Its visual format enables a shared understanding of the project and its requirements, facilitating teamwork and communication.

Importantly, the canvas supports rapid iteration, enabling teams to update it easily as they gain a better understanding of the problem space or encounter new constraints. Finally, it serves as a useful documentation artifact, offering a high-level overview that preserves institutional knowledge for current and future team members.

Let's go through the 10 building blocks of the Machine Learning Canvas, starting with the Value Proposition section.

Value Proposition

In accordance with backward thinking, we start with the business question. When creating an AI product with a business- and human-centered approach, the most important considerations are: Who are our users? What values do they hold? What problems are we solving for them?

The Value Proposition section of the Machine Learning Canvas is where these questions are addressed. It should emphasize the importance of understanding and addressing critical user needs or business objectives, identifying the target audience, and articulating the specific value that the system will provide. A clear value proposition should define the target audience, address their significant need or challenge, articulate the offered value, and highlight what sets the offering apart from competitors. Here's a suggested template for an effective value proposition statement:

> **For** [target customer]
> **who** [statement of the need or opportunity].
> **The** [product name] is a [product category]
> **that** [statement of key benefit—compelling reason to buy or use].
> **Unlike** [primary competitive alternative]
> **our AI product** [statement of primary differentiation].

Using this template helps to clearly outline the target audience, the main problems the product solves, its competitive edge, and the unique benefits it offers. This structured approach enables effective communication of the value proposition to potential users.

Here's an illustrative example to demonstrate how the template can be implemented for a hypothetical AI-powered personal finance app, SmartFinance, indicating who the target audience is, how it satisfies those users' needs, and its unique benefits/how it distinguishes itself from traditional solutions:

> **For** individuals seeking to optimize their finances
> **who** need a simple, effective way to track spending, budget, and save money.
> **The** SmartFinance app is an AI-powered personal finance app
> **that** provides personalized budgeting and saving recommendations based on your spending habits and financial goals.
> **Unlike** traditional banking apps or manual budgeting methods
> **our AI product** uses advanced AI algorithms to analyze your financial data and offers actionable insights to improve your financial health, tailored to your unique circumstances.

It's worth putting in the time to deeply understand the user or business problem—otherwise, you risk jumping to solutions without thoroughly grasping the challenge.

To craft a compelling value proposition statement, spend some time with the Value Proposition Canvas, shown in Figure A-3.

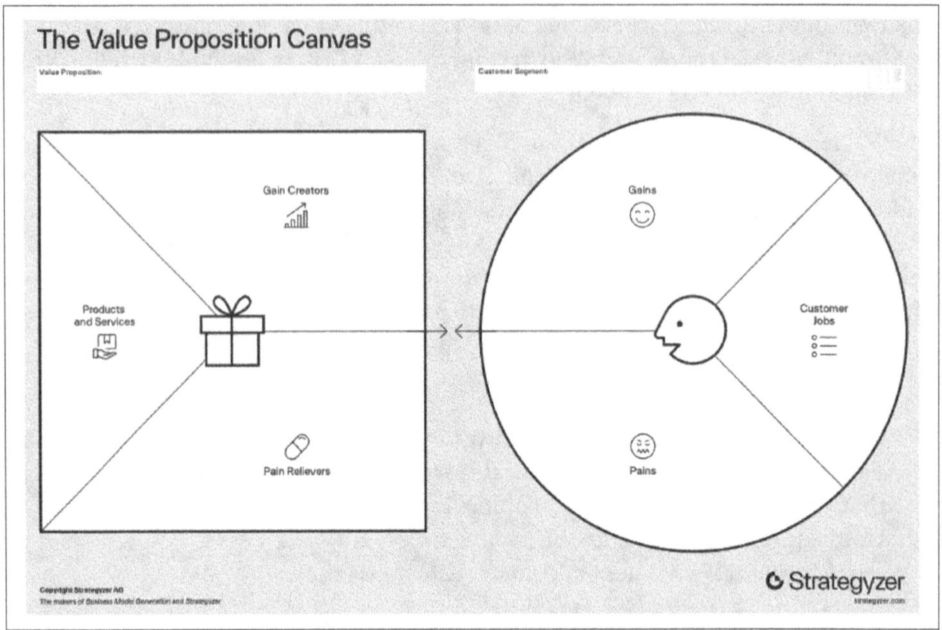

Figure A-3. The Value Proposition Canvas (source: https://oreil.ly/4pA9C)

The Value Proposition Canvas is designed to help organizations create products and services that align with customer needs. It enables teams to better understand user pain points and address them effectively by comparing identified needs and challenges with the value being offered, ensuring a strong fit between what customers want and what is delivered. Developed by Alexander Osterwalder as an extension of his Business Model Canvas (*https://oreil.ly/bhN5J*), it places a specific focus on understanding customers and crafting compelling value propositions. The Value Proposition Canvas has two sides: the Customer Profile on the right outlines customer jobs, challenges (pains), and benefits (gains), while the Value Map on the left illustrates how the proposed products or services create value by generating benefits and reducing challenges. The objective is to align the Customer Profile with the Value Map, guaranteeing that the value proposition meaningfully addresses key customer needs.

After clarifying the target audience, their problems, and that AI is the most suitable solution, the next step is to identify the success criteria. Let's transition to the Machine Learning Canvas's next building block: Monitoring.

Monitoring

The Monitoring section of the canvas should outline the metrics that are important for assessing value creation and determining the impact of the ML system in production. Since the model will function as a component within a broader software system, taking a holistic perspective on the success of the AI product is essential. This calls for a diverse set of metrics, which can be categorized as follows:

Business metrics
: Assess the business value generated from decisions influenced by the ML model's predictions. Ultimately, value is created through decision making, with predictions serving as inputs to improve those decisions. Examples of business metrics include conversion rate, revenue growth, and cost reduction. For instance, in financial operations involving extensive cloud usage, infrastructure cost is a key efficiency metric for technical teams.

AI product health metrics
: Vital for managing an AI product's effectiveness and long-term viability. A key focus area is measuring user engagement—for example, frequency and depth of interactions with AI features, as well as daily and monthly active users (DAU and MAU). Retention metrics, such as churn rate and cohort analysis, are essential for gauging user commitment and product stickiness over time. Another important metric is net promoter score (NPS), which measures customer loyalty and satisfaction by asking users how likely they are to recommend the AI product to others on a scale of 0–10.

AI technical metrics
: Evaluate the effectiveness of the AI model. Important metrics include model degradation, data drift, concept drift, accuracy, and standard performance measures like F1 score, precision, and recall.

System technical metrics
: Provide insights into the overall behavior of the system. Metrics such as robustness, scalability, and throughput are essential for understanding the system's technical health.

Including metrics from all of these categories in the Monitoring section of the canvas enables a comprehensive analysis of the AI product's success, capturing business impact, user engagement, and technical performance.

The remaining parts of the Machine Learning Canvas reflect the two main phases of every ML project: the training and prediction phases. Let's begin with the latter.

The Prediction Phase

Following the backward thinking strategy, start by planning how the machine learning model will be integrated into the larger software system. The Prediction section of the Machine Learning Canvas should reflect how the model will be used, even before it has been trained. The objective is to prototype and evaluate how the AI system will solve the business problem defined earlier.

Prediction Task

When working on a machine learning task, you need to define the input, output, and problem type. Inputs represent real-world objects or features, and outputs are the answers to specific questions the model aims to predict. In supervised learning, the system learns from example inputs paired with known outputs. The output is usually provided after a certain time delay, and predictive models are trained to predict it in advance.

When defining a prediction task, consider existing human baselines and alternative prediction methods. These can provide valuable insights for data preparation and model building. When creating a new model without an existing production method, start by establishing a basic benchmark—something intuitive and easy to calculate. This "heuristic" benchmark might be based on constants, rules of thumb, or aggregate statistics.

Avoid using a simple machine learning model, such as linear regression, as your benchmark; instead, opt for a more interpretable and easily explainable approach. For example, for anomaly detection, you might decide to use the 99th percentile value calculated from the training dataset as a heuristic benchmark. In a recommendation system, you could suggest the most popular item in the category of the customer's last purchase.

Decisions

In any prediction-based system, value is ultimately delivered through the decisions it informs. AI's successful alignment with business goals depends on how well the ML model integrates into the complete workflow—the model provides predictions or probabilities, but the real impact comes from how those predictions are used.

To connect the work in the Prediction Task part of the canvas to actionable outcomes, you need to consider how the predictions will influence decisions. How will those predictions generate the intended business value? Asking, "What if I had perfect predictions?" can make it easier to reflect on this before investing a significant amount of time in model building.

Table A-1 provides examples that clarify the distinction between predictions and decisions. Prediction generally involves estimating or forecasting unknown values based on data, while decision making involves taking actions informed by those predictions.

Table A-1. The distinction between predictions and decisions in machine learning contexts

Use case	Prediction	Illustrative decision
Credit scoring	Probability that a customer will default on a loan	If the probability of defaulting is greater than 20%, reject the loan application.
Healthcare	Probability that a patient has a particular disease based on symptoms and test results	If the probability exceeds a defined threshold, recommend a specific treatment plan or further diagnostic testing.
Retail inventory management	Forecasted demand for a product in the next month	If the predicted demand exceeds current inventory levels by 10%, order additional stock.
Automated trading	Forecasted price movement of a stock in the next 10 minutes based on market data	If the stock is predicted to rise by more than 2%, buy a specified number of shares.

Decisions always follow predictions. In this way, prediction results and subsequent actions are integrated into the broader workflow. Simply put, you can describe how the ML model is embedded into business processes by defining the upstream tasks, identifying the ML-driven solution, and specifying the downstream tasks. See Figure A-4 for a visualization of workflow integration.

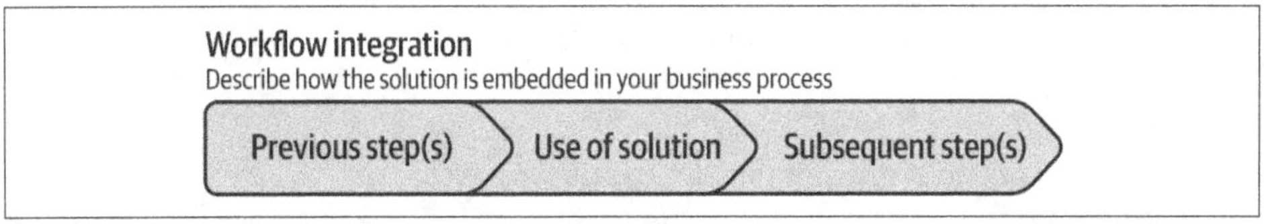

Figure A-4. Workflow integration canvas to specify the upstream and downstream tasks or processes and the usage of the ML model output (source: idalab.de)

Making Predictions

Filling out the Decisions part of the canvas helped you determine how predictions and decisions should be made. This section specifies the requirements for prediction serving. *Serving* refers to the process of deploying a trained machine learning model into a production environment, where it can receive input data and generate predictions or outputs. The goal of any serving architecture is to meet requirements for consistent and efficient outputs (considering performance, availability, and operational SLAs, as well as prediction volume), while minimizing unnecessary features, complexity, and cost.

The information you provide in this part of the canvas serves as the foundation for designing the serving architecture, which is always use case–specific. What is the expected frequency and volume of predictions? Are there constraints related to data recency or the time required to compute features?

Answering the question of how predictions should be computed will clarify the preferred prediction consumption paradigm, such as batch or real-time. Batch model serving processes data in batches periodically, while real-time serving generates predictions on individual data points as they arrive. For example, batch serving might be used for demand forecasting, where a model periodically analyzes historical sales data to predict future product demand for inventory planning. Real-time model serving might be used in anomaly detection, where IoT sensor data streams are monitored continuously to identify issues as they arise. Real-time serving is necessary when low-latency responses are needed to trigger actions or immediately enhance user experiences.

The appropriate serving architecture—whether batch, real-time, or hybrid—depends on latency, throughput, and scalability needs. It may also require optimizing the model for efficient inference using techniques such as quantization, pruning, or distillation. Compute resources (e.g., CPU/GPU) must be provisioned, and scaling strategies may need to be implemented to meet performance demands. Serving mechanisms might include exposing models via REST APIs, Kubernetes deployments, or serverless functions, depending on the infrastructure.

It's crucial to understand these technical aspects to ensure robust and reliable machine learning model deployment and serving in production environments. To that end, you should answer questions such as:

1. When do we need to generate predictions?
2. What latency and frequency constraints do we have?
3. Where will predictions be generated?
4. What does the prediction generation (serving) pipeline look like?

By completing this part of the canvas, you will determine whether you need real-time or batch predictions and identify the serving metrics to monitor in production. Next, you'll outline your strategy for deploying the model into production.

Impact Simulation

This part of the canvas focuses on establishing methods and metrics to evaluate the system before deployment. The goal is to answer the question, "How well would the system perform on these test cases?" It's important for the simulation to be reliable, which means it should be tested on scenarios that are representative of real-world use cases.

Similarly, during training, the data should accurately reflect the conditions the system will face in production. However, you shouldn't give the system too much prior information about what it will be tested on. When selecting a test set, it is crucial to ensure that it produces meaningful, interpretable results within the AI system's domain. A common approach is to use the most recent data as a test set, to assess how well the system would have performed if it had been deployed days, weeks, or months earlier.

In the Impact Simulation section of the Machine Learning Canvas, you should answer the following questions:

1. How will we evaluate system performance pre-deployment?
2. What metrics best reflect value generation?
3. What should the model audit pipeline look like?
4. What model governance steps are needed?
5. What model guards need to be implemented?

It's essential to evaluate the system's performance prior to deploying it into production. You should use both offline metrics (accuracy, precision, recall, F1 score, etc.) and online metrics (conversion rate, latency, availability, etc.) for this. These metrics will help you determine how the model performs in real-world scenarios and whether it meets the desired business objectives.

The Training Phase

As mentioned previously, every ML project consists of two main phases: training and prediction. We covered the prediction phase in the previous section; now it's time to consider training. This phase includes all the tasks involved in building an ML model: data preparation, new data collection, feature engineering, and training (and retraining) the model itself. Following the backward thinking process, you have finally arrived at the true origin of any ML system—data.

Data Sources

AI systems fundamentally rely on data. Creating an inventory of all possible data sources is one of the most critical steps in an ML project, because data availability often determines the project's feasibility and success.

Key questions to address about data sources include:

1. What internal and external data sources can we leverage?
2. How can we access and collect this data?
3. What will the data ingestion pipeline look like?

The output of this step should be a list of potential data sources, relevant APIs, and access methods. If the required data isn't currently accessible, this may signal the need for a separate data engineering project to enable model development. This stage often reveals hidden costs that may make an ML project unfeasible.

The Data Landscape Canvas (*https://oreil.ly/hsXsZ*) by Datentreiber is a useful tool for conducting a data inventory in your organization. It might also be used as part of the workshop for AI product design.

Data Collection

Data usually mirrors the world. As the world changes, ML models need to be updated to reflect these changes. This is done by collecting and incorporating new data. Retraining a model involves both gathering and labeling this new data. In this section of the Machine Learning Canvas, you should clarify how data will be continuously gathered and labeled.

The following questions are essential for ensuring a reliable retraining process:

1. How is new data for model rebuilding collected?
2. What is the labeling process?
3. What does the data collection pipeline look like?
4. What does the data preprocessing pipeline look like?

Completing this section increases the project's feasibility and helps you anticipate the cost of building the necessary data infrastructure.

Building Models

In this section of the Machine Learning Canvas, you reflect on architectural decisions for the model training subsystem (in addition to the model serving subsystem). Here, you should answer the following questions:

1. How frequently do we need to update models?
2. How many models do we need in production?
3. What time and computing constraints do we have for model training?
4. What does the ML model retraining pipeline look like?

The output should be a clear set of requirements for the model-building process. It's important to recognize that the frequency and approach to model training depend on several factors. Different strategies can be used depending on the use case, data velocity, and business needs:

- *Ad hoc model building* involves training models on demand to answer specific business questions or address unexpected issues. For example, a retailer might analyze recent sales data using clustering to identify emerging customer segments for a targeted marketing campaign. Ad hoc analysis allows organizations to quickly gain insights from data to adapt to changing circumstances. These models are typically one-off and not put into regular production.
- *Scheduled model building* involves updating ML models at regular intervals to ensure continued accuracy as new data becomes available, without the need for manual intervention. The update frequency depends on the rate of data change and business requirements. For example, for an ecommerce demand forecasting model, weekly updates might be sufficient for business needs.
- In *event-driven model building*, models are automatically trained in response to triggers such as data volume thresholds or drops in accuracy. For example, a fraud detection model might be retrained when the percentage of flagged transactions exceeds a specified threshold, indicating model drift. Event-based approaches require robust MLOps infrastructure to monitor performance and orchestrate retraining workflows.

Outlining the complexity and frequency of model training helps guide the design and implementation of the training subsystem and ensures alignment with the operational requirements of the ML system.

Features

The final building block of the ML project is feature engineering. This part focuses on creating input representations from raw data sources that will be available at prediction time. Key questions to consider include:

1. What attributes of the input data are useful for the ML task?
2. Will we need additional features that are not present in the raw sources?
3. How can we represent the raw data as features?
4. What strategies can we implement to handle sensitive data such as PII?
5. How are sensitive attributes (race, color, gender, religion, origin, age, pregnancy, family status) protected?
6. To what extent might features become discriminatory in the AI product?
7. What does the feature engineering pipeline look like?

The output should be a list of potential features to extract from the raw data or obtain from elsewhere. You should also consider aspects such as data preprocessing, feature creation complexity, feature selection and dimensionality reduction, and evaluation routines, because all of these impact the architecture of the feature engineering subsystem.

Domain knowledge plays a crucial role in feature engineering for machine learning projects, as it guides the selection and transformation of meaningful features. Involving subject matter experts in the feature design process increases the likelihood of building a reliable and effective AI product.

APPENDIX B

Data Products and Data Contracts

Data products and their contracts are becoming popular as lightweight mechanisms for scalable data management, helping ensure that data quality is not an afterthought but a fundamental consideration at every stage of the lifecycle.

Data Products

Data products are curated outputs derived from raw data that provide value to end users, typically in the form of insights, actionable information, or analytics. They are created through various stages of the data engineering lifecycle, including ingestion, storage, transformation, and serving. Data products can take many forms (*https://oreil.ly/x9hlV*), such as reports, dashboards, machine learning models, or APIs.

Figure B-1 illustrates a general structure for designing a data product using the Data Product Canvas (*https://oreil.ly/x9hlV*). This framework supports scalable data governance by guiding the creation of consistent, reliable, and well documented data products. Each data product consists of eight key building blocks:

1. Domain name
2. Data product name
3. Consumer and use case
4. Data contract (more on this in a moment)
5. Documentation of data sources
6. Data product architecture, including transformation pipelines and lineage

7. Ubiquitous language, to establish a shared understanding of terminology
8. Classification of the data product (source-aligned, aggregate, or consumer-aligned)

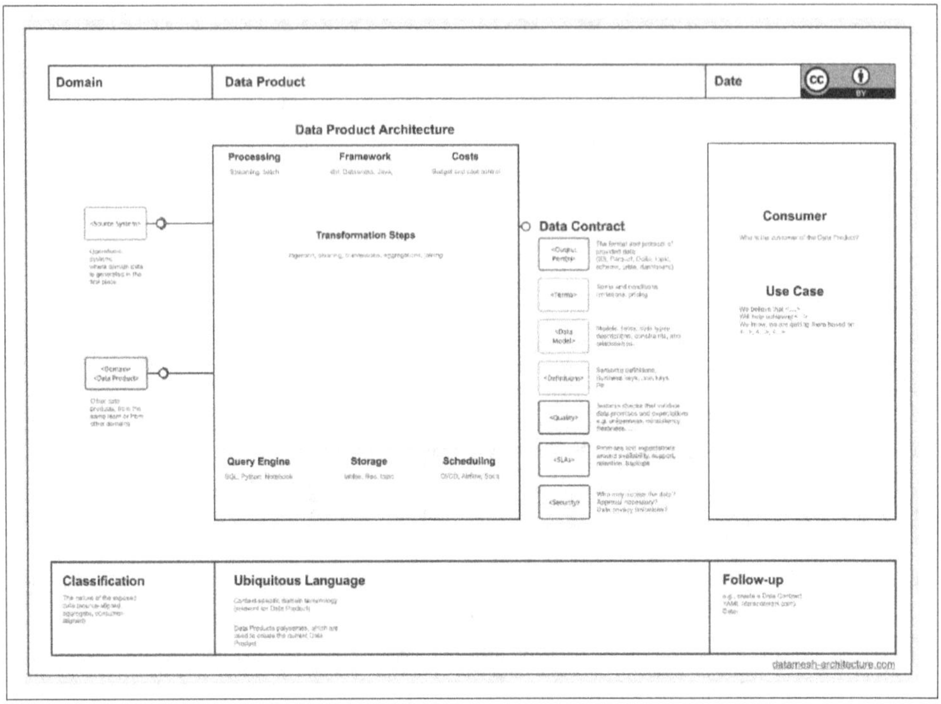

Figure B-1. The Data Product Canvas provides a structured approach to designing data products across an organization

Data Contracts

A critical component of data products from a data governance perspective is the data contract (*https://oreil.ly/WxikE*). Data contracts are formal agreements between data producers (e.g., source system owners, data engineers) and data consumers (e.g., analysts, data scientists, business users) that define the expectations, responsibilities, and standards for data exchange. They ensure that data consistently meets specific agreed-upon quality, format, and delivery requirements.

In their book *Data Contracts* (O'Reilly), Chad Sanderson and Mark Freeman define these contracts as "a mechanism for expanding software-oriented collaboration to data teams, bringing quality to data through human-in-the-loop review, just as the same systems facilitated code quality for product teams."

The key components of a data contract that will ensure effective data governance for your data product include:

Data schema
: The data contract should clearly define the structure, types, and relationships between the data fields. It should link to relevant data policies and standards and specify metadata requirements for each field.

Quality standards
: The data contract should establish standards for data accuracy, completeness, and consistency. It should also assign the roles responsible for data quality monitoring and improvement.

Delivery schedule
: The data contract should specify when and how frequently data will be delivered, ensuring alignment with established data retention policies. Include governance-approved processes for handling late or missing data.

Service level agreements (SLAs)
: The data contract should define performance metrics and response times for data delivery and issue resolution and incorporate governance-approved metrics for data availability and accessibility. It should include escalation procedures for SLA violations and processes for governance review and approval of SLA changes.

Security, privacy, and governance
: The data contract should ensure that data handling complies with relevant privacy laws and security protocols. Reference specific data classification levels as defined by governance policies and include requirements for data masking and encryption of sensitive data. Specify access control policies and procedures, data handling guidelines for different privacy classifications, and relevant compliance requirements (e.g., GDPR, CCPA, HIPAA). Clearly define the roles of data owners, stewards, and other governance stakeholders.

Change management
: The data contract should outline procedures for managing schema changes, data source modifications, and other alterations. Include governance-approved change control procedures and specify required approvals for schema changes or data transformations. Define communication protocols for notifying stakeholders of changes and processes for updating related documentation and metadata.

APPENDIX C

The Integration of AI Governance and MLOps

Integrating AI governance into the MLOps Stack Canvas (Figure C-1) enables teams to proactively identify and mitigate risks related to bias, fairness, privacy, and security, while also supporting compliance with relevant regulations and standards. This integrated approach enhances model quality, promotes reliable predictions, and reinforces responsible AI development. It scales alongside technical capabilities, encourages cross-functional collaboration, and facilitates audits and accountability.

In this appendix, we'll review the components of the MLOps Stack Canvas (introduced in Chapter 2) and extend the framework to incorporate key AI governance concepts.

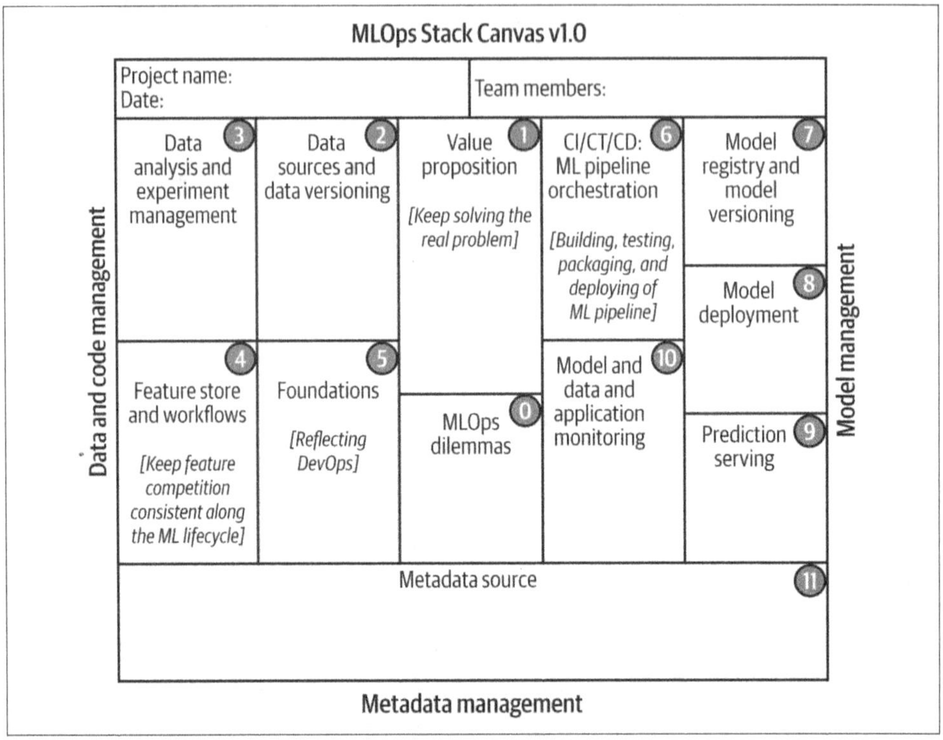

Figure C-1. The MLOps Stack Canvas framework

Value Proposition

In addition to formulating a general value proposition and data governance goals for the MLOps platform, consider how AI governance contributes to the overall value of the ML project. For instance:

- Add a "Compliance Requirements" section to outline applicable regulations and standards (e.g., the EU AI Act, GDPR, industry-specific AI regulations).
- Include a "Risk Classification" component aligned with the EU AI Act categories (unacceptable, high, limited, or minimal risk) to assess the potential risks and expected benefits of the AI system.
- Add an "Ethical Impact Assessment" section to evaluate the potential societal and ethical implications of the AI system and ensure that the project aligns with the organization's AI ethics principles.
- Incorporate a Stakeholder Analysis component to identify all parties affected by the system, paying particular attention to vulnerable or marginalized groups.

Data Sources and Data Versioning

While considering data sources during the MLOps process, you'll also need to take AI governance into account. To that end, you should:

- Ensure data sourcing complies with ethical guidelines and legal standards.
- Include data quality and bias assessment protocols to identify and mitigate potential biases in training data.
- Incorporate a data ethics review process to evaluate the ethical implications of data collection and usage.

Data Analysis and Experiment Management

To keep the AI governance focus while developing processes for data analysis and experiment management, integrate ethical guidelines to prevent biases:

- Use experiment management tools to log all experiment details, ensuring transparency and accountability in model development.
- Incorporate fairness metrics and bias analysis in experiments.
- Document decision-making processes and rationale.
- Implement version control for analysis scripts and notebooks to ensure the reproducibility of experiments.
- Implement explainable AI (XAI) techniques to ensure model interpretability.
- Include ethical experiment documentation requirements to create an audit trail.
- Incorporate an ethical review process for experiment design and results.

Feature Store and Workflows

Maintaining AI governance in the Feature Store and Workflows component requires policies that ensure data privacy and security. Standardize feature engineering workflows to make them reproducible and transparent, documenting all transformations and their intended purposes. Furthermore:

- Add feature importance analysis to support transparency, interpretability, and identification of potential ethical implications.
- Implement feature bias detection and mitigation strategies.
- Include privacy-preserving feature engineering techniques.
- Add feature documentation and requirements for auditability and governance.

CI/CT/CD: ML Pipeline Orchestration

This part of the canvas is a natural fit for embedding governance automation. To integrate AI governance into continuous integration, testing, and deployment processes, align these workflows with ethical, legal, and organizational standards from the start:

- Integrate ethical review checkpoints at critical stages of the CI/CD pipeline, such as before and after model training and deployment. For example, a healthcare company might include a review checkpoint after training to evaluate whether model predictions adhere to ethical standards concerning racial or gender bias.
- Ensure traceability between code changes and model versions.
- Implement automatic model card generation after each training pipeline to document model limitations, potential biases, and intended use cases.
- Use gradual rollout strategies with human oversight to minimize risk.
- Add model robustness and security testing, including adversarial testing and input perturbations. Frameworks like CleverHans or the Adversarial Robustness Toolbox can be used to strengthen models against manipulation and attacks.
- Conduct pre-deployment ethical impact assessments and include model fairness and bias tests as part of the CI/CD testing suite. Tools like IBM's AI Fairness 360 or Google's What-If Tool can be integrated to automatically detect and report bias in model predictions during the testing phase.
- Automate compliance checks for data handling and model behavior. Implement automated compliance checks in the CI/CD pipeline. For example, include automated scripts to verify that data anonymization and pseudonymization techniques are correctly applied before any data is used for training or testing and to support compliance with regulations such as the EU AI Act, GDPR, and HIPAA.
- Include governance approval gates in the continuous deployment process. Before deploying a model, add validation steps where stakeholders (such as ethicists, legal advisors, and target community representatives) can review and approve the model based on ethical considerations.

Model Registry and Model Versioning

To ensure model versioning aligns with data versioning and governance policies, include ethical metadata and governance information in the model registry. The following practices are recommended:

- Establish approval workflows for model deployment.
- Maintain an audit trail of model changes and approvals.

- Implement model lineage and provenance to document the entire lifecycle of each model and the accountable individuals.
- Include model risk assessment documentation.

Model Deployment

Maintaining AI governance in model deployment requires several key actions:

- Implement canary releases and A/B testing with ethical considerations.
- Ensure human-in-the-loop processes for critical decisions. Include human oversight mechanisms for high-risk AI systems.
- Conduct post-deployment monitoring for ethical concerns.
- Add gradual rollout strategies for careful monitoring of deployed models.

Prediction Serving

To keep the AI governance focus in the Prediction Serving part of the MLOps Stack Canvas, integrate the following steps:

- Provide mechanisms for users to contest or appeal decisions and gather user feedback to identify potential issues or biases. Implement rate-limiting and abuse prevention controls.
- Apply ethical input validation to guard against misuse or biased inputs.
- Monitor model outputs in real time to ensure fairness.
- Maintain comprehensive audit logs of all predictions.
- Incorporate model explainability interfaces for end users and auditors.

Model, Data, and Application Monitoring

To maintain AI governance in the Model, Data, and Application Monitoring component of the canvas:

- Establish continuous fairness and bias monitoring.
- Set up alerts for ethical breaches or unexpected model behavior.
- Monitor for data drift and concept drift, with attention to ethical implications.
- Implement automated detection of shifts that could impact fairness or performance.
- Configure automated alerts to flag governance violations.

Metadata Management

Metadata management is a crucial aspect of AI governance and is covered in depth in Chapter 3. For now, here are some key practices to incorporate into your MLOps processes:

- Maintain comprehensive documentation of AI governance practices and policies, with proper version control.
- Establish traceability between models, data, and governance decisions.
- Maintain an inventory of AI systems and their governance status.
- Include metadata for regulatory compliance (e.g., EU AI Act, GDPR).
- Add traceability for critical model decisions.
- Collect metadata related to model interpretability and explainability.

By incorporating AI governance concepts into the MLOps Stack Canvas, you create a comprehensive framework that not only addresses the technical aspects of machine learning operations but also ensures ethical, responsible, and transparent AI development and deployment. This adapted canvas promotes trust, accountability, and sustainable development of AI systems throughout the entire ML project lifecycle.

Integrating Data and AI Governance into MLOps

An emerging trend in the context of the EU AI Act is that data and AI governance are becoming closely intertwined with MLOps. A promising development is the integration of MLOps platforms with internal audit and risk management systems to enhance governance processes. This helps organizations ensure that AI models comply with regulatory requirements and organizational policies throughout their lifecycle. Table C-1 summarizes the data and AI governance processes that should be incorporated across the MLOps tech stack.

Table C-1. Summary of integration of data and AI governance into MLOps processes

MLOps Stack Canvas component	Data governance	AI governance
Value Proposition	• Compliance requirements	• AI regulation compliance requirements • Ethical AI values
Data Sources and Data Versioning	• Data catalog • Data access control • Data lineage and provenance • Data privacy and security	• Bias assessment • Data ethics review process

MLOps Stack Canvas component	Data governance	AI governance
Data Analysis and Experiment Management	• Data privacy and security • Data access control • Data handling monitoring	• Fairness metrics and bias analysis • Experiment reproducibility • XAI techniques • Experiment documentation • Ethical reviews of experiments
Feature Store and Workflows	• Feature versioning • Cataloging features with metadata • Access controls for feature store • Feature lineage and feature provenance • Feature documentation	• Feature assessment for potential bias and non-discrimination • Feature documentation • Privacy-preserving feature engineering • Feature importance analysis
CI/CT/CD: ML Pipeline Orchestration	• DataOps • Automated data profiling • Automated anomaly detection mechanisms • Governance checks in CI/CD pipelines • Automated compliance checks for data • Data security in CI/CD pipelines • Data quality checks and validations in CI/CD pipelines • Sensitive data protection • Data drift detection and alerting in the CI/CT workflow	• Traceability between code changes and model versions • Documentation (model card generation for transparency) • Pre-deployment ethical impact assessments • Gradual rollout strategies with human oversight • Automated compliance checks • Model fairness and bias tests • Governance approval gates
Model Registry and Model Versioning	• Access controls and permissions for the model registry • Model versioning aligned with data versioning • Version history of models	• Ethical metadata • Governance information in model registry • Approval workflows for model deployment • Documentation of model limitations, potential biases, and intended use cases • Model lineage tracking • Model risk assessment • Model audit trail
Model Deployment	• Deployed models adhere to data privacy and security regulations	• Canary releases and A/B testing with ethical considerations • Human-in-the-loop processes for critical decisions • Responsible AI checklists (pre-deployment verification) • Post-deployment monitoring for ethical values
Prediction Serving	• Input data validation • Sensitive output protection • Data privacy during prediction serving • Data usage monitoring and auditing during prediction serving for compliance • Auditing and logging of prediction requests and responses • Detecting and alerting on any deviations in prediction quality, performance, or fairness metrics	• Real-time monitoring for fairness and bias • Prediction explanations • Ethical input validation • Predictions audit logging

MLOps Stack Canvas component	Data governance	AI governance
Model, Data, and Application Monitoring	• Monitoring for data quality, bias, and drift in production ML systems • Processes for investigating and remediating data governance issues	• Monitoring for data drift and concept drift with ethical implications (continuous fairness and bias monitoring) • Performance monitoring against ethical KPIs • Alerts for AI governance violations
Metadata Management	• Data taxonomy and metadata schema • Data governance metadata (data lineage, provenance, compliance checks, access logs)	• Inventory of AI systems and their governance status • AI regulatory compliance metadata • Version control for governance policies • AI governance documentation • Traceability between models, data, and governance decisions • Metadata that captures model purpose, data used, performance metrics, compliance checks, and approvals

APPENDIX D

Emerging Roles in Organizations for EU AI Act Compliance

Compliance with the EU AI Act is operationalized on two levels: the organizational level and the individual AI system level. As organizations increasingly adopt AI technologies, new roles are emerging to support compliance efforts and manage associated risks. This appendix explores those roles and common team topologies.

Emerging Roles

The *AI ethics specialist* plays a crucial role in ensuring that AI systems are designed and implemented in alignment with ethical principles. Their responsibilities include developing AI ethics values, guidelines, and frameworks (see the Values Canvas (*https://oreil.ly/c79Xu*)), as well as conducting ethical impact assessments for AI projects. They address concerns related to bias, fairness, and transparency in AI systems and work closely with legal, compliance, and AI development teams. Staying up-to-date with AI ethics research and best practices is also a key part of their role.

The *AI internal auditor* is responsible for independently assessing AI systems to ensure compliance with ethical and regulatory standards. This involves conducting audits to evaluate the fairness, transparency, and accountability of AI systems and benchmarking them against organizational policies and external regulations. The auditor provides recommendations for improving the compliance of AI systems and develops AI-specific audit frameworks and methodologies. Collaboration with AI ethics specialists and compliance officers is a vital aspect of this role.

The role of a *legal AI compliance officer* or *AI regulatory affairs specialist* is to ensure that AI systems comply with applicable laws and regulations. This requires staying informed about evolving AI legislation, developing compliance strategies for AI initiatives, conducting legal risk assessments, and providing guidance on data privacy and AI transparency. They work closely with legal teams, AI development teams, and AI ethics specialists.

The *data and AI governance specialist* develops and implements policies that ensure responsible management of data and AI assets. This includes creating data and AI governance frameworks, enforcing compliance with data protection regulations (such as GDPR and CCPA), establishing data quality and metadata management practices, and developing policies for AI model versioning and lifecycle management. They collaborate closely with data engineers, AI teams, and compliance officers to ensure the effective implementation of these policies.

The *AI risk management specialist* is responsible for identifying, assessing, and mitigating risks associated with AI systems. This includes conducting risk assessments for AI projects and deployments, developing risk mitigation strategies, and continuously monitoring AI systems for potential risks and vulnerabilities. They collaborate with AI security specialists and compliance officers and provide risk-related insights to leadership to inform decision making.

The *AI security specialist* ensures that AI systems are protected against threats and vulnerabilities. They implement security best practices in AI development and deployment, conduct security assessments of AI models and systems, and develop defenses against AI-specific threats such as model poisoning and adversarial attacks. They also monitor AI systems for security anomalies and collaborate closely with cybersecurity teams and MLOps engineers to maintain the security of AI systems.

These roles are embedded with broader organizational structures such as cross-functional teams or governance boards.

In the next section, we'll explore Team Topologies (*https://oreil.ly/ZW6OJ*), a framework for organizing and structuring software development teams to optimize workflow and delivery. We'll extend this concept to ML teams and examine how the emerging roles related to EU AI Act compliance can be integrated effectively.

EU AI Compliance for ML Teams

Matthew Skelton and Manuel Pais developed the core concept of Team Topologies and introduced it in their 2019 book of the same name. The framework defines four fundamental team types (see Figures D-1 and D-2):

- *Stream-aligned teams* are the primary team type, focused on delivering value directly to customers or users. They work on a specific product, service, or feature set aligned with a business domain.
- *Platform teams* provide internal services and tools to support and accelerate stream-aligned teams. By offering self-service capabilities, they aim to reduce the cognitive load for other teams.
- *Complicated subsystem teams* handle complex components or areas that require specialized expertise, which stream-aligned teams may not possess.
- *Enabling teams* assist other teams in adopting new technologies or overcoming obstacles. They provide specialized knowledge and coaching.

Team Topologies also defines three core interaction modes between teams (see Figure D-1):

- *Collaboration*, where teams work together closely for a defined period
- *X-as-a-service*, where one team provides a service that another team consumes
- *Facilitating*, where one team helps another team learn or develop a new capability

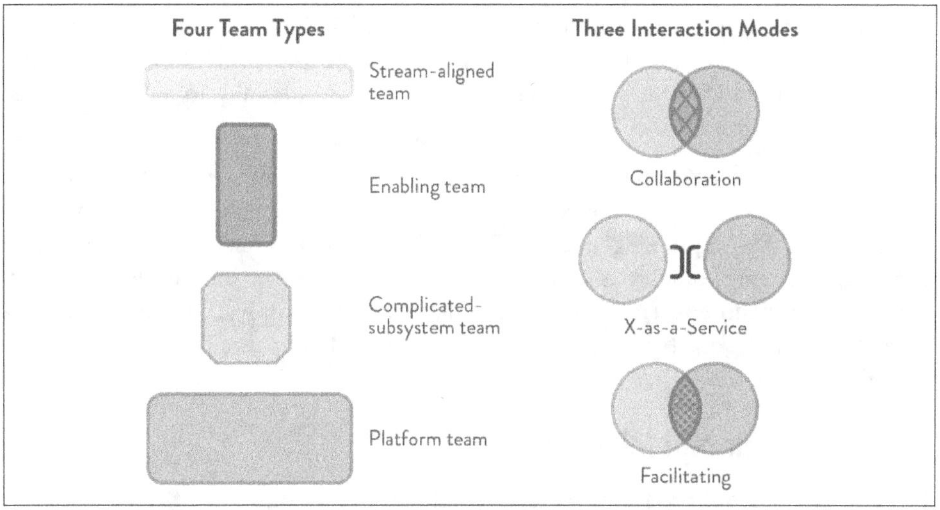

Figure D-1. The four team types and three interaction modes. Image from the book Team Topologies *by Matthew Skelton and Manuel Pais (IT Revolution). Used with permission.*

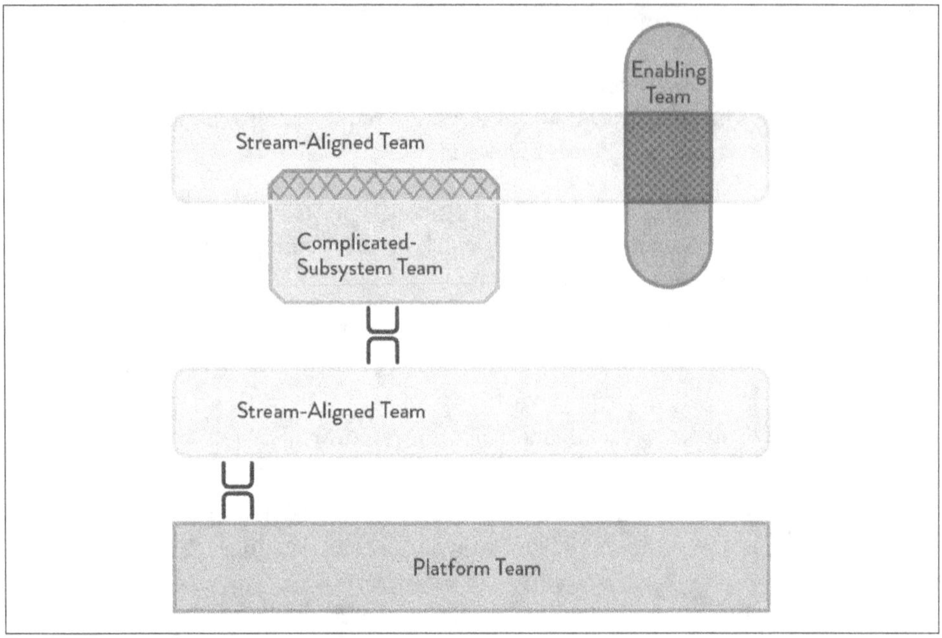

Figure D-2. Primary interaction modes for the four fundamental Team Topologies. Image from the book Team Topologies *by Matthew Skelton and Manuel Pais (IT Revolution). Used with permission.*

The core principles of Team Topologies guide effective team organization and dynamics. A key principle is Conway's law, which states that "organizations design systems that mirror their communication structures"—in other words, the structure of those systems tends to reflect the way teams are organized and interact. This highlights the importance of designing team structures intentionally to support desired system architectures.

The Team Topologies framework also emphasizes the need for teams to handle only as much complexity as they can effectively manage, to avoid excessive cognitive load. Prioritizing collective intelligence over individual capacities encourages a team-first mindset. Team Topologies also promotes defining natural boundaries for team responsibilities and ensuring team encapsulation, with clear, well-defined interfaces. Finally, evolving team structures are essential to adapt to changes in technologies and organizational needs.

Team Topologies for ML Teams

With the rapid adoption of ML/AI technologies, it has become clear that data science and ML teams don't all fit neatly into the complicated subsystem team category. In practice, they often span multiple team types. David Tan, Ada Leung, and David Colls explore this idea in their book *Effective Machine Learning Teams* (*https://oreil.ly/zK4s0*) (O'Reilly), where they distinguish between four types of teams in the ML space:

- *ML product teams* (stream-aligned) deliver user-facing ML features with minimal dependencies on other teams.
- *ML domain teams* (complicated subsystem) focus on complex ML applications tailored to specific domains.
- *ML and data platform teams* provide foundational ML and data capabilities to support other teams and reduce duplication of effort.
- *Enabling ML teams* specialize in particular aspects of ML product development and provide assistance to other teams.

As visualized in Figure D-3, the ML domain team's interaction modes range from collaboration to as-a-service delivery of ML solutions. With its expertise in advanced ML models and domain-specific tasks (e.g., retail forecasting, content recommendation, churn prediction), it operates as a collaborative unit within the organization. It also provides ML models and capabilities as a service to multiple stream-aligned teams, ensuring that teams across the organization can leverage ML expertise without duplicating effort.

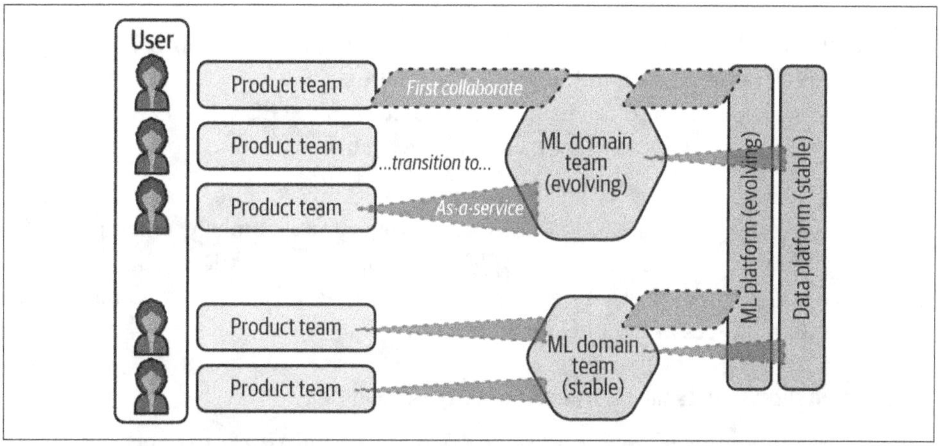

Figure D-3. Visualization of typical topologies for ML domain teams. Image from the book Effective Machine Learning Teams *by David Tan, Ada Leung, and David Colls (O'Reilly). Used with permission.*

Aligning Team Topologies with Ethics, Compliance, and Governance Roles

Now that you have a sense of the core team topologies and how they relate to AI teams, let's see how this ties in with the EU AI Act. Team structures in AI teams are not static; they evolve based on the organization's needs, scale, and maturity. As discussed earlier, ensuring compliance with AI regulations and supporting the development of trustworthy AI systems requires the introduction of new, specialized roles. The following subsections give a few examples of how these emerging ethics, compliance, and governance roles can be integrated into the Team Topologies framework as enabling teams or complicated subsystem teams.

Enabling team: AI ethics and governance

This team functions as an enabling team in the Team Topologies model, focusing on AI ethics, compliance, and governance. It might include roles such as:

- AI ethics specialist
- Legal AI compliance officer or AI regulatory affairs specialist
- Data and AI governance specialist
- AI risk management specialist

The AI ethics and governance team will support other teams (such as ML product or domain teams) through facilitation and collaboration. Its goal is to help these teams navigate ethical considerations, ensure compliance with the EU AI Act and other data and AI regulations, and implement effective governance practices.

The organization's data and ML platform team could incorporate some of these governance and compliance capabilities into its offerings, for example by embedding ethical AI guidelines and checklists into ML development workflows, implementing automated compliance checks in ML pipelines, or providing preapproved, regulation-compliant data sources and model architectures.

Complicated subsystem team: Data and AI security and auditing

This team handles the complex and specialized aspects of AI security and auditing. It will include roles such as:

- Data and AI security specialist
- AI internal auditor

The team primarily operates in the X-as-a-service interaction mode, providing security and auditing capabilities to ML teams across the organization.

By integrating the emerging ethics, compliance, and governance roles described here into the Team Topologies for ML teams framework, organizations can embed proper data and AI governance directly into their development workflows. This approach supports compliance with the EU AI Act and related regulations while preserving the benefits of fast flow, clear ownership, and reduced cognitive load that Team Topologies is designed to enable.

Index

A

B

C

D

V

About the Author

Dr. Larysa Visengeriyeva has a PhD in data quality management and is the former head of data and AI at INNOQ. As the creator of *ml-ops.org* and coauthor of *datamesh-architecture.com*, she's helping advance the field through knowledge sharing and community building.

Colophon

The animal on the cover of *The AI Engineer's Guide to Surviving the EU AI Act* is a white-bearded manakin (*Manacus manacus*), a small bird found in the tropical forests of South America. This book's cover depicts a male manakin, who sports iridescent black plumage with a bright white neck and fluffy chin feathers that he puffs out as a courtship display. Females are a more subdued olive green color.

White-bearded manakins primarily feed on fruit, berries, insects, and spiders found in the forest. They forage in the lower levels of the forest canopy, flitting from branch to branch in search of food. These birds prefer dense, mature forests with a thick canopy for roosting and building nests for their young.

This species has a fascinating behavior known as *lekking*, where males gather in specific locations (called *leks*) to attract a mate. Each male sets his stage by clearing part of the forest floor, and then puts on a display of jumps, elaborate movements, vocalizations, and loud wing snaps to attract females. Groups of up to 70 males have been observed lekking in the breeding season (the rainy time of year when food is abundant). After mating, the female builds a nest, lays 1-2 eggs, and nurtures her chicks alone while the polygynous male will continue to look for additional partners.

Many of the animals on O'Reilly covers are endangered; all of them are important to the world.

The cover illustration is by Monica Kaamsvaag, based on an antique engraving from *Lydekker's Royal Natural History*. The series design is by Edie Freedman, Ellie Volckhausen, and Karen Montgomery. The cover fonts are Gilroy Semibold and Guardian Sans. The text font is Adobe Minion Pro; the heading font is Adobe Myriad Condensed; and the code font is Dalton Maag's Ubuntu Mono.

www.ingramcontent.com/pod-product-compliance
Lightning Source LLC
LaVergne TN
LVHW080037210926
848481LV00011B/3219